BEE COUNTY COLLEGE
DATE DUE

SEP 1 6 1977		
SEP 2 1 1977		
AUG 2 1978		
AU		

20322

F
802
.L7
K55

Klasner

My girlhood among
outlaws

20322

F
802
.L7
K55
1972

Klasner

My girlhood among outlaws

My Girlhood Among Outlaws

EDITED BY EVE BALL

*My
Girlhood
Among Outlaws*

by Lily Klasner

THE UNIVERSITY OF ARIZONA PRESS

TUCSON, ARIZONA

About the Author and the Editor . . .

LILY CASEY KLASNER was truly a child of the New Mexico nine-teenth-century frontier, encountering its turbulence and hardships in westward migration and later in Indian raids that robbed her family of most of their possessions. Although her formal education was intermittent, Mrs. Klasner attended the New Mexico Highlands University at Las Vegas and became a teacher and telegrapher as well as a rancher. She also became a writer, and from a meticulous diary, reinforced by letters, clippings, pictures, and documents, she fashioned an autobiography, further guided and shaped by historians Maurice Garland Fulton and Eric Bruce. The Klasner manuscript, lost after the author's death in 1946, showed up twenty years later in a trunk in an adobe hut in New Mexico. In 1968 Eve Ball, teller of tales about territorial New Mexico *(Ma'am Jones of the Pecos* and *In the Days of Victorio),* undertook the editing and annotation that resulted in the present volume.

THE UNIVERSITY OF ARIZONA PRESS

Copyright © 1972
The Arizona Board of Regents
All Rights Reserved
Manufactured in the U.S.A.

I. S. B. N.-0-8165-0328-1(cl)
I. S. B. N.-0-8165-0354-0(p)
L. C. No. 77-165206

Contents

ILLUSTRATIONS

My Girlhood Among Outlaws

Introduction

FOR MANY YEARS, persons interested in the history of Lincoln County, New Mexico, have been on the trail of a manuscript written by Mrs. Lillian (Lily) Klasner about the experiences of herself and her family. Lily, third child of Robert Adam* and Ellen Eveline Casey, was born in Mason County, Texas, in 1862. When she was five years old her family moved to the Rio Hondo in New Mexico, bringing with them about 300 cattle, 200 sheep, and a large remuda.

While still in her early teens, Lily planned to write the story of these pioneer experiences and toward this end she hoarded every bit of information she could obtain -- news clippings, old letters, documents, records, and interviews with many people who had participated in historic occurrences or had witnessed important events. Especially did she value papers and documents given her by Sally Chisum Robert, daughter of James Chisum, most valuable of which was the diary kept by Sallie's uncle, John Chisum, during his detention in the Las Vegas jail. In this he wrote detailed explanations of the charges preferred against him, their origin, and his innocence of these allegations. Following the death of Sallie's husband, Sallie and Lily shared a home in Roswell for many months. Will Keleher, in his *Violence in New Mexico,* wrote:

For many years the original John S. Chisum narrative was in the possession of Chisum's niece, Sallie Chisum Robert. Sallie Chisum Robert and Lily Casey

---

*Because military discharge papers and a land deed did not carry the name Adam, family members question its being their grandfather's name.

Klasner, daughter of Robert Casey (killed in Lincoln County on August 2, 1875), were intimate friends for many years. The two women visited Santa Fe together on or about September 1, 1904, and while there discussed a plan to collaborate in writing their recollections of early days in Lincoln County. The project was never completed. For a time Mrs. Klasner had possession of the narrative.

Apparently Mrs. Robert lost interest in the project and later gave to Mrs. Klasner all that had been preserved.

Mrs. Klasner did most of the work on her manuscript between 1925 and 1929 and was well past sixty-five when she completed it. She wrote with lead pencil on large tablets such as used by school children of the time. Failure to interest a publisher in this original draft caused Mrs. Klasner to seek skilled assistance. Upon the recommendation of Mrs. John William Poe, Mrs. Klasner contracted with Maurice Garland Fulton to rewrite and publish her manuscript. Colonel Fulton was unable to complete this contract for publication so the contract was dissolved in 1929, and the manuscript lay untouched for many years.

In the early 1940s Mrs. Klasner accompanied her niece, Mrs. Ola Casey Jones (then county superintendent of schools), to consult with Eric Bruce, an old acquaintance who was then principal of the Lincoln School. An arrangement was made for him to undertake completion of the manuscript. Mr. Bruce was told that when he finished with the contents of a suitcase and box in which her papers were kept, he was to give these to Mrs. Jones. Mrs. Klasner stressed the fact that after her death this niece was to receive a trunk containing much of historic interest and also a certain large, black satchel that she had carried for years, in the bottom of which would be found something of great value. This satchel was conspicuous because it was so much larger than those in vogue at the time. Originally designed to be carried behind a saddle, these satchels usually carried dance frocks for young women to change into after reaching their destinations. What this particular one contained, nobody ever learned because shortly after the owner's death in 1946 the satchel and many other articles of value were lost in a fire. Though the trunk and its contents did not impress the family as being of any value, it was saved and stored in an abandoned adobe on one of the farms along the Ruidoso now belonging to Mrs. Jones.

I first heard of the manuscript from Col. Fulton, but not until early November, 1968, was any serious attempt made to find it.

It was my privilege to be present during a visit between Mrs. Jones and her old friend, Mrs. Edith Coe Rigsby, daughter of pioneer Frank Coe. Their reminiscing brought to light the existence of the manuscript, and the possibility of its being stored in an old adobe house. It was agreed it might pay to investigate. It did! Mrs. Jones' husband, Elliot, and son, John, found the very old and very large domed trunk, covered and lined with heavy canvas, which Mrs. Jones could identify as the one Mrs. Klasner took with her to the Upper Peñasco when she was seventeen.

The trunk was crammed, the top layer consisting of Mrs. Klasner's clothing including her wedding dress. Underneath were oilcloth book satchels, and below them heavy Manila envelopes into which papers had been crammed, apparently at random. If they had ever been classified, which is very probable, someone had searched through them and replaced documents indiscriminately. Mice and water had damaged both containers and papers, and some had obviously survived a fire. Fortunately the typing was uninjured, probably because, being closely packed, oxygen could not penetrate. But the margins were crumbled.

Perhaps the most important page was one giving the table of contents indicating divisions into parts and chapters; Fulton had begun and discarded several versions without indicating a reason. Because of his remarkable memory he sometimes relied upon it rather than upon records. Also found were chapters he had intended using; although no finished drafts of these were found, many carried marginal corrections for final typing along with instructions to a Miss Webb.

There also were chapters or accounts of incidents in Mrs. Klasner's handwriting. Some are illegible in places, but many had been copied as written by her, and were preserved. Of the controversial ones there is enough of her draft to clearly indicate her sometimes biased conclusions.

It would be hard to find two collaborators more unlike in background and training. Lily's early existence was both crude and hazardous. Shootings and murder were so commonplace that the Casey children took them for granted until their own beloved father was the victim. After his death Mrs. Casey probably could not have survived without the help of John Chisum in combating injustices and dishonesty and of James Chisum as guardian to the Casey children. In this close association, John Chisum chose to make of Lily his confidante because she was "so long-headed and had plenty of hoss-sense." The obituary which appeared in *The Roswell Record* of June 1, 1946, states of Mrs. Klasner,

She was truly a woman of the West living here when there were only a few people and no law and order; where most of the travelers were outlaws and Indians. She was able to hold her own with any of them, as people had to be in those days. She was fearless and would think nothing of riding a horse all day and doing a man's work.

After the death of her father Lily developed a protective coloration in defending her mother, and she soon learned to pit her wits and her six-shooter against desperate characters she encountered.

Maurice Garland Fulton, son of Robert Furwell Fulton, chancellor of the University of Mississippi, was reared in a scholarly atmosphere. After doing graduate work at two universities and completing his service in World War I, he taught at the University of Indiana until advised because of his health to go West. He joined the faculty at New Mexico Military Institute at Roswell in 1922 and soon made research in the colorful history of southeastern New Mexico his absorbing avocation. History lay at his doorstep and he soon was recognized not only as a writer of college textbooks but as an authority on such diverse subjects as Shakespeare and Billy the Kid!

Fulton recognized that Mrs. Klasner's reminiscences contained much vivid information as yet unpublished. He was impressed with her knowledge of people and events and with her excellent memory, but her writing lacked organization and he felt that in some instances it lacked verification. But her writing was colorful as shown in these excerpts:

Robert Casey served in the U.S. Army as Union Soldier, Guide, Guard, and Scout in the Texas State Troops and Texas San Saba Home Guards.
He was sent to the frontier of Texas, where he suffered all kinds of privations, exposure hardships, and great dangers of life as only the old pioneer of bell metal could endure. I have heard him tell many times of loved ones killed and scalped, scenes that drew heart's blood and tried the very soul of man. I myself have been in Indian fights. . . .
Father . . . with the aid of my Grandfather, four of my uncles, all ex-Union soldiers and other good brave men set to work at once to organize a band of men to go a way out West, cut sign, and fight the Indians back from scalping these poor old pitiful men, women, and children; until the legislators could make laws for State Troops or some kind of protection.
They banded together under the name of Home Guards, and called their Camp San Saba, it being on the San Saba River.

Each man had to furnish his own mount, arms, equipment, and feed. No pay for a long time. It was do this or be butchered and scalped.

I tell you we all had many narrow escapes "Taking the West."

Colonel Fulton had found raw material for what he considered the creation of a vivid account of frontier life, but to him it lacked form. He attached much importance to what he termed the architecture of a book, and to him is due the credit for organization and limitation as well as verification of account.

He made a blueprint; he selected material and background and drew up plans, dividing them, like ancient Gaul, into three parts.

Part One, "From Texas To New Mexico," dealt with the Casey ancestry and the migration of the family into New Mexico. It depicted a people with the courage and determination to face dangers and overcome obstacles almost incomprehensible today.

Part Two, "The Reign of the Six-Shooter," recorded events leading to and following the Lincoln County War, but was not a repetition of accounts given in Fulton's *History of the Lincoln County War*. In some details the two are contradictory. How much of the differences are owing to Mrs. Klasner's strong convictions, and how much to the many subsequent years Fulton continued research after rewriting this manuscript, are difficult to determine. It should be remembered that here he was presenting Mrs. Klasner's conclusions, not his own.

However, it is Part Three, "John Simpson Chisum," that is peculiarly Mrs. Klasner's contribution to the history of her time. The collaborators agreed that until that time (1929) there had been no comprehensive account written of John Chisum. The intimate friendship of the families provided Lily an opportunity to know much of the activities and the problems of the Chisums. She had spent weeks visiting at their South Spring River Ranch, first in the enormous adobe built around a hollow square, and later in the famous Long House. She was visiting there when John left to find medical aid for the malignant tumor on his neck, and she stayed on while members of the family went to Paris, Texas, to attend the burial of their brother and uncle.

It was readily admitted that John Chisum indulged in decorous flirtations with young women, but most of them, including Lily, understood his attentions. It was country where, as Sam Jones said, "They was maybe thirty to thirty-five young men to every girl; when a new one come to the country the cowboys married her before she lit offen her hoss." Every young woman received much attention, and many married at fourteen and fifteen, but Lily Casey was not one of these. Perhaps her years at the Ursuline Academy in San Antonio during her teens prevented an early marriage. She no doubt missed the many suitors to which she was accustomed, but this did not prevent her making excellent grades in school. Nevertheless, it was rumored that had she so wished she could have married John Chisum. Others mentioned in the role of her suitors were Abneth McCabe, Bob Olinger, and several others. Lily Casey was a true pioneer in that respect — she "did not talk."

The complicated question of "squatter's rights" contributed much to the conflict that almost wrecked Lincoln County. Early settlers may have known little about legal aspects of gaining possession of land, but they ordinarily recognized a man's right to ownership of the plot on which he made his home, even if he did no more than stake his horse and spread his bedroll. He could obtain 160 acres if he filed on it, made it his home for three years, and made certain "improvements" such as house, corral, cultivated fields, irrigation ditches, and other manifestations of permanency.

Robert Casey purchased the mill and a two-room adobe in 1866 and in 1867 obtained a quit-claim deed guaranteeing him the right of ownership of the buildings and peaceable possession of the land. But to obtain a patent it was necessary to comply with the Homestead Act. By 1877 people began having their land surveyed and filing on it. An additional quarter section could be obtained on a tree claim — holding it by planting trees. Land could also be obtained by paying script issued by the Territory. But a hundred years ago land was of little value and if a man owned the source of water he could and did make use of the land without owning it. John Chisum controlled range extending two hundred miles along the Pecos, but just how much he really owned is not known.

Governor Ross's report made in 1886 to the Secretary of the Interior indicates the unscrupulous nature of land grabbing:

It is notorious that possession of large quantities of the public lands has been obtained under the form of preemption laws through the boldest perjury, forgery, and false pretenses, and that in some instances this has been done, if not with the connivance at least through the inadvertence and carelessness of public officials. If these lands had been obtained for actual occupation and cultivation, the results would not be so disasterous to the Territory, but in many cases they have been absorbed into great cattle ranches, merely for the purpose of getting control of water courses and springs, and to thus keep out settlers and small herds; and in others, the lands have been stolen for purely speculative purposes.

Lily Klasner felt that "squatter's rights" constituted the fairest claim to possession. For almost eleven years the Caseys had regarded their land along the Feliz as their own; they had complied with all requirements of the Homestead Law except filing on the land. It is possible Mrs. Casey planned to have her sons file on the land when they became twenty-one. Lily had built a monument of stone on her plot of ground and apparently neither she nor her family anticipated that their ownership would be challenged. But James Dolan annexed their land on the Feliz, and Lily spent most of her inheritance in litigation over it, losing consistently. From these experiences she developed a keen dislike and mistrust of attorneys that colored much of her thinking. This feeling was shared by many others who had suffered from the unscrupulous practices of many lawmen. Inability to substantiate many deep beliefs may have contributed to Mrs. Klasner's disinterest in finding another collaborator after she and Colonel Fulton abandoned their project.

Mrs. Klasner seems to have kept alive a desultory interest, for she did send out a chapter now and then to some person she hoped to interest in completing the manuscript. It is not certain that all of these were returned.

When Eric Bruce began work on the manuscript he was handicapped by not having the source material upon which it was based. Extensive research was necessary, and in pursuing this he found much published or officially recorded material, authenticated and accepted by historians, that was at variance with Mrs. Klasner's accounts. It is understandable that Mrs. Klasner would continue to believe her versions, told directly to her by people who had participated in or witnessed the incidents, were more nearly truthful than some of the recorded versions that could very easily have been "doctored" for political expediency.

Again no accord could be reached, so the second major attempt to collaborate was discontinued. Mr. Bruce scrupulously returned all papers entrusted to him and very generously gave Mrs. Jones his incomplete draft of the book.

Letters and other documents preserved by Mrs. Klasner give much insight into the personalities of the people and provide a sketch of her life in the years following the close of her book. Discouraged

Working as a telegrapher on the Mexican border, Lily Casey met and married Joe Klasner in a formal ceremony at Laredo, Texas.

by persistent attentions of bachelors on the Peñasco and also a murder which had horrified her, she decided to go into another line of work, telegraphy. Though she kept in touch with her sister Ellen (Mrs. John Moore of Balmorhea, Texas), her relatives on the Hondo heard from her infrequently. It was during the time she worked as a telegrapher along the Mexican border that she met and married Joe Klasner. Her niece treasures a photograph taken at Laredo, Texas, showing the couple in their wedding garments.

This marriage terminated in divorce, and Mrs. Klasner again returned to teaching. Because she spoke and understood Spanish excellently she decided to work among people who needed a teacher with knowledge not only of their language but of their customs and psychology. She enrolled at the New Mexico Highlands University at Las Vegas and qualified for teaching by taking the annual examinations held at the county seat (at that time Carrizozo) and worked under the administration of her niece, Mrs. Jones.

A renewed interest in having her book published led her to take courses in writing, although as yet she had no publishing contract. When age forced her retirement from teaching, Mrs. Klasner lived for several years at San Patricio and became largely dependent upon her niece for both care and income. She was later moved to a one-room adobe house at Tinnie which belonged to Robert F. (Buster) Casey, son of Adam Casey.

A short time later she became ill and was taken to St. Mary's Hospital at Roswell where she died on May 31, 1946. She was buried in South Park Cemetery where her mother, her brother Adam, and his wife and their daughter Helen had been buried. It had been the expressed wish of her mother, Ellen E. Casey, that the bodies of her husband and their four children be moved here from the family plot on the Hondo ranch, but because of the great lapse of time, this was never done.

The years of research I had done on the family of Heiskell Jones, contemporaries and friends of the Caseys, interested Colonel Maurice Garland Fulton in urging me to find Mrs. Klasner's manuscript and obtain the owner's permission to prepare it for publication. Mrs. Ola Casey Jones acquiesced in the idea and has been very cooperative in supplying information to supplement that given by her aunt.

EVE BALL

PART I

From Texas to New Mexico

I

My Pioneer Ancestry

IN HEREDITY AS WELL AS ENVIRONMENT I may claim to be a child of the frontier. My mother had a pioneer genealogy covering several generations in this country. Successive migrations brought them west and south until they eventually reached Texas. My father's family, the Caseys, were comparative newcomers. Devout, "fighting-Irish" Catholics, they came first to Mamramcock, New Brunswick, Canada, moving later to Massachusetts where my father, Robert Adam Casey, was born.*

Young Robert, imbued with the spirit of pioneers and his ancestors, ran away from home when he was only sixteen. He, like many boys who enlisted for the war with Mexico, misrepresented his age. Recruiting officers undoubtedly suspected this, but accepted Robert as a farrier, or horseshoer, and sent him with the first recruits to Fort Mason, Texas, where he served for five years in Troop G, 2nd U.S. Dragoons. He was honorably discharged at the end of his first enlistment, but military life was in his blood and he served in later campaigns.

My Grandmother Shellenbarger visited us often, and tales of her girlhood experiences captivated my youthful mind. I especially

---

*Mrs. Klasner thought her brother Adam (Add) was named for their father; but Robert F. Casey, son of Adam Casey, thinks that is erroneous. There also are some conflicting data on the time and place of his birth.

liked hearing about the falling of the stars in 1833. Her father happened to step out of the house for wood one night and saw the whole sky illuminated with falling objects. He called his family, then ran to tell the neighbors. Everyone was terribly frightened by these thousands of stars, and it was easy to believe the world was coming to an end!

Grandmother told me, too, of trouble between the Mormons and the Gentiles in Illinois. Gentiles, critical of the plurality of wives their Mormon neighbors had, wanted to force them to conform to the laws of Illinois. Grandfather was very influential in that part of the state. Once when Grandfather was away, Joseph Smith, leader of the Mormon colony, rode to Grandmother's home and asked for her husband. When told that he was away, Smith asked her to tell him that the Mormons would not leave the country as they had been warned to do. He said that before running they would fight until their bridle reins swam in blood. She admired his fighting spirit and told him that she did.

She told me, also, of a big tower built by the Mormons for use as a tabernacle. It was rumored that when it was finished Joseph Smith would ascend to Heaven from its top. Instead, their leader was murdered, and his people chose Brigham Young as his successor. Discouraged by the persecution they underwent, the Mormons decided to migrate westward.

Another account that impressed me vividly was Grandmother's story of the black wolves that infested Illinois. The country was sparsely settled and houses were far apart. During a very cold winter one of her neighbors was on his way home with a sleigh load of food when a pack of fifteen or twenty black wolves pursued him. He pulled off his overcoat and threw it out. They tore at it for awhile, then renewed their attack on the sleigh. The team was running as fast as it could, but the pack drew near a second time, so he threw his coat to them, gaining a little time for him. Fortunately he was close to a house, and when he drew up at the door the wolves slunk away into the darkness.

Grandmother was seventeen when she married Samuel Shellenbarger, a man of Dutch descent, and after their marriage they moved from Danville, Ill., to Ohio. There my mother, Ellen E. Shellenbarger, was born in 1837.

Indians were still menacing that part of the country, but some were friendly and willing to trade with the whites. When Mother was about six she traded some red calico and brown sugar for an Indian baby girl. She kept the child for the day, but in the evening the mother returned and demanded her baby. Mother hid behind the door with her new possession, but Grandmother made her return the child to its mother. The Indian woman surrendered the calico, but had eaten the sugar. Mother cried at having to give up her newly acquired toy. Her first experience with the Indian concept of bargaining stood her in good stead in dealing with the Apaches in later years. When Indians sold their land they had no concept of their agreements being final, in the same way the Ohio Indian woman regarded trading her baby.

Shortly before the family left Ohio for Texas, Mother fell from a swing causing injury to her hip that handicapped her all her life. In her later years she was compelled to use a crutch, and this infirmity endeared her to her family, especially to her father. Although Mother never used this to rouse sympathy, it undoubtedly caused others to appreciate even more her courage and physical endurance.

Grandfather was an Episcopalian deeply prejudiced against Catholicism. He attempted in every way to prevent his five daughters from becoming interested in members of the Roman church and was alarmed when Mother became interested in Robert Casey, solely because he was a Catholic. Mother knew she was her father's favorite child, and exceedingly disliked opposing his wishes; but she was so deeply in love with Father that she felt that she could never marry anyone else.

At the beginning of their courtship Mother's family lived at Fort Mason where Father was in military service, but not long after, the Shellenbargers moved to McClennon County, near Waco. If Grandfather hoped that this move would end the love between his daughter and Robert Casey, he didn't know the Irish. As soon as Father secured his discharge he went to Waco and resumed the courtship. By that time Grandfather was ill. He realized that he might not recover and wished to see his daughters "settled," especially Mother, because she was crippled. He received Robert Casey courteously and consented to Ellen's marriage, provided the ceremony be performed by Judge Stubblefield. Father agreed, but was not satisfied until a second ceremony was performed according to the rites of his church. Mother enjoyed saying she had been married twice without being widowed!

Soon after their marriage the young couple went to Escondido

Robert and Ellen Casey, the parents of Lily Casey Klasner,
established their family in the midst of hardship
and turbulence in frontier Texas and New Mexico.

Station (later, Escondido Springs) about two hundred miles west
of Fort Concho. There Father had charge of the Stage Stand of the
famous Butterfield Overland Mail, which ran westward from San
Antonio through Fort Mason, Menardville, Fort Concho, Centralia
Station, and on to Fort Stockton. Thence its course continued
through Barella Springs (later, Barrel Springs), the San Augustin
Ranch, San Elizario, and on to El Paso del Norte.

Escondido was considered the most dangerous station on the
hazardous road. Only a foolhardy Irishman would have taken his
bride there where he had to hobble and side-line the mules used
on the stages, and stand guard over them with his Spencer cocked,
constantly alert for an Apache attack. Much credit is due to a
young woman willing to risk her life to be with her husband.

There Will, my oldest brother, was born. The family moved
to Frio County, stayed a short time, and then to Peg Leg, where
Robert Adam, their second child, was born in 1861. When many
men left the country to serve in the Confederate Army, the Indians
became aggressive, causing Father to move back to Fort Mason
where there was protection for his family.

Both my grandparents and parents suffered at the hands of the Comanches in 1866. My grandparents felt fairly secure from attack since they lived within two miles of Fort McKavitt. However, there were only one or two companies at the fort — a very insufficient force for adequate protection of the settlers. The Comanches were uncanny in their ability to piece together information on where the white men were, in what they were engaged, and when they would return. Branding time was an especially vulnerable one for the whites, as the men doing the work would be far from home and might be away several days. Those remaining in the country had to attend not only their own cattle, but those belonging to friends and relatives serving in the army.

It was on such a mission that Grandfather embarked one morning before daybreak. The horse he had borrowed could not be led so Grandfather was riding a slow, lazy one and leading his own fast one. He had ridden but a short distance from the house when Grandmother went to the cow pen and Aunt Clara started to the garden to get a watermelon. Aunt Clara had hardly gone through the gate when she heard a horse. She was only fourteen and so nearsighted she thought the man approaching on a run was a neighbor. When he got near enough for her to see that he was an Indian she started for the house, screaming as she ran. Without slackening his pace he stuck his lance* into her back and knocked her to the ground. When she tried to get up, she couldn't see and let her head fall as though she were dying, so the Indian rode on.

After several attempts she did get up and found that she could see. She managed to reach the fence, a worm one made of rails, which she tried to climb rather than take the longer route by the gate. Weakened by the loss of blood, she fainted and fell into the yard. From here Grandmother half carried and half dragged her into the house. Grandmother had hardly barred the doors when the Comanches were pounding on the back one, demanding admission.

Grandmother grabbed the shotgun and pointed it through a crack in the wall, keeping up a conversation as though there were others in the room with her. By moving from one opening to another,

---

*Some of the Casey family think Clara was wounded by an arrow instead of a lance.

she was able to deceive her attackers and they soon withdrew, leaving only one to stand guard at the cow pen.

The other Indians rounded up most of Grandfather's stock, including the milk cows, and did not come near the house again until they were ready to leave. Then they discovered Grandmother's feather bed and pillows which had been left in the yard overnight and proceeded to rip them open. Feathers flew in all directions and Grandmother thought they were plucking the geese, ducks, and chickens. After doing all the mischief they could, they rode a short distance from the house and fired one shot which struck the door.

Meanwhile Grandmother had dressed Aunt Clara's wound. All day she had been terrified not only by her daughter's condition but by having recognized among the horses hidden by the Comanches the two that Grandfather had taken when he left. She had no doubt that her husband had been killed. Toward evening a neighbor, who knew that there was no man with the two women, slipped through the bushes and got close enough to the house to call to Grandmother. She recognized his voice and told him to come in. She told him of the happenings of that terrible day and her fears for Grandfather.

Runners were sent among the friends of Grandfather and a number came to the house to organize a search for him. It was decided that the party divide and part be sent in pursuit of the Comanches. The Indians had been gone for hours and the pursuers did not overtake them. The searchers surmised that the Indian who had attacked Aunt Clara had been watching the house from a *motte* [grove], and had seen Grandfather leave with the two horses. The men found the tracks of four horses whose riders had followed Grandfather to the river. He had been shot twice in the back, dragged from the water, stripped of his clothing, and left on the bank, unmutilated.

A neighbor took Grandmother and Aunt Clara to the Fort where the surgeon found the lance had been poisoned, which delayed Aunt Clara's recovery. Some time later she married Charles Merganthaler, lived in San Antonio, and reared a large family.

This attack left Grandmother in a tragic position, without a husband and stripped of most of the resources for making a living — the 900 cattle that would have sustained the family. She learned that at the first camp the Comanches had killed 14 animals, stripped the meat from the bones, and jerked what they could not eat. Signs indicated there had been over 300 in the raiding party.

Among those who pursued the Comanches was Pat Coglan [Coglin], later of fame at Three Rivers, New Mexico. It was reported to Grandmother that when he learned how large a party of Indians they were trailing he said, "There are so many Indians that if we should overtake them, they could eat us Whites for breakfast and still be hungry." The civilians gave up the pursuit, and there were no soldiers to follow.

About a year after Grandfather was killed, Grandmother married a Mr. McDougal.

2

Earliest Recollections

I WAS BORN IN 1862 amidst the perils and vicissitudes of the Texas frontier during the Civil War. Our family lived near Fort Mason in Mason County, and my father was away from home at Camp San Saba serving in the Home Guards. These were companies of men organized to protect the defenseless women and children left alone while the men were in the armies of the North or South. There was constant danger not only from roving bands of Comanches, Kiowas, Kickapoos, and Lipan Apaches, but what the southern women feared even more than Indians were the Jayhawkers drifting in from the North.

An experience Mother had with one shortly after my birth frightened her terribly. Before leaving, Father had found a Mexican couple, Pete and Sarah, to stay with her and the little ones.

Our house was a "dog-trot" log cabin, consisting of two rooms with an open porch between them. The passage was used for hanging saddles and other gear, and afforded a cool and comfortable outdoor living room in summer. The room Pete and Sarah used for sleeping also served as kitchen and dining room for both families; the other was our bed-sitting room.

One day just before dinner (the noon meal) while Sarah was clearing the table and Mother sewing and rocking my cradle with her foot, a horseman rode to the outside kitchen door. He was a formidable looking person who wore pistols in open holsters on either side, and carried a rifle. Mother answered his "Good day,

Madam," with "Good day, Sir," and added, "get down and have a chair. Have you had dinner?"

He replied that he was hungry and took his seat at the table. Mother heaped a plate with food and set it before him. He had taken only a few mouthfuls when he caught sight of a bottle of bear's oil on a shelf. He asked gruffly, "What's that?" Mother told him. "No it ain't," he replied, "you're just saying that so as you won't have to give me any." Knowing that he believed it to be whiskey, Mother said, "Taste it, Sir. You're welcome to it if you want it."

He grabbed the bottle and drank from it greedily, then rushed to the door and spat it out. He turned back and started to the head of the bed in which Sarah and Pete slept. People were accustomed to keep what little money they had between feather bed and straw tick. As he turned his back on Mother, she took a shotgun from the wall, cocked both barrels and threw down on the man. She ordered sharply, "Now, you git!" He turned and finding himself looking into the muzzle of the weapon, promptly decided to abscond the field. He said, "Don't shoot, Madam; I'll go." And he backed toward the door.

Keeping the gun on him, Mother said, "If you don't I'll pull the trigger." Still facing her he stepped out the door and mounted. As soon as he got out of range he began swearing. Then he shouted at Mother, "I've a notion to come back and kill every one of you." She replied, "If you haven't had enough yet, just come back." Before he could accept her invitation, Pete came in with a sharp ax upraised. The Jayhawker decided that his best course was to *vamoose*.

Mother learned that a band of desperate carpetbaggers had come into the country and had robbed several homes. She took no credit for protecting hers, admitting that she had been frightened, and said she thought that the screaming of Sarah and the two boys had probably scared the man as much as she had.

The constant menace of Indians influenced much of their daily life. Mother and Sarah wore dresses during the day but at dusk would change into men's clothes so a lurker might think there were three men in the house. They did all the milking, feeding, and bringing in wood and water well before dark, then bolted the doors and windows and did not open them until morning. No lights were used and, except in cold weather no fires were built — people went to bed early and arose before daylight.

Father was at Camp San Saba when one of our neighbors went there and told him he had a baby girl, so he got a furlough and came home to see me. En route he had to cross a little stream at a point where there was a pecan grove and much underbrush. He knew there might be Indians concealed there but, six-shooter in hand, pushed through. As he anticipated, marauders were hidden in the brush. He fired six shots while his horse was running, and the Indians disappeared. Unhurt, he had a memento in the form of an arrow that hung in his saddle blanket but did not injure his horse.

Miss Kate Crosby was visiting us when Father arrived. She went to the cradle, covered me, and told Father that he was not to see me until he promised to educate me, and to buy a piano for me. He laughed and promised. He looked at me and said I was so white that he doubted that I had a drop of blood in me. He suggested that for that reason I be called Lily. Mother compromised for Lillian, but family and friends called me by the name Father chose.

Fortunately I was a strong, healthy child. Mother was very busy with the two boys, both of whom were "puny." In later years she said, "Lily, you were a regular little pine knot; nothing ever seemed to hurt you."

When I was past two a little sister was born and named Ellen E. for my mother. I was delighted and loved sitting at the foot of the cradle and rocking her while crooning the old lullaby, Rock-a-Bye-Baby.

It was as though Mother had three babies, for Add, the stronger of the boys, had an accident when he was three, and for a long time was a constant care. He had followed Mother to the cow pen and disobeyed her order to remain outside. When he crawled under the fence to pet a calf, its irate mother charged, knocked him to the earth, and struck the back of his head with her hoofs. The blow fractured his skull, and for three days he lay in a coma. It was impossible to obtain a doctor because toward the end of the War Between the States the country had been stripped of physicians. Although the neighbors thought Add was dying, he miraculously recovered, but the right side of his body was paralyzed.

Will was very frail, and little Ellen a sickly child. Small as I was, I could carry her without difficulty. Mother said seeing me do so reminded her of a mother cat with a kitten.

Later another brother was born. I helped care for little John S., as I was almost five and could do more for him than I had for Ellen. As I stood by his cradle rocking him to sleep I saw a large centipede crawl over the end of the pillow toward his head. Before I could stop it the centipede was in the baby's hair. I knocked it off and screamed. Both Mother and Grandmother, who lived with us, rushed to me. Mother was armed with the fire tongs and Grandmother with the poker. I pointed to the horrible crawling thing that had regained the pillow. Mother siezed it with the tongs, mashed its head, and carried it out of doors. She laid it on a rock, and to prevent its being blown away, placed a stone on its head. She wanted Father to see it, but before he arrived one of our roosters ate it. He had been intended for chicken and dumplings, but the family was afraid to eat him.

Our closest neighbors, the Vaughns, lived four miles away. There was a grown daughter whom I called Miss Mollie, and a girl named Ida, only a year or so older than I. There was a son about eighteen, Moody, who teased me and of whom I had deathly fear. I thought that if I were given my choice of having him or a Comanche about, I'd choose the latter. Undoubtedly he had no idea how afraid I was of him, or I am sure he would not have persisted in scaring me as he did. He would rush at me threateningly, and I usually took refuge under the bed. Though others laughed at my fright it was real and terrifying to me, even more terrifying than an Indian raid I experienced.

While we lived at Little Elm, Menard County, Texas, Grandmother went to visit Aunt Clara, who returned to our home with her. Aunt Clara was, understandably, afraid of Indians, but I do not think Grandmother knew the meaning of fear. She was never known to shed a tear, regardless of what occurred.

At that time we had three dogs, Tige, Prince, and Rover; Father had got Rover for me when I was nine months old. One night the dogs charged and barked in a manner that made Mother sure that Indians were prowling about. We heard loose horses runing but did not dare open the door, though Grandma urged us to investigate. Toward midnight the dogs were quiet and we dropped to sleep. At daybreak Mother awakened and peeped out. She saw a fine brown horse in a little *motte* of pecan trees about fifty yards from the house. She told Grandma and Aunt Clara that the horse was milling about as though in pain. He would start to lie down, go to his knees, and then get up and begin pacing about again. As the light increased Mother thought she could see something sticking high in his side, but she would not permit Grandma to go to the animal. All she ventured was crossing the porch to the kitchen so she could cook breakfast.

About ten that morning Mose Taylor, a neighbor, came over and found his brown horse, one of his best, with an arrow in its side. Indians had made a raid and, since they could not drive the animal, had left it behind as they made off with the others they had stolen.

3

Journey to New Mexico

EARLY IN 1866 Father took to New Mexico for James E. Ranck
and Ben Gooch* of Fort Mason, Texas, a herd of cattle for which
he was paid a third of the proceeds. During this trip Father spent
the winter on the Hondo where he became interested in the mill
and ranch owned by Leopold Chenny [Chene]. He bought the place,
then started on the long journey of over 800 miles back to Texas
to get his family.

For the return trip he bought a large ox wagon of the type
known as the Murphy, made by special order for the mountainous
country of New Mexico. At that time there were only trails made
by Indians or buffalo that could hardly be called roads. He bought
eight yoke of well-trained oxen to draw the heavy load he planned
to bring back to the Hondo. Rather than make the trip with an
empty wagon, Father considered possibilities for carrying back some
commodity that would sell readily in Texas. There always was a
demand for salt so he detoured by the Salt Flats south of the Guadalupes and filled his wagon with salt. This cost nothing but the work.

He engaged a Mexican boy named Julian to make the trip with
him. Neither spoke the other's language when they left the Hondo,
but during the three months they traveled together each learned a
sufficient number of the other's words to make himself understood
in routine work.

---

*In one note Mrs. Klasner says the cattle belonged to Ranck and Lockhart.

Drivers of ox teams walked beside their wagons and controlled the animals by command, well-trained oxen responding to "Gee" and "Haw." The teams could be urged forward by command or whip, but without reins to check them, the only means of stopping them was to shout "Whoa!" For that reason several tribes of Indians referred to cattle as "Whoa-haws."

Before leaving, Father wrote to Mother at Fort Mason and told her he was coming home. By government post dispatch his letter went to Santa Fe and from there by stage to San Antonio. Another stage carried it to Fort Mason, and still another to Menardsville. The time required for the delivery of it was long, but much shorter than the trip Father made by ox team. He warned her that he would probably be three months on the road and tried to lessen her apprehensions concerning him.

Upon the day of his arrival Mother had gone to town to take the butter and cheese. When she returned she gave the children their lunch and told my older brothers that she could not hear their lessons until she had rested awhile, then sent us out of doors to play.

As we were leaving the porch we heard a whip pop and we called to Mother that someone was coming. She got up, and we all watched the two wagons, one trailing the other. There were two men, one of whom walked and drove the many yoke of oxen. She got her sunbonnet and started to meet the wagons and we followed. As they approached she looked closely to see if the driver were Father, but did not recognize the tall, bearded man walking beside it. Disappointed she told us to return to the house.

At this point there was a short turn in the road which required careful driving to get eight yoke of oxen and two wagons around it. The man gave her no greeting or indication he knew us. But when he got his outfit into a straight road he left the wagon and came forward. Still thinking him a stranger, Mother stood in silence with us huddling behind her. The man smiled, then began to laugh. But even then Mother did not recognize him until he said, "Don't you know me, Evy?" Because of his dusty clothing, long hair, and tanned and unshaven face, she had not until she heard his voice. Then she exclaimed, "My God, Robert, I never saw you look like this before!"

He kissed her and turned to us but we were afraid and would not come near him. Add screamed when Father knelt beside him, and even Will, the oldest, shrank back from the strange-looking man. But Father had prepared for this by stopping in Menard and bringing a paper bag of peppermint sticks, which did much to reconcile us to his endearments.

Father saw to unyoking the steers before he would go into the house. Mother started preparing a meal for him and the Mexican boy while we climbed upon the wagon and began digging in the salt.

When we were called to the table he was already seated and I remember his saying, "I have been gone nearly a year and in all that time have not slept in a house nor seen a white woman. I have seen very few white men, but many Mexicans. I did not have a tent — just camped out and took the weather as it came, rain or shine, wet or dry."

He promised Mother that he would take us to New Mexico and never leave us again. There was, he said, no money in cattle in Texas, but a good chance to do well in New Mexico. He had bought a place there, one where we would be together and happy.

Father finished preparations for moving in the late fall of 1866. Because of the probability of finding a better supply of water in winter, it was considered the best time for the trip. He gathered about 1800 head of cattle, packed our clothing and bedding in a new wagon, and household equipment and food in the one in which he'd made the trip home. Each had a strong canvas cover to protect both the cargoes and those who rode in them. We had little furniture but Mother was careful to include the iron cook stove, cooking utensils, garden seed, and several bolts of cloth which she had woven.

Our food consisted of unparched coffee, bacon, yellow corn meal, and some flour. Beef was no problem for a calf could be killed as needed. Mother had skillets, a Dutch oven, a coffee pot, a thick frying pan, an iron teakettle, and some tin plates and cups to be used on the way. Her precious dishes were not to be unpacked until we reached the ranch on the Hondo.

There was one piece of equipment of which Mother was very proud, and which required careful packing — her sewing machine. I am sure that she had a good supply of needles, thread, buttons, and other equipment for sewing, for I well remember her using them after we reached our home.

I was five, and to my care had been entrusted responsibility for the two younger children, Ellen and John, whom Father called the "Yearling." These two were frail, and neither Will nor Add was sturdy.

In addition to the family there were eleven men, several of whom were Mexicans. I remember Julian, Miguel, Juan, Flores, and Ramón. Charlie, an American, had decided to join the emigrant train, and there were two more Americans whose names I do not recall. And, of course, Father.

For protection on the trip Father joined forces with another outfit in charge of Lace and Joe Bridges, brothers. They too, were taking a herd to New Mexico for its owner. They had fewer cattle than we.

During the early part of the trip Father used two-horse wagons but when one broke down he traded both off for a large prairie schooner drawn by six oxen. He used three yoke one day and another three the next, thus giving a team a day's rest to graze and recuperate from the hard pulling. I remember the names of some of those steers: Tom and Jerry were his lead team; Whitey and Whiskey came next; and the wheelers were Spot and Lip. In the alternate team were Duke and Diamond, Red and Rowdy, and Buck and Berry. I can remember seeing Father hold the yoke and call "Come, Buck! Come Berry!" The oxen would walk to him, thrust one horn through the bow, turn their heads, and carefully slip the other into position. The wheelers were yoked first, and the leaders last.

Father carried a long, rawhide whip with a short stock and could flick a fly off the lead team with it. He seldom struck an animal, but the popping of the whip caused them to increase their speed. Of course if they decided to run there was no way to stop them. He could give a command but there was no way to enforce it.

The oxen traveled at about the same pace as that of the slowly moving herd and that gave us time to keep the " 'possum-belly" filled. This was a big dry hide for carrying fuel. When we saw a dry stick or cow chip we ran, picked it up, and threw it into the 'possum-belly swung beneath the wagon so that when we camped, dry fuel would be available. At the beginning of the trip wood was no problem but the farther west we went the scarcer it became. We used it sparingly so that if there were snow on the ground we did not have to dig around in it for a supply.

We came by way of the old emigrant trail, well known to Father who had traveled it before. Along it we found mesquite which gradually decreased in size from trees up to twenty feet high to mere bushes. The roots make excellent wood, though they are usually covered with soil. Mesquite makes a fine, hot fire but smokes cooking utensils badly so that cleaning them is almost impossible. For that reason our pots and pans were usually carried with the fuel.

When mesquite was not available, buffalo chips made a quick, hot fire but quantities were required for cooking. Sometimes we had to depend upon bear grass, which produces more blaze than heat.

The 'possum-belly served another useful function — that of providing transportation for calves dropped along the trail. Sometimes one had to be carried two or three days before it was strong enough to follow its mammy. Then it was necessary for someone to watch so that it would not be left behind. If one gave out, a man picked it up and carried it on his horse to the wagon for another ride in the 'possum-belly.

There was a similar problem with the sheep which Mother had refused to leave behind. She had raised this small flock from dogie lambs given her by neighboring ranchers. They had learned to come at her call of "Lamby, Lamby," for food or salt. She had sheared them, carded the wool, spun it into thread or yarn, woven cloth for clothing and blankets, and knitted our stockings. No wonder she thought them indispensable.

It was well we made that long, dry trip in winter, for had heat added to our miseries we might have been unable to stand it. Long before we reached the Horsehead Crossing of the Pecos our supply of drinking water was exhausted and we were suffering from thirst. Think how much greater was the need of the animals that had gone without water for two days! When the cattle first scented water I think we must have been at least two miles from the ford. The herd began to move at a fast walk and in spite of efforts of the men to slow their pace, burst into a run before reaching the river. Father turned the oxen loose for fear they might stampede with the wagon and he rode ahead to attempt to prevent the cattle's piling up in the water and drowning. Only a few of the weaker animals were lost.

We stayed at the crossing about three days and it was while there that we came upon evidence that brought forcibly to us the uncertainty of life in those times of lawlessness. One evening Julian and Miguel came into camp very wrought up over something they had difficulty in making us understand. Father understood some of their words but they spoke too rapidly for him to know just what had occurred. He left Miguel with us and went with Julian to investigate. At the river he found a body in shallow water. When he got it to the bank he found that the man had been stabbed five times. A piece of rope had been tied to the body for dragging it to the water's edge. On the bank there was no sign, and Father concluded that the corpse might have floated down the river, possibly for a long distance. He and the Mexicans dug a shallow grave, wrapped the body in a piece of canvas, and buried it.

A short time later he learned from men at Fort Stockton of two men who had left there to go to Fort Concho, where San Angelo is now located. Only one reached his destination. He reported that a band of Indians charged him and his companion, and that the partner was killed. We assumed that his was the body we found.

Then, as we drove up the Pecos, on the east side to avoid a surprise attack by Apaches, Father came upon the dead body of a horse with its throat cut. That was unusual. His explanation was that the survivor of the two travelers who had started for the Concho had killed his companion and "made Injun sign" either to conceal his guilt or to warn those who came that way of danger.

Horsehead Crossing was indelibly impressed upon my mind both by this occurrence and another. Close to the ford we found a new-made grave. The headboard was the endgate of a wagon with a girl's name and age scrawled upon it. At Fort Stockton Father was told that an emigrant train headed for California and camped on the Pecos because of the illness of this girl. She was buried the day she died and the wagons moved westward.

On our way north we followed the winding river and it was in Pecos Bend that I suffered from hunger for the first time. Charlie went to sleep on guard and let the cattle wander into the river, noted for its dangerous quicksand. Many of the animals were bogged; and when Mother arose for preparing breakfast she discovered what had happened and called Father and Will. With some of the men they hastened to the river to attempt to rescue the cattle. Mother joined him, and left us asleep. When we awoke we were puzzled at their absence but we stayed with the wagon.

Four hours of uncertainty led to hunger. It was increased by our having gone to bed without supper. Ordinarily that did not occur, but Father had not stopped to camp until late, and as we were asleep in the wagon he did not disturb us.

Ellen and I decided to go the short distance to the Bridges' camp and ask their cook for food. Errands were usually assigned to us because of Add's infirmity. Johnnie, the baby, was too young to help. When we reached the wagon we were ashamed to say that we were hungry, and returned without asking for food. Later I took a small pitcher and went back to buy milk; but again my courage failed, for I had been taught that self-respecting people did not ask for food, and that without money nobody could buy anything.

At noon the cattle that could be rescued were driven back and Mother prepared a bountiful meal for us.

4

Attack by Apaches at Black River

DISTANT SMOKE INDICATED APACHES were following us as we drove up the Pecos. Frequently when we saw a column in the west there was an answering one to the east. This continued for about three weeks. At each camp precautions were taken against a surprise attack, but it was not until after we crossed the river at Pope's Crossing that Father was greatly disturbed.

Travel was necessarily slow because cattle cannot move fast, especially when there are many young calves following. In addition we encountered much snow. At one camp we were forced to stay six days during which we could see neither the sun nor the ground.

Because of the danger of an attack the trains kept close together and at night men from each train stood guard. It was at Black River that the Indians struck. The night before the attack Mother sent me to the other train to ask Mr. Joe Bridges to join us, and to circle the wagons for our mutual protection. He laughed and replied that he did not think there were any Apaches near. Again separate camps were made, perhaps fifty yards apart.

After we had cooked supper, Father suspected that the Apaches were close because when looking into the darkness he thought he detected indistinct figures of men in motion. He walked over to the Bridges' camp and told them of his apprehensions. Bridges replied that if he had seen any people they must be members of another train that had overtaken ours; and he offered to bet Father a yoke of steers that he was right.

The usual guards were posted but after the others had gone to sleep Mother slipped out to see if our two Mexicans were alert. As she feared she found one asleep with his gun. She slipped it away from him and brought it to camp. In a few minutes the man came to the wagon, excited. Mother returned his weapon and tried to make him understand that he must not go to sleep on guard again.

The following morning she arose early and found herself in a dense fog. She began cooking, but did not call Father and Will because they had stood late guard and needed rest. Gradually those on early guard started the cattle on the day's drive by letting them swing out in the direction they were to travel so that they could scatter and graze during the day with the herders bringing up the rear. The work oxen were not turned out but kept near the wagons and permitted to graze until we were ready to start. For them, grazing opportunities came early in the day and late in the evening.

When this had been done the Mexicans came to the wagon for their breakfast. They were excited and talking rapidly to each other. Though Mother could not understand them she was alarmed. She waked Father so that he might eat and get ready for starting. When he sat up she picked up a rope and said, "Robert, hadn't you better catch up the horses?" She added some suggestions because she feared an attack. She asked him to rope our fastest race mare for Will, and to take the next most fleet one for himself. She added that she hoped he would keep the herd close to the wagons.

Father peered through the fog and said to Will, "If the Apaches attack, turn the cattle loose and you and the Mexicans make a run for the wagons where we can fort up and fight. Remember that if we lose the cattle we have many more in Texas, and that one life is worth more than all the cattle in New Mexico."

Mother knew that Father was a fighter and feared he would risk his life for the herd, thereby leaving the train at the mercy of the Apaches. He listened to her and then jokingly called, "Listen, Will! You have a brave mother. She has it all arranged for us to run, for she doesn't want us to fight."

As she finished speaking the Indians struck with the suddenness of lightning. They had been able to get very close because the fog limited visibility to about thirty feet. Father heard the terrible war whoop as he was pulling on a boot. Quickly drawing on the other he shouted, "Great God! They're here!" He grabbed his gun and shouted to the Bridges' outfit to turn their wagon over and use it for a breastwork. This they were unable to do because it weighed more than a ton. Later he admitted that he suspected they would have abandoned their cattle to the Indians rather than risk their lives. Father said that he had not only to protect his family but to save his animals for their future support.

Charlie Thomas and Joe Bridges of the other train, standing by the wagon, permitted the Apache leader, José La Paz, to come close enough to fire two shots from a pistol, one of which went between them. Then both started running toward our wagons. Lace Bridges told us later that he thought of his suit in which he had been married, and which was in his trunk in the wagon, and that he would not abandon it. His wife had died, and that possibly influenced his decision. Strangely, he was not injured.

Father went to the aid of those left in the other camp and helped turn the wagons over for a barricade. In the excitement, the owners threw their guns into the vehicles, and when the wagons were upset the weapons were covered with bedding.

After driving off many of the cattle and horses the Apaches continued to circle at a distance but made no further attack, so we could regroup.

Some amusing things had occurred: A Dutchman with the Bridges' outfit had a fine horse which he hobbled each night as a precaution against its being stolen. When the attack began he ran to his mount, loosed him, and started him down the trail. He said to his companion, "I'll bet no Apache catches that horse!" The fog was beginning to lift and they could see the animal stop, and the Indians catch him.

In our group there was much concern about the sheep Mother had brought with us. The animals were pets and their loss would have been distressing to us. I remember seeing old La Paz, a brilliant red blanket flapping from his shoulders, ride toward the little huddled bunch to start them down the trail. As the frightened animals started Mother gave the familiar call, "Lamby! Lamby!" To them it meant salt, and they turned and ran back to her. La Paz followed close enough to shoot and break the leg of his horse. Later we learned that the Apaches got the animal to his hide-out, but that the Indians were unable to save its life.

During the fight some of the horses of the Bridges' party —

five, I believe — were cut off and ran toward our wagons. Mother wanted to go after them, but Father would not let her try it. She said, "I'm not afraid; I have a gun." She did, a shotgun which she had loaded. Disregarding Father's orders she ran, headed the horses, and got them back safely. Upon examining the weapon Father found that in her excitement she had put both charges of buckshot into one barrel and all of the powder into the other. She had used only one cap and got it in the barrel loaded with buckshot.

Taking inventory, Father found he had one yoke of oxen left, but had been robbed of all his horses and all but about 300 head of cattle. The Bridges' had lost all their cattle except their oxen. Both trains were in desperate straits in the midst of hostile country — very little ammunition, no food except beef, and had difficulty starting the wagons with the remaining oxen and horses.

Before we attempted it, Father started a horseman to Fort Stanton who undertook to make his way to the Hondo. Reaching our home there required weeks of hard work and constant vigilance. Twenty-five days had elapsed when the attack was reported at the Fort. The soldiers were unable to get out until months had passed. Not until April did a detachment reach the site of our camp on Black River. It, as well as the Apache camp, was easily identified. The Indians had stopped four miles above the trail. The stolen cattle had been driven up Dark Canyon into the Guadalupes, which seemed to be the favorite retreat for the Indians.

Some of our cattle were found in an almost inaccessible canyon, later called the McKittrick because of its Anglo discoverer, Felix McKittrick, who camped at the famous spring and for years made it his headquarters. The soldiers found fifteen tepees had been pitched near the water and later abandoned, so they burned them and continued searching for our cattle. No more were found and the cavalry believed the rest had been killed and the meat jerked for future use.

Jesús Sandoval, an old guide employed by the military, had led the soldiers to Black River. He told Father that a large number of cattle had been carried off by being driven off the trail the cavalry had followed, and that the soldiers did not wish to separate in order to follow both. This side trail, he said, "was just like a wagon road and wide enough and smooth enough that a government freight wagon could have been driven over it."

5

The Casey Mill on the Hondo

FATHER'S PROBLEM now was how to proceed to the ranch with the one yoke of oxen. The only feasible idea was to use, if possible, some of the unbroken steers, yearlings, and two-year-olds. It was no easy job to convert these raw, untamed steers into patient, docile substitutes for the well-broken oxen we had lost. Father and the men roped them, threw them, then hogtied them until the yokes could be put on their necks. Even then it was uncertain whether they would work to the wagon. As one yoke of such young calves was not strong enough to draw as much as a single yoke of full-grown oxen, it was necessary to have about four yoke for our big wagon. One team he named Grant and Sherman.

Another problem was what to do with the Bridges' wagon. It seemed best to tie it behind ours as a trail wagon, but doing that would increase the load our young steers had to pull; and it still remained doubtful that they could move the vehicles. Father tried to insure the safety of the wagons and their contents by putting the gentle yoke of steers at the wheel — on the tongue of the wagon — and the other yokes in the lead. Even when this was done Father did not feel that it was safe for the children to get into the wagon, for there was a probability that the unbroken young animals might turn it over. So we walked, small though we were. By then I was six, Tricks (Ellen) four, Johnny two, and Add, though older, handicapped by his crippled leg. But we set out even though Johnny had to be carried. The men walked by the steers, doing all they could to get the unruly animals quieted down and settled to their new task of drawing the wagons. Our herd, or rather the remnant of it, was kept closely in front of the wagon so that the hitched steers would be induced to follow the herd and travel with it.

In this fashion we started, for Father felt that we must not remain at Black River another night. When we had gone several miles Father had sufficient confidence in the young steers that he put the children in the second wagon. This he considered safer than the first one, and we were overjoyed at being relieved of the difficult and tiring walking. I well remember how tired I was from trudging those long miles. That first day we managed to go at least ten miles before making what was called a "dry camp" — one in which no fires were built.

The next morning we discovered that we had left one of the ox chains at Black River and also one of our skillets. We were badly in need of both and sent back two of the Mexicans; they returned without the articles and reported that they had seen Indians circling about our campsite. Whether or not their report was true we never knew. We proceeded to put as many miles as possible between us and the danger the next day.

We realized well that we had before us a long stretch to the next settlement, Missouri Bottom [Plaza], on the Rio Hondo. We knew also that in our crippled condition the journey would be much longer than ordinary. We went on for seventeen days with our food supply short, facing the possibility of hunger. We had eaten our last bread the morning of the attack by the Indians, and we had no more until we got close to Missouri Bottom. During this interval we met an outfit returning to Texas after having driven a herd somewhere westward — Arizona, I believe. At sight of them our hopes of securing additional provisions rose but when Father tried to buy some breadstuff they were unwilling to sell even a small amount for fear they might run short. Not even for the children would the owner consent to sell, but his cook had a kinder heart. He gave Mother one of the big loaves of bread such as was baked in Dutch ovens and she husbanded it for several days, giving us just a small piece with our meals. She did not touch it herself, nor did Father.

When we got near Missouri Bottom, Father decided to send a

Mexican ahead to get some breadstuff, but when he came back all he brought was corn meal. Although it was late Mother immediately cooked several skillets of corn bread, enough for each person to have all he could eat. Never in all my life had bread tasted as delicious as that, even though it was made with water and soda and cooked in a Dutch oven.

Father thought it best to stop and rest at Missouri Bottom for a week or so before proceeding. As this old settlement — one of the oldest in the Pecos Valley — has been obliterated by time, I think it should be described.

The village was simply a cluster of angular, flat-topped adobe houses scattered along the Hondo, a crooked road serving as the main street. There was, I think, but one store, a general one, carrying supplies of dry goods, groceries, hardware, and whiskey. It was run by Colonel Buster and Major Voce, Confederate officers who were refugees in the area after the close of the Civil War. Their clerk was Frank Reicken [Reagan?] who will be mentioned later. In the community were two other American families, those of Heiskell Jones and a man named Scran about whom I know little. There was also a Frenchman, Lalone, who had married a Spanish-American woman, and John Newcomb, who also had a Mexican wife. The rest of the community was composed of Mexicans.

Everything was primitive and crude. The people had a few goats and a few yoke of oxen; some were rich enough to own a cow or horse. The stock was put in a village herd and one or two boys were set to look after them as they grazed on the luxuriant gramma grass that surrounded the town. One of the chief duties of the herders was to see that none of the animals strayed far enough away to become the prey of lurking Indians. Adjoining the town were small fields in which a few necessary crops were raised, being cultivated mainly with old, wooden-beam plows pulled by oxen. In some cases, however, the owners of the little plots had not risen above cultivating them with forked sticks used as plows.

The people were Mexican in dress. I remember how astonished I was at seeing all the native women going about with *rebosos* [shawls], draped over their heads so as to leave but one eye visible. Until that time I had seen only one Mexican woman, Sarah, and she had been in Texas so long she had discarded Mexican head covering and wore a bonnet like the Anglos. My childish reaction was to think that the Mexican women had but one eye.

Very fertile soil accounted for the existence of Missouri Bottom. In those days the Hondo was a good-sized stream so full of water that it rose almost to the top of the banks. This made irrigating easy and the crops grown on the fields surrounding Missouri Bottom were as fine as anyone could wish. What business activity the town had came through the herders who drove their cattle through on their way west, and from the few American farmers scattered over the country.

During the first part of our stay at Missouri Bottom we enjoyed the hospitality of the Heiskell Juneses, who were friends of Father's, but after a few days, Father decided to take us a mile or so further to where another American family, the Hollands, lived. This family, I believe, later moved to Texas. They had been driving cattle into New Mexico to sell and had planned returning; now that their cattle had been taken by the Indians, they went back. They had their wagon, a yoke of steers, and five horses which they traded for enough of an outfit and provisions to enable them to make the return trip. They probably joined another outfit returning to Texas, and threw in with them for mutual protection, for I doubt that they would have undertaken the trip alone.

Father had cherished the ambition of settling in New Mexico and was undaunted by the disasters and discouragements he had encountered, so he was eager to get on to the ranch. He employed brothers, Felipe and José Miranda, to take us there. The Mirandas ran a freight wagon between Missouri Bottom and the little town of La Placita (later called Lincoln) which was some fifty miles farther up the Río Bonito. Felipe Miranda brought down a large load of freight for the Buster and Voce store, and was glad to take advantage of Father's offer of pay for taking us and our few belongings to our new home.

I remember that his wagon was much larger than ours, and when Mother and we children got into it, it seemed much warmer and more cozy than ours had been. The trouble with our wagon was that it had been overloaded; consequently we were perched above the bed of it where we felt the wind and cold. Mother discarded what she did not need badly and took her bedding, consisting largely of blankets she had woven.

Felipe's wagon bed was so high, and the big sheet top tied down so well that the children could satisfy their curiosity about the outside only by peeping through the cracks. The road wound through a narrow canyon between hills rocky and devoid of trees. Every few miles, it seemed, the road crossed the Hondo.

As Felipe had an extra yoke of oxen, Father arranged to have them hitched to our wagon and take it up for us. This made it possible for Father to turn back into the herd the raw steers he had used in getting our wagon up from Black River to Missouri Bottom. Father and the Mexicans came along with our wagon and cattle. The road we took made the 40-mile journey in three days, the gentle oxen of Felipe Miranda allowing us to travel in comparative comfort. In all that distance there was no settlement, not even a house. When Father had come out with the herd of cattle owned by the other men, he had taken them up into the country around what is at present the town of Picacho. The ranch he bought from Chene had been first settled on about 1855 by another Frenchman, Lalone, whom I have mentioned as living at Missouri Bottom, and sold by him to Chene.

As the deed indicates, all that Father bought from Chene was the improvements, together with the right of peaceable possession. This was all that could be conveyed in those days in a land purchase, for no government survey had been made in that part of the country; consequently there was no such thing as patented land. At the same time Father purchased a ditch and some improvements on the south side of the Hondo, which had been made by Charles Blanchard, a brother-in-law of Chene. Chene claimed the right to sell these, and there is on record another deed executed by him conveying them to Father.

The grist mill mentioned in the deed was a most important factor in Father's selection of the place. He was long-headed enough to see the business possibilities in the ownership of it and, at the same time, it satisfied his mechanical turn to be in charge of the machinery of a mill. The building itself was two stories high, about a hundred feet long, and perhaps forty wide. It was made of adobe, and as the adobes used in it were much larger than usual — about eighteen inches wide and two feet long — the building was very strong and substantial, strong enough to withstand Indian attacks. The portholes in the walls were evidence of the intention. On more than one occasion in subsequent years we ourselves had to "fort up" inside those strong old walls of the old mill, when Indians were bad.

Because of the danger from Indian attacks, no one ever thought of putting into a building any more doors and windows than were absolutely necessary; so this mill had only one door in the front, and but two windows, one on each side.

An unusual feature of the building was the roof. Nearly all roofs in that part of the country were flat ones made of dirt, but our mill had somehow come to have a roof made of wide planks laid side by side and sloping to the ridgepole. In a country where lumber was as scarce as it was then, it was strange to find such a roof. The planks must have been brought from as far away as Las Vegas, for I do not think there was at that time any saw mill nearer.* The mill, located on the top of a small elevation, was the most conspicuous building on the Casey ranch.

On the east side of the mill was a large irrigation ditch, or *acequia*. Thirty yards north of the mill was a two-room adobe dwelling which became our home for the time being. The rooms were about fourteen by sixteen with dirt floors, and the roof was the usual flat dirt one. To procure logs strong enough to support the roof without sagging, it was necessary to go into the mountains and bring down pine logs large enough to extend from one wall to another, and small enough ones to lay across these larger ones. Then a lot of branches would be cut from the many willows growing on the banks of the Hondo, and the pine poles covered with these. Next, over all this was laid a thick layer of wheat straw and mud. When this had dried, a large amount of dry soil — clay was regarded as best — was spread over the top, and the roof was complete. It was protection enough in wet weather, and thick enough to afford insulation from the hot rays of the sun.

Near the house was a large irrigation ditch, and on the other side of this was a small adobe where the renter usually lived. Close to this was a log corral for cattle, and about five hundred yards below the corral was a dugout, or *chosa* as the Mexicans term it; and across the river was another little one-room adobe. Both of these were generally occupied by some of our Mexican renters.

All over the ranch were ditches for irrigation. On each side of the river ran two large "mother" ditches about three feet deep,

---

*There was a mill on the Tularosa River, later bought by Dr. Joseph C. Blazer.

with a top width of about nine feet, sloping to a bottom width of six feet, thus preventing the dirt from caving in. Each of these ditches had its dam in the Hondo to divert the water from the river into it. The north ditch being the older, had its point of diversion higher up than the later one.

We found a considerable part of our land already broken up and under cultivation. When Father bought the ranch, he had equipped it with plows, hoes, reap hooks, scythes, and the like, and had left it in charge of Ignacio Padillo, who had added, in Father's absence, to the amount of land under cultivation. It had taken Father nearly a year after he arranged for the purchase of the ranch to bring his family.

There were few trees on the place, but we had brought some pecans with us and planted them soon after our arrival. In a few years they gave us a nice grove, although some foolish boy who was working for us once cut down a good many of them before Mother discovered what he was doing.

Such was Casey's ranch when we reached it — unpretentious, but it really meant home to us. We lost no time in bestowing ourselves and our belongings as best we could. Mother put her equipment into the room that was to serve as kitchen, and the other became Father's and Mother's bedroom. Tricks and I slept in this room on a trundle bed. My two older brothers, Will and Add, slept in the mill with the men. We found ourselves a part of the frontier in an even more definitive sense than we had been when living in Texas, for life in New Mexico was fraught with more danger from Indians and lawlessness than our old home had been.

6

Pioneer Activities and Makeshifts

MY FIRST IMPRESSION of New Mexico was that it was a foreign land. There was a marked difference in the manners and customs of the natives at Missouri Bottom from those we had known in Texas. I noticed especially the difference in the manner of carrying weights on their heads. All houses were usually some distance from the river, the main source of water supply, because Indians might hide in the timber bordering the streams. During spring and summer irrigation, water for domestic use was taken from the *acequias* one of which was close to the houses. In the fall and winter when the ditches were empty, water had to be carried from the stream. By that time there were few leaves on the trees, consequently less danger to those carrying water. And it was the women to whom this task fell.

The Mexicans had few buckets; instead, they used earthen jugs, *ollas,* which held from three to five gallons. A woman could take one of these on her head, and with a bucket in each hand, go to the river and fill all with water. Then she put the full olla on her head, picked up both buckets of water, and walked to her home, perhaps a half mile away. During that proceeding she could carry the load without setting down a bucket. The secret of this was her skill in balancing the olla by use of a twisted ring of grass or reed which she placed on her head to support the jug. I practiced attempting to stand with a small jar of water on my head but never mastered the art.

Their manner of washing, too, was strange. Few had soap, and to me that was surprising for in Texas everybody made quantities of it from fat treated with lye. The Mexican women found an excellent substitute for soap by use of the roots of the *amole,* or Spanish dagger. They laid the roots on a flat rock and pounded them with a smaller one until the tubers gave up a liquid much like soap. This made a fine lather and was exceptionally good for bathing and washing either clothing or hair. It seemed to bleach cloth and intensify color in dyed fabrics.

Washboards, too, were unknown; flat paddles were substituted for their use. Clothes were soaked in the amole juice, laid upon a flat stone, beaten with the paddle then dipped into the stream. This process was repeated until they were clean enough for rinsing in the river.

Both clotheslines and clothespins being unknown, laundry was laid on the bushes. For an ironing board, Mexican women spread blankets on the earthen floor, and, squatting beside the piece to be ironed, used an old-fashioned flatiron which had been heated over coals in the fireplace. Impossible though it may seem, a Mexican woman could iron a fine white shirt with a pleated bosom beautifully, and she took great pride in her skill.

I found their methods of cooking strange until I became accustomed to it. We had brought a small iron cookstove from Texas, and so far as I know it was the only one, except possibly at Fort Stanton, in the whole country. Mexicans cooked in a corner fireplace. For supporting cooking utensils made of clay they used a *tinamaste,* which could be triangular, circular, or square. It was a piece of flat iron, supported by legs about six inches high. Placed over the coals, the cooking pots (also called ollas) were set upon it. Ollas used for drinking water were suspended where the breeze could strike them, cooling the water by evaporation. Crude as their methods were, Mexican women were excellent cooks and their food delicious.

They preferred to simmer nearly all their meat dishes. For their savory soup they usually diced meat into bite-sized pieces to be sautéd. When well browned it was stewed slowly until almost done. Then they added onions, chili, and salt. This dish, called *cadillo,* was as appetizing a dish as I ever tasted, and it did not take me long to learn to make it.

Everybody made strong coffee — boiled, then set aside for the grains to settle.

Frijoles (beans), were cooked in an olla with a very small neck tapering from a wide vessel. The opening served to hold steam in the vessel, thereby making the pinto (spotted) beans tender. The secret of cooking frijoles lay in keeping them covered with water while simmering, and in replenishing the water with more boiling water.

Fried cabbage was a favorite dish and it was much more palatable than that cooked by boiling. Potatoes and beets were baked in an *horno* (outdoor earthen oven), and were of a flavor much superior to those boiled.

The *tortilla,* a thin cake made of corn, was a staple article of diet, and Mexican women vied with each other in their skill in making them. Corn was soaked in water, into which a small amount of lime was placed, and then boiled. That softened the grain until it could easily be ground to a fine paste on a stone called a *metate.* A *mano,* a smaller stone, was used for crushing the grain. Kneeling behind the metate and taking the mano in her hand the Mexican woman used the latter to roll the softened corn and mash it into a dough. She took a small quantity of this *masa* between her palms and patted it until it was very thin and round, with a diameter of from six to eight inches. She cooked it on a heavy piece of iron called a *comal.* The tortilla was made without any leavening agent or fat, and was very wholesome. Even today I prefer tortillas to any other kind of bread.

Tools and implements used in raising crops were also of the crudest type. Plows were made of wood with iron points for the shares. Hoes and spades were of cast iron. Vehicles in common use in farming and hauling were called *carretas,* and were a rude form of cart, usually equipped with only two wheels. I remember very well the first I ever saw. It was driven by Indians from Isleta, who came through the valley of the Hondo peddling apples and grapes they had raised. They stopped the oxen in front of our house, and in pantomime indicated that they wished to exchange their product for some of our wheat, corn, and frijoles. To our great delight Mother traded with them. There was no fruit in our area and those little shriveled apples tasted delicious to us. They were the first we'd ever seen.

We speedily imitated the Mexican methods of farming. Father rented land to the natives for half the crop. He had so few tools that he was glad to have them make some of their devices. Harvesting and threshing wheat was a major problem, and the Mexicans taught us methods used, I think, in Bible times. When we first came Father and the boys cut the wheat either with a scythe or what was called a reap hook; later they bought cradles. For threshing the grain the first necessity was a threshing floor. A circular piece of ground was leveled and a mortar made of mud, straw, and water spread upon it. To harden the mortar, sheep or goats were put upon it and made to trample it down compactly. When the floor was ready, wheat was hauled to it and scattered over it. Goats were turned in and made to run around by men standing at the edges for the double purpose of keeping the animals on the floor and keeping them moving. When the grain had been tramped from the straw the goats were driven off and the wheat turned. Again the trampling process began and was continued until the grain was separated from the stalks.

In the next process the wheat was thrown with pitchforks against the wind so that the straw might be blown away. The grain fell and "winding" was repeated until the grain was free from straw. With long-handled shovels the grain was again tossed into the air until free from dirt. If one were very particular as to cleanliness, it was washed and spread on canvas to dry.

Corn was handled a bit differently. Our land was well adapted to its growth and we produced big crops of it. Every grain was plowed into the earth with steers, and though we did not use wooden plows as did our Mexican friends, we were little better equipped than they. Though we, as did everybody else, had some tools for sharpening implements, it was impossible to keep them in good condition. Corn was cultivated with heavy iron hoes, very dissimilar to those in use today. Methods for gathering corn were primitive. For hauling corn from the fields, the carreta was again used. This is a small two-wheeled cart, the wheels being made of cross sections of logs with the centers burned out to carry the axle. With nothing for lubrication but leaves of the prickly pear, this refinement was used only when there was danger of friction charring the wheels, as on long journeys. For short trips the screeching of dry wheels could be heard great distances. For shelling it a *serenda* was used. This was made by taking four poles, preferably walnut saplings because they did not break easily, and using them to form the supports of a platform. Thin poles were laid along the four sides and rawhide straps woven to form a network with small openings. When the serenda had dried it was taken to a pile of ears of corn and placed upon forked sticks to fasten it about three feet above the ground. The ears of corn were thrown upon it and beaten with sticks or clubs until the grains were detached from the cobs, and fell upon a piece of canvas laid under the device. Corn was winded much as wheat was, a shovel being used for tossing it.

Though Father was a cowman he loved farming and was ambitious to produce crops and vegetables. Each year he got seed from the store of a post trader at Fort Stanton, and especially of those vegetables he had not previously raised. Mother, too, loved gardening, but was more practical than he. What she wanted was to raise root crops that could be buried and kept during the winter for cooking. Because of the very good soil in a bend of the river about a mile from the house, they planted a garden there. When the garden needed cultivating she took my brother, Will, about eleven at that time, and spent the day in the garden. She took a lunch and left me at the house with the other children. Johnnie, the baby, was small and I had the care of him in her absence. Though Add was older, it was I who took the responsibility for the rest.

Mother always took the Spencer, and Will carried the hoe, lunch, and a bucket for drinking water.

The garden produced great quantities of vegetables and when we had more than we needed for ourselves, Father found a ready market at Fort Stanton for the surplus. Though some of the officers had gardens planted in good soil with plenty of water from the Bonito, they never seemed to raise enough vegetables to supply their own needs.

There was also a ready demand for great quantities of butter and cheese at the store, and Mother supplied the post trader with what we did not use.

The mill, however, provided most of the income for the family. It was built on the brow of a small hill in which a deep hole had been made for the overshot water wheel which furnished the power. Water was brought down through a ditch, then through the millrace where it fell into what were called the buckets of the wheel. Connected to the water wheel was another called the drum wheel; about twenty feet above the latter and connected to it by a leather belt was another called the pulley wheel. The latter in turn was connected with a small iron wheel that was geared into the burrs. The burrs were the most important factor of the mill because it was they that ground the grain. Ours were French burrs made of flint, and when they wore smooth from grinding, were "picked"; that is, sharpened by hand. That was a tedious process and a painful one, also, for we had to be very careful, working in gloves and trying to prevent bits flying and stinging our skin.

Fascinating to the children of the family was the cataract of water falling over the rocks when the mill was not in operation and the head gate in the millrace closed, turning the stream away from the wheel. It was a great source of entertainment during warm weather. Though we had no bathing suits we were not concerned, for we did not know that such garments were in existence. We substituted old clothes and enjoyed the water as much as anyone could. Regardless of danger, we loved getting inside the wheel, and then, as it slowly turned, walking up it until the force of gravity sent us tumbling to the bottom as the wheel went around. Sometimes Mother added to the excitement by slipping to the head gate and opening it slightly. This sent a little water into the wheel and caused it to revolve more rapidly, but this only added to our enjoyment.

We knew, of course, that the mill did not exist for our amusement but that it afforded our main source of income, and we valued it accordingly. So far as I knew, nobody, not even a small child, could ignore the importance of making a living.

Though the pioneers had their faults and weaknesses, few could shirk work or indulge in idleness. In a very literal sense work was a life preserver, and every member of a family had his tasks. Not one had Rip Van Winkle's "insuperable aversion to all kinds of profitable labor."

Business required that Father be away much of the time. Because I was the strongest and healthiest of the children it became my obligation to do much of the riding and caring for cattle that ordinarily would have evolved upon my older brothers. Neither failed to do all he could, but I realized in later years that it was I upon whom my parents depended. I did not resent that but was proud of my ability to ride, rope, brand, and perform the various functions of a cowboy.

While Father was away in Texas, acquiring a herd to replace that lost in the Apache attack at Black River, and upon many other occasions when he was gone for weeks, I did much of the herding. When Father was there he was busy inspecting and supervising the cultivation and the mill work, so I continued to herd cattle as I did in his absence. In addition to the mill he had a carpenter shop and a blacksmith shop in which the work needed at home was done; but his employees also did much of the repairs for the neighbors, and were a small source of income. At times he employed men to work cattle, but much of the time I did the most of it, aided by my brothers when they could.

The farming was done primarily by renters. The difference between these and his "hired men" was that the latter were paid only wages, but the former were furnished chosas and received a percentage of the proceeds of the crops they raised.

Mother's household and its care was a big undertaking. She did the cooking and sewing for the family; she raised a garden; she made butter and cheese; she raised chickens; in Father's absence she supervised the operation of the mill and most difficult of all, she reared six children ranging in ages from eleven to one year. Any one of these activities would have been a full-time job for a woman of today, and how she ever accomplished what she did is still a mystery to me.

For clothing she had brought from Texas a bolt of cloth — good, sturdy, long-wearing homespun — so she did no more weaving, for when this bolt was exhausted she bought from the store what was required for clothing the family. That necessitated cutting and stitching, and fortunately she had a sewing machine. She also did much knitting. I cannot recall having seen my mother sit down without some kind of work in her hands. The mending, which was always needed, occupied much of what she called spare time. Of course, she was seldom in bed after four in the morning; and seldom quit before ten at night. And she did this day after day, year after year, with seldom a break from the routine.

When Will took over the care of the sheep, Add and I continued to herd cattle. After we had driven them into the corral in the evening we each had definite tasks to perform with the chores.

The cattle were determined to invade the fields, and preventing their destroying the crops was a major operation. Sheep gave little trouble in that respect for they were content to graze on the lush grass about the place. But cattle! They were a constant menace, and required constant care during the day.

For years there was always a baby in the home whose care was my evening work. I loved my little brothers and sisters but at times resented the responsibility for them. Ellen was supposed to help with this, but she was not strong, and seldom did much to assist me.

Another of my tasks was the care of the seed for planting. We bought little except that of new vegetables that Father wanted to try. We collected seed from the garden, put it into little sacks, labelled them, and for protection against mice, suspended them from rafters in the mill.

We even helped in the mill, holding the sacks while the ends were whipped tightly together. The meal and flour were put into sacks made of *manta* (cloth woven by the Mexicans) much like unbleached muslin. One end and the edges were stitched, but the open end into which the ground product was put was sewn by hand. And that was a tedious job. At times the mill was in operation day and night, which meant that the filling and closing of sacks was also a twenty-four-hour-a-day task. And though a man did the sewing, the children took turns holding the sacks for him.

I can still hear Mother call after supper, "Come, children, get your books and study your lessons." That was after we had fed the chickens and cooped each brood in its home; had fed the hogs; had carried in the night's supply of water, cobs, wood, and chips; had helped with the evening meal and the dishwashing; had washed crocks in which the milk was strained; and had put the younger children to bed. Then we studied.

Because there was no priest closer than Manzano, we went to church only when he made his semiannual trips to the country. On Sundays we worked only until the noon meal had been eaten and the dishes washed. After that we bathed in the river in summer, and in a wash tub in the kitchen in winter. Then we saddled up, and dressed in clean clothing, rode to visit either the Fritz or Chávez children and ran horse races.

7

Early Settlers: Upper Lincoln County

IN ORDER TO GIVE a general impression of the people living in Lincoln County when we settled in it, I shall try in this chapter to speak of those who were there at that time or who came in shortly afterwards. The location of our ranch was so central that we easily became acquainted with everyone whether a permanent resident or a mere passer-through. We were on the route taken by those who drive cattle from Texas to Arizona, and the trail men of these outfits always stopped at our place. Until about 1873, there was not an American settlement — not even a cow camp on the Pecos River — and the only settlement to the west of the river was the Mexican town of Missouri Bottom. Forty miles further to the west was our ranch and mill, and it is no wonder travelers were glad to stop awhile and become acquainted. It was necessary for them to have meals and lodging, and we were glad to let them have what they needed, with no charge made for man or beast.

Until about 1855, this whole southeastern section of New Mexico that afterwards became Lincoln County was altogether in the hands of the Indians, no Mexicans having come in. But in that year, according to Roman Aragón, who is unquestionably one of the oldest settlers as well as one of the oldest inhabitants, for he reckons his age at 97 years,* he and some others from Old Mexico

---

*Keep in mind, Mrs. Klasner was writing this in the 1920s.

came into this part of the country on a buffalo hunt, and liking the appearance of the land, water, and climate, went back to their homes with the idea of inducing a colony of their relatives and friends to move out. About the same time some Mexicans living up in the Manzano country decided to come into this section, and so from these two sources — the El Paso del Norte on the south, and the Manzano section on the north — there came in enough Mexicans to establish small settlements at La Placita (later Lincoln), La Placita de Missouri (Missouri Bottom), San Patricio, Ruidoso, and Tularosa.

The Indians at that time were friendly and did not molest the Mexican settlers in any way except by pilfering occasionally, but by 1865 the Indians had changed their attitude toward newcomers. The story of how this change came about is an interesting one, and I shall give it as I got it from Old Man Clene, who was one of the first Americans to settle in this section. With Clene were two other men, Dick Ewing, and another whose name I do not recall. This third man became sick and died, without his partners' knowing the exact nature of the disease he died of. Not wanting to keep his bedding, Old Man Clene and Dick Ewing traded it to some Indians; and soon afterwards the Indians who got it developed very bad cases of smallpox. In a short time the disease had spread widely among the Indians.

The Indians with their strong superstitions, put the blame for the smallpox on the newcomers. They believed that somehow these new citizens had used witchcraft, and with an Indian, once such a conclusion was reached, the inevitable sequel is retaliation. Soon they were stealing horses and cattle from the Mexicans and Americans, and making trouble generally. But in spite of this there were new settlers brave enough to come, and the population slowly but steadily increased.

I do not know just exactly who were the first Americans to come into the country or why they happened to come, but I think they began to come in about 1865 or 1866. Some, I suppose, were of the restless, westward-pushing type who simply wandered further and further from civilization until they found a place such as Socorro County.*

---

*At that time Lincoln County had not been organized and this section was part of Socorro County.

There they took up their abodes. Others I know were discharged soldiers who became acquainted with the section during the Civil War, being stationed at Fort Stanton. The Fort had been burned in 1861 by the soldiers stationed there in order to keep it from falling into the hands of the Confederates, but about 1865 the Government decided to rebuild it because soldiers were needed in the Mescalero Apache country.

Adobe buildings were put up to serve as barracks, and in 1873 Captain Randlett ordered an irrigation ditch dug for watering gardens. It would be altogether impossible to mention the early settlers in anything like the order in which they came on the scene. I shall, however, try to present them according to the locations in which they lived. Elevation of the land steadily increased as one went from the Pecos Valley to Lincoln and other places in the mountains, so old timers always spoke of going "up" to Lincoln and "down" to Seven Rivers and other points on the Pecos. In this way "up" and "down" came to denote the two divisions of the county, and I shall make this the basis of my division of the early settlers.

In 1868, Lincoln was not known as Lincoln, but was called simply La Placita (the village). It was not then the county seat, because all the southeastern part of the Territory was Socorro County and the county seat was at the town of Socorro. When Lincoln County was established in 1869, La Placita became Lincoln.

I distinctly remember my first visit to La Placita. One day in 1868 Father announced that he was going there the next day for a meeting of the citizens of that section on some matter of business, and he offered to take Mother and the children along. Of course we were eager for the excursion, and started our preparations. The original plan was to devote simply a day to the trip and to return home by bedtime. But we were longer in getting there than we had expected — the roads were very rough and some of the hills were so steep a climb for even a good team such as ours that drawing a wagon with nine passengers was difficult, and we did not reach La Placita until late in the day. On the trip we saw an Indian hidden between rocks. Father reached for his pistol, but the Indian did not let himself be seen again. The business that Father had to attend consumed more time than he anticipated so by the time we could start home he felt it was too late, and the best thing was for us to stay the night there. Alec Duval had a sort of hotel in connection with the

La Placita branch of L.G. Murphy & Co.'s store, and we took accommodations there for the night. We children did not object to the continuation of our visit, for it gave us time to ramble around and see something of the town.

Scattered along the two sides of a crooked stretch of road were twelve or fifteen houses which might be credited with a certain degree of pretension. They were adobe, flat-roofed, angular in shape, and one story in height. In the rear of the houses fronting on the street were a number of *jacals,* that is, houses of a simpler type made by standing up cedar or juniper posts and daubing them together into walls by applying mud. Both sorts of houses were plastered on the outside with mud and whitewashed inside with a gyp [gypsum] solution, called by the Mexicans *jaspe.*

The population of the town was predominantly Mexican, most of them getting their livelihood by farming tracts of land up and down the valley of the Bonito which flows by the edge of the town and furnishes abundant water for irrigation. The business section of La Placita consisted of a few stores. José Montana had a store and saloon, and Jacinto Sánchez a store in which Antonio Aván Sedillo worked. Captain Saturnino Baca, who later became one of the conspicuous citizens, had not then moved to the town, but was living some miles to the west in the vicinity of the old Antonio Torres place. Mariano Trujillo was the most prominent citizen of the village; he was what the Mexicans call *jefe,* or big man.

There is a story of his burial that is worth recording. When he was about to die, he asked to be buried under a large rock on the outskirts of the town, for fear the Indians might molest his body. Trujillo told his friends that if they did not fulfill his request he would come back and haunt them, and such a threat was sufficient to insure full respect of his wish. When the old fellow had paid his debt to nature, his friends dug his grave as nearly under the rock as possible, and after putting his body in it and refilling it with the earth, they hitched fourteen yoke of oxen to the stone and with the aid of leverage from long logs, they turned the stone over on top of the grave. This rock, which was supposed to be a meteorite, is still to be seen in the disused old graveyard at Lincoln.

Gradually the town began to receive American accessions, and when it became the county seat more and more Americans began to filter in. Alec Duval ran a saloon which was also a branch of the

L.G. Murphy & Co.'s store. Pete Bishop, a large, bald-headed old man, ran a regular saloon in the town; that is, his place was exclusively for the dispensing of alcoholic liquors. The Boltons might rightfully claim to be the first American family to move into the town. Up to that time the few Americans coming in had been men who at the time of their coming had no families, but who afterwards acquired them by marrying native women.

John Bolton had served as quartermaster's clerk at Fort Sumner when the Navajo and Apache Indians were kept on the reservation at the Bosque Redondo, but was transferred to Fort Stanton when Fort Sumner was abandoned by the Government. He soon brought to the Fort his wife and three children — a son, Johnny, and two daughters, Amelia (afterwards Mrs. J. P. Church) and Ella (afterwards, Mrs. Davidson).*

After acting as quartermaster's clerk at Fort Stanton for a few years, Mr. Bolton had to give up that position when an Army order required that all quartermasters' clerks be enlisted men. As Mr. Bolton was beyond the age limit for enlistment, he was unable to qualify under the new regulation. He then removed his family to Lincoln where Mrs. Bolton conducted a hotel (boarding house) for awhile. When in the winter of 1873 or 1874 Lincoln attained recognition enough from the Post Office Department to have a Star mail route, the mail being brought from Las Vegas, Mr. Bolton became the first postmaster.

Among the American settlers was a Jew, Philip Bowski(?) who was later county clerk. Living on a farm in the vicinity of Lincoln were two other American settlers, George Van Sickle and Henry Farmer. Also a man by the name of Calvin Dodson lived just on the west edge of town.

When I made my first visit to town, the old *torreón* (tower) was already a conspicuous landmark. It was built by the first Mexican settlers about 1855 for protection from the Indians. Old Jesús Miranda, who lived for a long time in Lincoln and whose descendants are still living in the town, always claimed that he was one of those who built the tower. The torreón was intended to be a sort of watch tower, originally two-and-a-half stories high with a *peretil,*

---

*His family had not been with him at the Bosque Redondo, but after going to Lincoln he had them make the trip from Ireland to Fort Stanton.

or parapet, on the top. A guard was stationed in it to look out for Indians, while the rest of the men were working in their fields along the Bonito. The story goes that in the lower part was kept a horse, all saddled and bridled, and if there was any indication of the approach of Indians, the watchman could ride posthaste, spreading the alarm among the men in the fields. Doubtless in the days when old Cadete (Cadette) and his band of Apaches took much delight in swooping down on the settlers in the country, the old torreón served its purpose well.

It was an epoch in the history of Lincoln when in the summer of 1873 L.G. Murphy & Co. brought their business down from Fort Stanton, where they had conducted the post trader's store and combined it with a branch they had operated in Lincoln for several years. This store became the controlling influence, both commercially and politically, and was thought to be responsible for much of the crookedness and lawlessness that reigned in Lincoln County during the next ten years.

In the Bonito Valley to the east of Lincoln there were a few American settlers. Major William Brady lived at the old Vorwick place about six miles east of Lincoln, on a site still known as Brady Hill.

Just to the east of Brady Hill, Florencio Gonzales, who was afterwards probate judge, lived in a substantial rock house. A little further to the east was a small Mexican settlement known as Las Chosas (the dugouts). José Miranda was the big man of that community and claimed virtually all of that country. The only American in the settlement was Jake Woods who had married one of the daughters of José Miranda.

About three miles further to the east was the famous Spring ranch so conspicuously associated with the Fritz family that it is sometimes known even today as the Fritz ranch. The remarkable supply of water on this place made it one of the most coveted locations in that section. Colonel Emil Fritz, while he was associated with Murphy in the post trader's store at Fort Stanton, succeeded in taking it up as a claim in about 1868 by putting it on what was called "soldiers' time." At first he and Murphy held the ranch jointly, but in 1873 or 1874 Col. Fritz bought out Murphy's interest. By that time Col. Fritz was in bad health, and longing to visit his old home in Germany before he died, he tried to get his brother,

Charlie Fritz, to come from Pennsylvania and stay on the ranch while Col. Fritz was away. The story was that Mrs. Charlie Fritz refused to come as long as Major Murphy had an interest in the ranch, as she was fearful that complications might develop. So in order to get his brother Charlie out to New Mexico, Col. Fritz got Major Murphy to sell out to him.

While Col. Fritz was still at Ft. Stanton his sister Emilie and her husband, Mr. Scholand, had come from Germany to make their home with the Colonel. For awhile Mr. Scholand clerked in the store of L. G. Murphy & Co., but he and Col. Fritz did not get along well together, and the story I always heard was that Col. Fritz drove him off. It was also said that the Colonel promised his sister that he would see to it that she and her children were always provided for if she would have nothing further to do with her husband. When the Fritz family first came to Lincoln they attempted lots of style in their mode of living. They had two cooks, a man and a woman, and drew much attention with their large, red, rockaway carriage drawn by four horses.

A few Americans had scattered themselves on the upper part of the Hondo. Ham Mills and his half-brother, Stephen Stanley, together with Jack Donaldson were living upon one of our places on the Hondo. Previously they had lived at Spring ranch. All three were Texans, said to live up to the reputation Texans had obtained. Both Ham Mills and Steve Stanley drank, and reportedly they drank exceedingly long and deep. On one such occasion they got into a dispute as to which was the better marksman with the pistol of the old cap-and-ball style, generally called a dragoon pistol. Finally they bantered each other to a test of their respective skills. Under the agreement Steve Stanley took the first shot, Ham Mills holding up his left forefinger for a target at a distance of twenty steps. Result: Ham Mills' forefinger shot off at the first joint.

Then Ham Mills took a shot, Stephen Stanley holding up the forefinger of his left hand. Result, Steve Stanley's forefinger lost at the first joint. This satisfied the two fellows that they were equally good shots. Such was the story they gave out, but whether or not it was true I am unable to say. But I am certain that both men had an incomplete forefinger on the left hand, and both swore to the veracity of the story.

On another occasion Steve Stanley proved himself a good shot.

He and Will S. Lloyd got into a fuss over something at Lincoln. Both were, of course, drunk, and soon they were ready to settle the affair by a shooting scrape which they proposed to conduct in somewhat the fashion of a duel. It was agreed they should stand back to back and then walk away until they had made the distance between them about thirty yards. At a given signal they were to wheel and shoot. Lloyd was too drunk to execute the maneuver skillfully, and so he missed his man. Steve Stanley did better, despite his being drunk, for he hit Lloyd on the hip; but Lloyd recovered.

When the sheriff, Jack Gylam, got killed in the Harrell War, Ham Mills was appointed sheriff. On a certain occasion he had a Negro under arrest, not for murder but for some crime serious enough to be called a penitentiary offense. This Negro was generally a bad fellow — what was described by the word "ornery" — and no one would have felt any regret had it happened that when the sheriff was making the arrest he had killed the Negro, a circumstance not infrequent in those days. Ham Mills had the prisoner on his hands literally, for there was no jail at Lincoln in those days and no money to pay for the keep of prisoners had there been one, for the county was broke and badly in debt. Lincoln County could redeem the script it had used only at twenty-five cents on the dollar. So Ham Mills had to keep the Negro a prisoner in a room at his own house.

The situation became more complicated by Mrs. Ham Mills, a young and pretty Mexican woman, desiring to go to a dance. It was not permissible for her husband to let her go alone; and he had to stay at home and guard a prisoner. The story told was that Ham Mills simply waited until after dark, went to the room in which he was keeping the Negro, and shot him. A few minutes later, the sheriff and his wife were on their way to the dance. The next day Mills gave out that the Negro had tried to get away and that he had been forced to shoot him in the line of duty as an officer of the law. Nothing was ever done about the matter. The people all accepted it as a good thing to get rid of a bad man, one that was hard to catch.

From the beginning the Ruidoso valley was very attractive to settlers. In the upper Ruidoso section was a family very prominent in Lincoln County affairs, the Dowlins. Paul Dowlin came in first and took charge of the post trader's store at Fort Stanton after L.G. Murphy & Co. had left. Later he was joined by his brother Will and they established a sawmill and gristmill on the Ruidoso. [It was not until several years later that grain was ground.] Will Dowlin was in charge of these, and Paul Dowlin was later killed in a shooting.

When Frank Lesnett was discharged from the Army at Fort Stanton he went to Dowlin's Mill, as the place was called, and became a sort of general manager for Will Dowlin. He afterwards bought an interest in the mill, and feeling himself settled in business, he went back to Chicago to be married, then brought his wife back with him. In addition to running two mills, Frank Lesnett kept a sort of hotel. This became a well-known stopping place for those making trips from Lincoln to Las Cruces or Mesilla.

At several points lower down in the Ruidoso valley there were American settlers, most of them married to Mexican wives. The Elijah Hughes place was one of the well-known ones in that section. Dave Warner lived about where the town of Tinnie is now. Chávez y Sánchez, who was part French and a highly respected citizen, lived on what was called Chávez Flat near the present town of Tinnie. About 1869 George Kimbrell came into the Hondo valley, living first in some caves that are there. Because of this, the Mexicans nick-named him Oso, the Bear.

At the point where the Ruidoso joins the Bonito to form the Hondo, was a community called in the early days, La Junta (the junction). Here lived Old Man Clene and Joseph Storms. The latter had won somehow the designation of Gallo, the Rooster. I suppose this came about from the old fellow liking to boast and crow over things, especially himself.

Going eastward from the junction the most important ranch on the Hondo was ours, known as Casey's Mill. In our vicinity and in houses belonging to us, lived at one time George Woods and Charlie Monroe, Jack Donaldson, Ham Mills, and Steve Stanley.

Our nearest neighbors were the Will S. Lloyds. Will had been an elderly sergeant at Fort Stanton, and after being honorably discharged, had settled in the country. Mrs. Lloyd had for many years followed her husband from army post to army post in Texas before they came to New Mexico. She displayed a considerable degree of culture and refinement, acquired no doubt from her association with the wives of the officers as maid; but if provoked it was said she could outstrip a sailor at cursing and swearing. About 1873 the Lloyd family moved from Lincoln to a place on the Pecos River that became known as Lloyd's Crossing. There Will Lloyd went broke, and the family then came back and settled about a mile from us. Their son Dick was a great friend of my brother Will. He was in reality Dick Kelly, being Mrs. Lloyd's son by a former marriage, but everybody called him by his stepfather's name. He was a good-hearted, hard-working boy about whom it was told that he would drink too much mean whiskey. He liked to go to Lincoln, get good and drunk, then race up and down the street firing his six-shooter. He always shot into the air, and never tried to hurt anyone. So far as I know, Dick Lloyd never killed anyone or stole anything. It was on one of these sprees in Lincoln that he managed to ruin a good race horse he had recently bought from Manuel Romero Kline who lived just below us. This beautiful, dark-red, bald-faced pony was the fastest in our community. Dick Lloyd wanted this horse so badly that he traded five horses to Manuel for it. After tanking up on whiskey, Dick proceeded to ride up and down the street pell-mell, lickety-split. It happened that just at that time a herd of milk cows and work oxen were being driven through the one street of the town. It was inevitable that Dick on his horse should collide with the herd, crashing into a large old brindle steer who insisted on keeping in the middle of the road. Result, both steer and horse knocked down, and Dick himself lying on the road unconscious. The steer and Dick suffered no permanent ill effects, but the horse was so badly stove up in the shoulder that he could never afterwards run.

A little later, Dick took a minor part in the early stages of the Lincoln County War. When Jesse Evans, Tom Hill, and George Davis had been arrested for stealing Tunstall's horses and placed in the jail at Lincoln, which was simply an underground cellar, Dick Lloyd was among the party of their friends that aided them to escape. I have always heard that the rescue party came up at night, tied the jailer, Maximiano DeBaca, took his keys from him, and then released the prisoners. Dick Lloyd was also with Billy Morton and Frank Baker when Dick Brewer chased them and arrested Morton and Baker. In the chase Dick's horse stumbled and fell, stunning Dick. The Brewer posse passed him up and did not try to capture him. Possibly they thought he was dead or perhaps there was no need to arrest him because he had not been in the crowd that killed Tunstall.

When I was about ten or twelve Mr. Lloyd gave me a dress. I went with the Lloyds to Fort Stanton and, since it was late when we returned, I spent the night there. Here is the story of that night as well as I can remember it. Mrs. Lloyd made a pallet for me on the floor, and as I was very tired from the trip I went to sleep immediately. Will Lloyd had drunk a great deal and after he got home he continued to do so. Mrs. Lloyd took possession of the bottle and refused to let him have more. That precipitated a family quarrel which became a fight. I was sound asleep and unaware of it until late at night I awakened to find Mrs. Lloyd on the pallet with me. Will Lloyd waked and resumed the quarrel with his wife. She continued to refuse to give him the liquor until he began to threaten her, and finally to kick her. Saying he was going to brand her on the foot if she did not get the bottle, he got a branding iron from the fireplace. She picked up a heavy whiskey glass and let fly at his head, luckily missing him by about an inch. She then called Dick and he quieted his father by giving him whiskey until he fell into a drunken stupor.

When he asked for breakfast Mrs. Lloyd refused to cook for him. He begged but she was so disgusted she continued to refuse. Mr. Lloyd turned to me and said, "Lily, she won't fix my breakfast. If you will, I'll buy you a nice dress. I want some chicken broth." I wanted the dress but was no cook. Mrs. Lloyd helped make the broth, and Will Lloyd kept his promise to me.

Later Dick Lloyd drifted into Arizona and met up with Curly Bill, a notorious leader of an outlaw band conspicuous in the early history of Tombstone. Walter Burns has given an account of this killing. Dick Lloyd came into Tombstone and got gloriously drunk. He wandered into a saloon where Curly Bill was playing poker with John Ringgo, Joe Hill, and others. Dick joined E. Mann, owner of the saloon, and drank a few times with him. But in one of those quick reversals of temper characteristic of the drunken man, Dick suddenly whipped out his pistol and threw it down on Mann. Then, without an instant's delay, he fired, the bullet cutting across the saloon-keeper's neck as the latter dodged behind the bar.

For some reason this performance did not provoke retaliation. Dick made his way across the street to his horse, mounted, fired a shot from his Winchester, flourished it above his head, and proceeded to shoot up the town. Bullets from his pistols crashed through windows and sent people scurrying to whatever protection was at hand. Dick's vagrant impulses next led him to appropriate a horse belonging to one of Curly Bill's band, Joe Hill, I believe. Mounted on the animal, Dick became inspired to ride into the saloon and break up the poker game. It seemed to be a good joke to play on Curly Bill and the others. The reception Dick got from Curly Bill's cronies was not what he anticipated. As he entered the room the players fired a fusillade from their revolvers. When the smoke had cleared, poor Dick lay sprawling on the floor, almost literally cut to pieces. I have always understood that after the interruption the game was resumed and Curly Bill remarked, "Dick didn't mean no harm, I suppose. He was just drunk and havin' a little fun. That's the reason, Joe Hill, he took your horse. He never meant to steal 'im."

8

Early Settlers: Lower Lincoln County

ONE OF THE EARLIEST FAMILIES to settle in the lower part of
Lincoln County was that of Haskell (Heiskell) Jones. When we
first came they were living at Missouri Bottom, and they continued
to reside there until the oldest boys were grown. Then the family
moved to the Ruidoso and two or three years later sold to the
Harrells. They also lived at Lincoln for a short time, but were driven
away from that town by the Harrell War. They took refuge at our
place and afterwards went to the Peñasco. They lived also at Roswell and Seven Rivers, and finally moved to Rocky Arroyo, where
the descendants of the family still live.

Mr. and Mrs. Heiskell Jones were truly pioneers of pioneers.
They moved from Iowa to Colorado about 1861, and from there
they came into New Mexico about 1865 [1866]. They located first
at Fort Stanton and later came down into the southeastern part.
Their coming made quite an addition to the census for there were
nine sons and one daughter. I can give the roll of the Jones children:
John, Jim, Bill, Minnie, Tom, Sam, Frank, Nib, Henry, and Bruce.
With such a large family on his hands it was of course impossible
in all this moving about for Heiskell Jones to accumulate much
property. Apparently the old man did not want to be burdened
with more than he could move easily. He seemed to wish to live
with the simplicity of the old pioneer who said that when he wanted
to move all he had to do was shoulder his gun, whistle to his dog,
shut the cabin door and be off.

Mr. and Mrs. Heiskell Jones raised their nine boys well. John was the only one who ever got into trouble, and that happened during the Lincoln County War. He was a fine looking fellow, tall, and without the slightest sense of fear — the type called in those days "fool-hardy brave." John was good hearted and inclined to be quiet and peaceable, and under other conditions he might have gone on through life without falling into trouble. He was, however, quick tempered and when angry was all for execution. It was this characteristic that led to his killing Bill Riley in a quarrel over land and John Beckwith over cattle.

Heiskell Jones was a good man and a good citizen. He was as honest as the days are long, and I know whereof I speak, for I knew him for fifty-odd years. In all that time I never knew him to cheat or take a mean advantage of anyone. In fact, I could not conceive of a more peaceful and law-abiding citizen than Heiskell Jones. In his case the only fly in the ointment was that all his life he was the victim of *wanderlust*. It seemed he could never settle down and stay in one place.

The community of Missouri Bottom came to an end when the Rio Hondo dried up. When I first saw the stream in 1867 it carried plenty of water. But as the settlers up toward its head drew off more and more water for irrigation, the stream diminished. I remember that in our first trip into the country, we crossed the Hondo about ten miles west of the present town of Roswell, using the only fordable crossing for wagons in a stretch of many miles. But by 1871 or 1872 the stream had become so low that those living at Missouri Bottom felt it useless to try to live there with practically no water.

They abandoned the town, some going to the Mexican settlement of Berrendo (antelope) a few miles east of where Roswell now is, and others to the Mexican settlements, El Redepente and La Boquía (Boquilla), which were farther up the Hondo where there still was a sufficient supply of water. A few of the Missouri Bottom people, the Anallas and Old John Newcomb, for example, sought locations as far west as the present town of Ruidoso.

About 1872 a group of people from Texas settled on land adjoining our claims on the east. In the party were the families of the two Rainbolt brothers, Liberty, or Lib, and Jim, and of the two Akers brothers, Amos and John. The Rainbolts bought the Francisco Romero place and the Akers what is now the Kimbrell place. Of course the expression "bought" simply meant in those days before the land had been surveyed, they merely purchased the improvements the former claimants had made as well as their right of possession. But these new neighbors of ours did not remain long; they came in the summer, made a crop, and then, having suffered from the lawlessness prevalent at the time, they returned to Texas. Later on, after things had become settled, Lib Rainbolt came back, tried White Oaks first, then San Marcial, and afterwards Roswell. It was in the latter place that he died, and his widow remained there. Amos Akers also returned and settled in Lincoln County, where in the course of time he died.

According to my best recollection, the first settlers on the Pecos were a few men who established cow camps. They generally made makeshift habitations for themselves by setting up an old A-tent or by building a chosa if enough timber could be found for making the roof, for at that time there was hardly a tree up and down the Pecos for sometimes a hundred miles. The rest of their equipment at a cow camp consisted of a wagon and ox team, a small bunch of cattle, and two or three cowboys who had drifted in from God knows where. Such were most of those early cow camps on the Pecos. The owners would stay there — you could hardly call it living — for two or three years before they would be able to hire Mexicans to come from Fort Stockton, Texas, or from Fort Sumner, New Mexico, the nearest settlements, and build them a one-room, adobe house.

The new camps began to spring up on the Pecos after the Mescaleros were made prisoners of war and put on the reservation at Fort Stanton. Before this, everybody had been afraid even to attempt to stay in the lower part of the Pecos valley for fear of Indian raids. But with that danger removed people quickly commenced to come in, because wonderful opportunities for cattle raising existed in the valley.

The first to have a cow camp there were Pearce and Paxton, partners who came about 1873 and located their camp above Pope's Crossing on the east side of the Pecos, claiming miles of river front as their ranch. They selected the east side so they would have a good lookout for Indians who always came from the west and supposedly could be seen as they crossed the river, giving the settlers time to prepare for the attack.

I remember both Pearce and Paxton well. Paxton used to stop at our house a good deal, and I have often heard him tell the story of his early life, especially that part relating to the loss of his sweetheart. He was a native of New York state and had become engaged to a girl back there. But he had formed the habit of drinking, and this girl refused to marry him unless he broke this habit. According to his account she gave him one chance after another but finally when she found he was unable to do so she told him plainly that all hope of her marrying him was at an end. Then Paxton struck out for the West, drifted down to Fort McKavett, Texas, and then into New Mexico.

When I knew him he had in some measure conquered his liking for intoxicants. I think he realized that drink was getting the better of him, and on that account went to live on the Pecos River where he was far removed from temptation except on the few occasions when he went to Lincoln. At such times the old craving reasserted itself and he went on a spree.

Milo Pearce was a different type of man. He was considered by everyone to be a dangerous man, but was not addicted to drinking. Pearce afterwards went to Roswell and entered the cattle business with Captain J. C. Lea. He married Captain Lea's sister, Mrs. Chalfee.

Following Paxton and Pearce came Jim Ramer and Joe Nash, partners in another cow camp just above Pope's Crossing, and also on the east side of the river. Then a little later came Buck Powell who worked for R. K. (generally called Bob) Wiley of Fort Worth who kept cattle down there. Yopp also worked for Wiley, although he was not a partner of Buck Powell. Dick Smith came into the Pecos about that time and met his death at the hands of Jim Highsaw. That about completes the list of the men who had cow camps — you could hardly dignify them by the names of ranches — down on the Pecos in 1873.

In the same year the town of Seven Rivers, which afterwards became notorious, got its start. Two men named Dick Reed and George Hoag seemed to have first realized that Seven Rivers, considered by all the cattle drivers as a good place to stop, would be an advantageous location for a general store, and their store became the nucleus of the town. Hoag was a single man, but Reed had a large family which included his son-in-law, Will Gray, who later, while acting as deputy sheriff, accidentally shot himself and subsequently died of his wound. In the course of a short time, two of Reed's brothers came to Seven Rivers and established themselves with their families. About 1876 Reed died of dropsy at our house, and was buried in our family graveyard. Later his partner Hoag sold out and went to Colorado.

Seven Rivers grew rapidly for a town in such a remote section. A short time later Henry L. Van Wyck, and then a little afterwards Herman Herrera (?) had a store at Seven Rivers, and others succeeded each other until there were some five or six stores.

About this time Will H. Johnson and Wallace Olinger started a cow ranch on the Pecos near Seven Rivers. Johnson's father-in-law, H. M. Beckwith, with his family settled on what was called the Beckwith ranch, one of the widely known places in the country. Old Man Beckwith was a well-educated Southerner who had come first into the northern part of the state and married into one of the *gente fina,* or best families, of the Territory. His wife was a Pino from the wealthy family of that name which still holds large ranches near Galisteo. The Beckwiths had afterwards moved toward the southern part of the state, but in a short time moved to Missouri Bottom, then when water got scarce went down into the vicinity of Seven Rivers. The present town of Lakewood is on the identical location of the old Beckwith ranch.

The Beckwith boys, John H. and Robert W., had a cow ranch near Seven Rivers on the east side of the Pecos.

Somewhat farther north from Seven Rivers, in fact about where the town of Artesia now is, a man named Blake had settled near a spring which still bears his name. About 1877, he sold to L.G. Murphy & Co., and the spring bore witness to the transfer of property by its name becoming the Murphy-Blake spring, by which designation it is known at the present time. L.G. Murphy & Co. had another camp down on the Pecos near Seven Rivers, but this one farther up they were said to operate for the express purpose of preying on the Chisum herd. It was when they acquired it that they began to use the arrow brand, a simple alteration made by adding tip and feathers to Chisum's long rail brand. The foreman at the Murphy-Blake ranch was Billy Morton, and it was near here that he was arrested by the McSween party, an account of which will appear elsewhere.

A little further north from the Murphy-Blake ranch lived an old man, by the name of Tarr. He had located by the side of a lake which was for a long time called Tarr Lake, but which was changed in later days to Lake Arthur.

When we came into the country, Roswell was practically non-existent. Some five miles south of the present site of Roswell at what later became Chisum's South Spring River ranch, there was living in a dugout a German by the name of Isenstein, who had an Irish wife. This woman was in size a whale — that is the only suitable word — and she further distinguished herself by wearing the reddest dresses she could buy. She was also perfectly fearless; nothing seemed to daunt her. Although the danger from Indians was great, if she had business to attend to at Lincoln, she simply saddled up her little bay mare, took her shotgun, and started. She generally made the 25 miles to Missouri Bottom during the first day and put up there for the night. The next day she made it up to our house and spent the second night with us. Then the next morning she continued her way to Lincoln, arriving some time on the third day. As the Isensteins were the first people to locate at South Spring River, the Mexicans called it El Ojo del Alemán, The Spring of the Dutchman. They still call it that, and even at this time they would not understand one who might speak of it as El Ojo del Sur, which would be Spanish for South Spring.

About two miles northeast of the present site of Roswell and at the head of North Spring River, lived an old man named Smith, whose habitation was a chosa. It was from him that this locality received among the Mexicans the designation El Loma del Viejo, or The Old Man's Hill. The fact that Old Man Smith's residence in that vicinity gave the title to these two spots shows how note-worthy was the presence of a single inhabitant in that otherwise unsettled land.

In the course of time Isenstein left South Spring and Old Man Smith left his place at North Spring River. It was then that a wealthy gambler and sporting man by the name of Van C. Smith and his partner, Aaron Wilburn [Wellburn] came down from Santa Fe and put up two buildings on the site of what has now become the town

of Roswell. One of these was a general store, the other a dwelling
intended to serve as a sort of hotel. Van Smith named the infant
town Roswell after his father, and got the Government to establish
a post office there. Smith and Wilburn planned to build up a town,
and they set about offering inducements to people to come and
settle. Smith's younger brother George came down and helped in
the management of the store. One A. B. Franks and his wife were
brought in to conduct the hotel, Franks acting as clerk and his wife
attending to the dining room and all the rest.

Owing to the Harrell Wars happening at this time the town
did not grow much, and Van Smith finally gave up the attempt to
develop a sort of gambler's paradise. After Smith left, Wilburn ran
the store with the help of Franks. Finally they had a falling out and
Franks shot Wilburn and wounded him so badly that he had to
be taken to Las Vegas for treatment. Then Franks disappeared
from the scene and Van Smith, who still owned the store, put F. G.
Christie in charge of it.

There were several families that came to Roswell when Van
Smith was promoting its settlement. One of these, the Teets, did
not stay long, but left for Las Vegas in order to send their daughter,
Belle, to school. A person by the name of Joe Hearn also lived at
Roswell for a time. I have good reason to remember the children
in this family, a little girl called Alice and her brother, Jack. I got
acquainted with them when they once stopped with their father and
mother at our place. What I recall most vividly about them is that
Jack, who must have been about fourteen, wrote me a letter when
he returned home and sent it out to me by one of Father's men,
Dee Sylvestre, who happened to go to Roswell with a load of corn.
The arrival of that letter was a notable event in my childish career.
I knew that grown men and women wrote letters occasionally, but
it had not entered my mind that children might do the same.

Also living at Roswell was another family of Smiths, not related
to Van. The plain and unadorned Smith who headed this family
was a blacksmith. We got to know these Smiths very well for they
often passed our place on visits to their great friends, the Ham
Mills family who lived on our section.

One of the first settlers in the Peñasco country was Charlie
Woolsey, who became famous as the man who came into the country with just an old wagon drawn by a yoke of steers, and with this

unpromising start in the cattle business was able to show at the end
of the first year an increase of seventy-five calves! Bill Riley and
W. W. Paul were also early settlers. They were partners and had
a ranch on the middle Peñasco. Frank Freeman and Billy Matthews
were another pair who settled in this section (the upper Peñasco)
at the time. Their place was near the present post office and store
known as Trail's End. As yet there were no settlers on the Lower
Peñasco.

This, I think, completes the catalogue of the American families
to the south and east of us, at least so far as permanent settlers
were concerned. Of course there were many families drifting through
the country who hardly tarried for more than a few weeks, or, at
most, a few months. These I have not tried to record.

The one who was unquestionably the foremost among early
settlers was John S. Chisum, the cattle king of the Pecos country,
whom I shall call Uncle John because he appears in these recollections under that name. I feel justified in this title, both because in
those days we usually addressed the older men of our intimate
acquaintance as "uncle" and because John S. Chisum was such a
staunch friend to our family and to me in particular during my
father's life and after his death that I have always thought of him
more as a relative than anything else.

When we came to Lincoln County, Uncle John's headquarters
was at Bosque Grande on the Pecos River some forty-five miles in
a northeasterly direction from our place. All my life I had been
hearing about John S. Chisum, for he and Father had been good
friends when both were living back in Texas. Very naturally when
I found myself in New Mexico, I had hoped that I would see this
man whose remarkable business ability as a cattle raiser and whose
powerful and attractive personality made him talked about and discussed everywhere. But it was much longer in coming about, this
visit of the great man, than I had expected. One reason was that
Uncle John's business matters took him to Fort Sumner or to
Las Vegas, in a different direction from our place.

But eventually he came. If I remember correctly it was in 1873.
He had bought a farm adjoining our place from George and Kelly
Hoag, and had come up to see about it. While he was there, he
decided to let us know that he was in our vicinity. So he sent one
of his employees over to our place with the message that he was

at the Hoag place. Father immediately rode over and brought his old friend up to our place to spend the night. As the Hoag ranch was only a mile or so away, the two walked over, Father leading the horse he had ridden down.

We children had heard the news that Father had gone to get his old friend and were so eager to see him that we awaited his arrival with our eyes popping out with curiosity.

The first to catch sight of them was Father's clerk, Abneth McCabe, who promptly came to the house and announced to Mother that they were coming. She asked, "Are you sure it is Mr. Chisum?" and McCabe, after another look, replied, "Yes, that's him." And he added out of knowledge gained from having worked for Uncle John, "I can tell his walk. Nobody else walks like him." Then when the two got close enough for us to catch the sound of their voices McCabe verified his identification by saying, "Listen to that laugh, everybody. That's him, all right enough; nobody else laughs as easily or as heartily as he does. You would think he never had a care or a sorrow in his life, but like everybody else he has them. However, it's his way to laugh them away."

To the children the coming of this man was an epochal event. In our eagerness to see all we could of him, we ran from the house and got down behind the mill, for he and Father were coming that way, and from our concealment, shyly peeped out to see what the much-talked-of man looked like. All we saw was a fairly well-dressed gentleman accompanying Father not a whit peculiar or distinguished in looks. We felt ourselves completely cheated out of our expectations and ran back to the house and inquired of McCabe, "Uncle Mac, where is he?" Uncle John, we meant. Then we added, "There is just another man with Father." Mother reassured us, saying that it was really John S. Chisum.

She laughed and told us he was not the sort of man to put on his back all he had. I am not sure just what costume we expected the cattle king to appear in; possibly something resplendent like the uniforms of the officers at Fort Stanton whom we had seen frequently at our place. But whatever may have been our expectations we did feel ourselves terribly defrauded of some ocular evidence of the greatness of the man who had come to be our guest.

When Uncle John reached the house, one of the first things he did was to attempt to get acquainted with the children. He seemed to be especially interested in us, not merely because we were the children of an old friend, but because we were about the only small Anglo children this side of Fort Concho, Texas. Any awe that we might have felt toward the man with the great reputation disappeared under his infectious good comradeship. I remember well how scared I was when I was introduced to him, but once he had taken my hand in his and said in his genial way, "Howdy, little girl. You look quite much like your father. Tell me your name, and how old you are, won't you?" Then there was no more shyness nor restraint.

In the interval between supper and bedtime, we children sat with the grown persons, listening to what they said, and gradually reached a more definite conclusion than before that Uncle John Chisum was just like the rest of us. This conclusion has remained with me always and served to put me, when I was a few years older, on terms of friendship with this remarkable man which I shall make the basis of the third part of this book.

The next morning Father and Uncle John rode all over our place and then came back to the house and talked until noon. I remember that Uncle John was struck by what a fine place Father had developed in a few years in that remote spot, and I heard him say several times, "Casey, you have done well. You certainly have got a fine place." After dinner Uncle John went back to the Hoag place and the next day to Bosque Grande. That visit was only the forerunner of many others in later times, especially when Uncle John moved his headquarters to South Spring River. That put him in Lincoln County, and on his frequent business trips to the county seat at Lincoln he invariably stopped at our place. We came also to know his three brothers, Pitzer, James, and Jeff Chisum, who were at that time in New Mexico helping Uncle John look after his extensive interests.

9

Apache Raid of 1867

THE THREAT OF INDIAN DEPREDATIONS hung over us constantly. When there was a prolonged period of quiet, we children tended to slack off our caution, but our parents were unflagging in their vigilance.

Livestock losses were frequent and costly. We had barely arrived at our ranch when Father found that three yoke of work oxen and several horses he had left on the Hondo had been stolen, presumably by Apaches. At that time no reservation lines had been established; even though there had been, the Mescaleros were inclined to go where they pleased, for from their point of view they owned all the land between the Rio Bravo (Rio Grande) and the Rio Pecos.

Father knew well that even more tempting to the Apaches than the cattle were his horses. He repeatedly warned the children that the hills surrounding the mesa on which the house stood might at any time conceal Indians. About the buildings there was a lush stand of sacaton (grass) in which Apaches could hide and wriggle their way toward the house without being detected. We were warned of the danger in getting even thirty yards from our door, and admonished that in case we saw an Indian we were to take refuge in the mill rather than the house.

Father exercised great care in protecting his herd. During the day the animals were close herded. At night they were driven into an adobe corral, built for protection. From the pine forest, thirty or more miles away, Father brought a quantity of long poles which were built into the walls near the top. They were pinned together with pegs to prevent the Indians from sawing the walls by the use of a rope. The corral was close to the house and proved to be an effective means of defense for the cattle.

Nevertheless, the Mescaleros made trouble for us. The first of their raids was made soon after we arrived. One night a band under the leadership of José La Paz slipped up to the ranch and with their butcher knives cut in two the pegs fastening together the poles near the top of a wide section of the corral, thus opening a gap through which they took about 325 cattle. Of these about twenty-five were fat, lazy, milk cows whose lethargy could not be overcome. Because driving them might entail noise, the Indians left most of them behind. This was unusual procedure for them, for they ran great risks on their raids.

They stole a sorrel horse we called Fox Walker even though he was kept tied with a rope of plaited rawhide just behind the chicken house which stood even closer to the dwelling than the corral.

We wondered how the Apaches managed without rousing us when we were so close. Later a Mexican boy, captive of the Indians, whom we took into our family told us how it was done. He said that the old chief, La Paz, was with the raiders and that he ordered this boy to watch the door of our house. La Paz and the others worked with great caution. After making the opening in the wall they made no effort to drive the cattle from the corral, for that entailed noise. They just waited for the animals to come of their own accord, and they came quietly.

The family knew nothing of the occurrence until early the next morning when Mother arose early and began cooking break-fast for the family. Ordinarily she surveyed the premises as soon as she could see well, but for some reason neglected doing so that morning. When she did find that the cattle were missing from the corral she did not think of Apaches at first, but that the animals had broken down the gate and escaped. This had happened pre-viously and the herd was found feeding outside.

When she discovered that the pins had been severed and that there were moccasin tracks outside the corral, she aroused the family. Father doubted the Apaches had taken the cattle, until he, too, inspected the premises. I remember his saying, "Well, thank God, they didn't get the other horses." Though I was only about six years old I remember this occurrence very vividly.

Fortunately some of the men who worked for Father had taken the other horses for a hunt in the Capitan Mountains. Otherwise the Apaches might have stolen them, also. Being left "afoot" in those days was a tragedy.

Father followed on foot the trail along which the Indians had taken the cattle. His familiarity with the management and driving of a herd enabled him to see that they had been driven in a compact body. Had they been permitted to scatter and graze as they usually did they would not have moved fast. The pony tracks were of unshod horses, and all led about a mile to the spot where the Apaches had crossed the Hondo.

While Father was at the ford, two mounted Americans came by from Missouri Bottom. He told them what had occurred and they said they were not surprised because news had come to the Bottom that a band of Indians was in our area and was apt to make trouble. The two men had made the trip by night to avoid contact with the Apaches who were known to dislike either fighting or moving in the dark. Father asked that one of them stay with us for protection and that the other go to the Fort with him for help. They readily agreed to this, and the one who stayed offered Father his horse for the trip.

As they rode toward La Placita Father and this man stopped at every house (there were very few) and warned the people to be on the lookout for attack. He told them he was going for a detachment of soldiers to follow the raiders. Two of the settlers offered to accompany him but he asked them to stay at home until he should return with the troop of cavalry.

Father told his story to Captain Chambers McKibbin under whom he had served as sergeant. The officer offered to use his forces in an attempt to recover the cattle and to punish the depredators. "Casey," said Captain McKibbin, "you are entitled to all the aid the Government can give you. I'll order a detachment of cavalry to get ready for the march as soon as possible. And I'll send in charge one of the best junior officers I have, Lieutenant Yeaton."

The troops were soon on the way. When they reached our

house they stopped to organize the pursuit. Lt. Yeaton told Father he had little knowledge of the terrain and asked if he would not act as guide for the scout. Father did not know the area to the south very well, but felt that he might be better qualified for the guiding than were any of the soldiers.

Taking the trail to the Hondo, Father led the scouting party as rapidly as he could. Tracks indicated that the Apaches had travelled as rapidly as they could move the cattle, and that they were headed for the Guadalupes, their favorite retreat.

They found the butchered carcasses of the cattle that had given out under the fast pace set by the Indians. Father's prize milk cows had been killed either by lance or arrows when unable to travel further. The choice meat had been cut and the rest left. Father was very indignant over the barbarity of this procedure because if the exhausted cattle had been left he could have gathered and returned them to the ranch.

The pursuit took Father and the troops into a country both difficult of travel and dangerous, owing to the many possibilities of ambush. Not only was it rough, it was also devoid of water. The soldiers experienced great difficulty in getting over the ground because they were mounted on large cavalry horses, animals unaccustomed to rough, mountainous country. Father and the man from Missouri Bottom rode small, wiry horses, well adapted to the terrain.

The pace was, of necessity, adapted to the slow horses used in the cavalry. Consequently on the first day the party made no more than the Rio Feliz, some twenty-five or thirty miles from our ranch. At the river they found indications that the Indians had stopped there about a day and had rested the animals where there was excellent grass and water. Right then Father decided that he would take that land and establish a herd there.

Next morning the pursuit was resumed with the party following a trail that seemed to lead directly to the Guadalupes. They followed for three days and not once during that time did they find water. This was a new and forbidding experience for the soldiers, none of whom had previously undergone such an ordeal under trying conditions.

Upon the evening of the third day they came upon the camp of the Indians who had no fear of their being pursued. The soldiers surprised the Apaches who were engaged in a feast and a dance, in celebration of their successful raid. Never before had a scouting party been able to follow them to their stronghold, and they had not anticipated that one could. Consequently they had not taken the precaution of guarding their camp.

As the soldiers drew near the Apaches their horses, famished for water, scented it and the men found it impossible to control their mounts. The horses took the bits in their teeth and dashed into the stream with their helpless riders. It is possible that the troops would have charged the camp had they been able to control their steeds. As the horses bolted for the water the soldiers fired upon the Apaches and when the animals entered the river the men remained in their saddles and continued shooting.

The Indians were not only surprised, they were stupefied with *tiswin,* a drink the women make of fermented corn, and offered little resistance. They rushed from their tepees and ran to whatever protection they could find.

When men and horses had drunk, the soldiers rode into the camp, knocked over tepees, and trampled under the horses' hoofs the prized baskets and pottery of the Indians' households upon which the woman had lavished much work both in construction and decoration. Many of the tepees were burned.

Had the Apaches been on guard the outcome might have been doubtful, for there was an abundance of cover, such as they use if they give battle, and they are formidable when cornered.

Some of Father's cattle were recovered but the remnant of the 325 had been driven so hard that it was out of the question to take them back to the ranch immediately. No one in the party, not excepting Father, knew where to find springs or water holes, and cattle cannot travel nearly so fast as horses.

Some Indian ponies were captured and among them was a little black mule the Apaches had stolen from us at Black River as we made the trip to New Mexico.

Casualties among the detachment of soldiers were few and of minor importance. Lieutenant Yeaton received a severe wound, perhaps the worst in the encounter. During the fighting he and Father were side by side. Upon seeing Old La Paz take deliberate aim at the young officer Father quickly reined up his horse and shouted a warning. It came too late, for La Paz fired and his bullet struck Yeaton in the hand, passing through it and entering his side. Father shot at La Paz and his bullet struck the old chief's leg and went on into the side of his horse. The Indian jumped from his mount, hid in the bushes, and got away. But Father got his horse, a fine, large sorrel, and brought him back to the ranch.

Old Sorrel, as we called him, was such a remarkable animal that he made a fine mount. He had been the favorite war horse of La Paz, or so we were told by the boy Father later rescued.

Old Sorrel had been well trained. If anyone attempted to drive him he would break back and run past, kicking both hind feet. If not disposed at the moment to do that, he would run at a person and try to bite him. We children were always afraid of him and if ordered to drive him up we would take either the longest whip on the place or a supply of stones with which to pelt this temperamental piece of horse flesh.

He would set back on any rope with which he was tied, and usually succeed in breaking it. Then, of course, he would run away. He hated a fence. Sometimes Will and Add would hobble and side-line him, give him a big feed, and say, "I bet you don't get away now." But Old Sorrel could always beat them at their own game. He would hobble as close to a rail fence as he could get, make a jump, and break it down.

Later we had another Indian scare and we took refuge in the mill, taking Old Sorrel in with us — knowing his peculiarities the men got the strongest rope on the place, doubled it, and tied him. They felt sure he could not get loose but during the night we were awakened by the noises he was making, playing ball with a stone. When we had lit a candle we discovered that he was loose. He had broken the rope by his master trick, i.e., sitting back on it, then had torn open several sacks of graham flour and eaten all he could. Then he played with the sacks. He tore open several and scattered their contents on the floor. He was so nearly foundered that the men worked all night to save him.

When he had recovered Father drilled a hole through each adobe of the mill and ran a chain through them. One end he made fast on the outside, and the other he put around Old Sorrel's neck and fastened it with a padlock. By this means we managed to keep him in the mill when we had to make it a place of refuge for ourselves and the horses.

We took Old Sorrel to Texas with us, and there he died of old age.

10

A Memorable Indian Scout

ABOUT A YEAR after the Indian raid Father went with a detachment of soldiers as their guide in the pursuit of a band of Apaches. It was on this expedition that he found and rescued the Mexican lad, Timio, who thereafter became a member of our household.

In the Indian troubles in southeastern New Mexico two tribes of Apaches are concerned. Old Cadete [Cadette] was the chief of the more warlike and murderous of these two tribes, while José La Paz was the chief of the other. [Both Cadette and La Paz were Mescalero Apaches.] While La Paz made numerous raids he and his band were not guilty of the atrocities committed by Cadette's band.

Cadette and some of his men added fuel to the fire by killing two soldiers, McGrath and Hoeffer, within a few miles of Fort Stanton. These two men had been sent out to haul in wood with six-mule teams that were said to be the best that had ever come to the Fort. They were driving their loaded wagons back to the Fort in the afternoon unsuspecting of dangers lurking in their vicinity. As the wagons ran down into the stream bed in crossing the Bonito Arroyo, the Indians charged from their hiding place in the willows on the bank and killed both drivers. The Indians, of course, drove off most of the mules, which were undoubtedly the chief objects of the attack, but two of the animals ran away and returned to the Fort with arrows sticking in them.

Naturally this attack caused great indignation. To have it occur right under the shadow of the fort made it seem an unendurable affront to the dignity and reputation of the Army, and aroused in the officers a determination to avenge speedily and thoroughly the death of those two soldiers. It was too dark to follow the trail that night, but about 3 A.M. the next morning a detachment of forty men started in pursuit.

Captain McKibbin made his first stop at our ranch. Father held at that time what was known as a forage agency contract which called for him to furnish to scouting parties — or for that matter, any party of soldiers that might pass on official business — what grain and hay they might need for their horses. Father and the officers at the Fort were always on the friendliest terms, and they made it their practice in passing about the country to make our ranch their stopping place.

Captain McKibbin not only wanted supplies, he had still another motive: he wanted Father to act as guide for his detachment. Father at first felt that he must refuse. He explained that he had just returned from an absence of nearly a year in which he had been in Texas and returned with another herd to replace that taken by the Apaches a year before. He said also that he was in the midst of building a new dwelling and did not see how he could well drop that project at the time. As a final reason for not leaving home, Father stated that he could not leave his family and his cattle exposed to another raid from the Indians.

Captain McKibbin, however, would not listen to Father's refusals. He even argued the matter, saying that Father ought to go in self-protection — with Father's aid they would unquestionably find the Indians and defeat them so decisively that they could not make further trouble. Captain McKibbin overcame Father's fears for the safety of his family and property by offering to leave at our ranch a picket consisting of one of his best sergeants, Abneth McCabe, and three other soldiers.

Father finally consented but made his doing so conditional upon his being left absolutely free in the choice of route. The reason for this stipulation was that Father knew that Army officers, even when quite inexperienced, were sometimes disposed to act in a self-sufficient way that frequently defeated the object of their scouts, and he did not wish anything of the sort to interfere this time. Captain

McKibbin gladly acceded to Father's stipulation, and the detachment moved the next day from our place.

After searching for three days in the general direction of Seven Rivers, they reached the rough country that surrounds the Guadalupe Mountains. At that time there were no inhabitants in that section and the detachment had to trust to luck for water. As they were riding down a very fertile canyon all covered over with heavily seeded grass, one of the officers discovered a large rattlesnake, which of course became an irresistible target. Captain McKibbin and Father each took a shot at the snake's head and each hit it. This incident, though seemingly trivial, played a large part in the subsequent happenings.

Some two or three miles further along, the detachment ran upon all kinds of fresh Indian sign. Captain McKibbin stopped the march and gathering his officers around him, held a council of war as to what the next move should be. He himself wished to mount a number of his best men on the better horses and send them in hot pursuit of the Indians, while the rest of his party remained behind with the pack mules. As it was then only about two o'clock in the afternoon, Captain McKibbin was very sanguine about his best men's being able to overtake the Indians by sundown, and he was also very confident that they would make such short work of the Indians that they would be back at camp by nightfall.

Father knew more about the ways and tricks of the Indians than anyone else in the party, for he had taken part in several fights back in Texas with the Comanches and Kiowas who were the most cunning among all the Indian tribes. He could not approve Captain McKibbin's scheme for he was extremely skeptical about the sign they had discovered. In his opinion it had been made simply to lead them off the real trail, for it went in a direction opposite to that in which the Indians were supposed to live. But Captain McKibbin was so confident of his own pet plan that he disregarded the promise he would allow Father to decide all matters connected with the route, and gave orders that were needed to put his plan in operation.

Although Father was greatly vexed at Captain McKibbin's course, he did not propose to fail in his duty and prepared to go along with the soldiers who were to ride ahead. But before starting, he happened to ride off a short distance to the side of the stopping place to examine a spot where the grass seemed freshly cut. To his surprise a boy of about fourteen jumped out of the grass right under the head of Father's horse. Thinking that the young fellow must be an Indian, Father drew his six-shooter and fired down at him. Immediately the boy began to yell *"Captivo! Captivo!"* But the meaning of his words was lost on Father who with his limited knowledge of Spanish, did not understand what the boy was trying to say. He shot at the boy a second time and called to Captain McKibbin, "Shall I kill him or take him?" As the Captain made no reply Father even shot a third time in the direction of the boy, still without hitting him. But by that time the old Mexican interpreter had realized the situation and he shouted to Father, "Don't kill him, Casey. He is a Mexican captive the Indians have had." Father ceased firing at once, and always thought it providential that he had missed the boy three times at such close range, for he was generally accounted a very good shot.

Though most certainly a Mexican, the boy was so black and sunburned that he looked more like an Indian than anything else. This was so much the case that when the officers gathered around him, there were some who insisted that he was an Indian buck who had got behind the rest of the Indians and had taken this means of playing off on them. Father would take no chances when there was every ground to think that the grass was full of Indians who might in the next moment jump out of ambush and wipe out the whole detachment.

The boy was at once rigidly cross-questioned with the aid of an interpreter. His answers were so frankly and honestly given that it was impossible to doubt their truthfulness. His name, he said, was Timiteo Analla,* and he told how he had been captured when a little boy in Aguas Lagunas, Old Mexico, by Victorio's band of Apaches and later sold by them to this band. When asked how he happened to be hiding in the grass, he said he had come there with a small party of Indians who were cutting the grass for the seed, but that when they heard the two shots that Father and the captain had fired at the snake, all the bucks had taken alarm, and mounting their horses, had ridden away as fast as they could. He

---

*Since no written version of the Mexican boy's name existed, no accurate spelling is assured. Others have spelled it Entimo Ansures, Timetio, and Timeo.

had then concealed himself in the grass, hoping in that way to escape detection.

When they inquired about the direction the Indians had taken, Timio said that the bucks had been cunning enough to make a fresh trail leading in a direction away from the camp where were the women and children. When pressed for information as to the location of this camp he indicated that it was in another direction, somewhat farther down and just behind some little hills to be seen in the distance. Some of the officers, however, were inclined to think Timio might be leading them off after all, but they finally concluded to use him as a guide to the Indians' camp. Mounting him on a large horse behind the Mexican interpreter, they ordered him to lead the way to the camp.

It turned out that he was telling the truth for, after a short journey, the party came in sight of the camp. Captain McKibbin promptly ordered his soldiers to charge the camp, and begin shooting at once, but to shoot high and try to avoid hitting women and children or any man who did not show fight. This was in accordance with instructions from the War Department which were not to kill the Indians but rather to take them prisoners.

Hardly had the soldiers begun their charge when one of the Indians was observed trying to leave the camp on foot. Captain McKibbin dispatched two soldiers after this Indian with orders to make him a prisoner if possible, but on no account to let him get away. The Indian dashed up a steep incline that was too precipitous for the government horses to climb, and the soldiers, thinking the fugitive was going to elude them, felt that their orders required them to open fire. The Indian fell dead, and Captain McKibbin then ordered the two soldiers to go up and bring the body down. To their great surprise, they found that it was a woman whom they had shot. Neither Captain McKibbin nor the soldiers themselves would have intentionally killed a squaw.

Father had charged the camp with the rest, but he always stated that when he became convinced that there were only women and children there, he realized that the soldiers ought not to be allowed to shoot to kill. As all the officers were either elsewhere or had their attention diverted, Father assumed authority to order the men to cease firing. The soldiers, not stopping to think whether Father had the right to give such an order, at once obeyed, and the shooting ceased. But they surrounded the camp, making prisoners of the women and children.

When the party reached camp, Father jumped from his horse, among the first of the crowd to dismount. No sooner had he done so than the little twelve-year-old daughter of the chief ran to him and throwing her arms about him, begged him to save her. The other women and children were so frightened that they could not do anything except express their fright by crying and screaming. Father indicated to the little girl that she need have no fears for her safety, and did what he could to reassure the others. Finally Captain McKibbin managed with the help of an interpreter to make the Indian women understand that they were not to be killed but were to be made prisoners. He also ordered them to get ready to move, and the squaws promptly commenced getting together their belongings which they had hidden when they discovered the approach of the soldiers.

Before starting from camp with his collection of squaws and children prisoners, Captain McKibbin endeavored to learn from them the whereabouts of the bucks. This was a very necessary bit of information since the bucks might either waylay the party of soldiers at some point, or by getting away from the vicinity might be able to gather together and bring back the rest of the tribe and so attack the soldiers with an overwhelming force. But the squaws would not say anything on this point. So Captain McKibbin and his officers concluded it would be the safer course to get supper where they were, and then to start on a night march down the canyon, guided as well as possible by the peaks of certain high mountains that could be seen. They intended to get the direction of those peaks by the compass and then to march east so as to strike the Pecos River which they knew must be to the eastward, as they had marched steadily west until they ran upon the Indian camp.

They traveled that night until about 10 o'clock, and then made a dry camp. Double guards were posted, and then the rest of the party went to sleep and slept soundly until daybreak. The next day's march began very early and was kept up until about 9 o'clock in the morning, when the party struck some springs the squaws had been willing to tell him about. There Captain McKibbin's detachment stopped and had breakfast as well as giving their horses a chance to graze, the first the animals had had for several days.

Father explained that because the soldiers were escorting the

Indian squaws and children it was impossible for them to make rapid progress, so it took four or five days to reach Missouri Bottom. Father felt the soldiers had no further need for him and at once started to his ranch, planning to cover the intervening distance of about forty miles as quickly as possible.

Captain McKibbin decided to turn over the command of the detachment to one of the junior officers, and he came along with Father, stopping at our place only long enough to have dinner, then pressing on rapidly toward Fort Stanton. The Captain was greatly pleased over his success on that scout and was eager to send the news on to Washington. As there was then no telegraph in our part of the country, it was necessary to send the dispatch by courier to Santa Fe and have it sent on to Washington by telegraph.

When Father reached home we children listened with openmouthed interest to his account of the scout. We were especially interested in the captive boy, Timio, who, as Father informed us, had been given to him by Captain McKibbin and was to stay with us and be virtually a member of the family. We hardly knew whether to be afraid of him or not. Recollections of our experiences at Black River with the Indians were still vivid in our minds. We remembered, too, what trouble they had made for us when they raided our cattle. We had not forgotten that they had taken a milk cow we children were especially fond of. When Father returned from the pursuit of the Indians we asked him if he had gotten back this particular cow, but he had to tell us that Indians had killed her and left her carcass by the side of the road. Now we faced the prospect of being added to our little group at the ranch one who had lived among such terrible creatures, and furthermore some of the Indians themselves were to appear soon at our home. Although we were made to understand that they were prisoners in the hands of the soldiers, we viewed the prospect with a good deal of childish dread.

When the soldiers and the Indians arrived within the next day or two, all that we could at first do was to peep at them from behind our corral. We were too afraid to go near them by ourselves, and it was not until after supper that, with Mother along as companion and protector, and with one of our American renters as interpreter, we mustered up enough courage to visit the Indian camp. When we reached it, we found that the Indians had all gone to bed, for the poor creatures were very tired from the long journey they had made in the past several days. But the squaw of the chief got up so we could see the child that Father had told us about as having picked him out as protector when the soldiers charged the camp. I remember that I thought her a very pretty young girl, dressed as she was in her buckskin jacket and short skirt, the seams of which were all fringed with buckskin and each point being tipped with tin, which jingled as she moved.

Our hearts went out to her, and we were seized with a wish to have her stay with us and become our playmate. In our childish way we reasoned that, as these Indians were captives, there would be no trouble in having her given to us, provided we made the request. Mother, ready to humor this whim of ours, asked the old squaw if she would allow her to keep the little girl and rear her as one of her own children. The reply of the Indian mother I have never forgotten for it summed up the submissive attitude characteristic of the Indian woman, while at the same time it diplomatically conveyed a mother's reluctance to part with her child. The squaw said, "We are captives, and, if the white man wishes, he can take my child. But her father is not here to say 'Yes,' and I could not say 'Yes' without his being here. He might get very mad to lose his child."

To our great sorrow we did not get the Indian girl as an addition to our family, but we did have the captive boy, Timio, or Tim as we usually called him. When we first saw him, he was most comically dressed in some of the officers' cast-off clothing which had been bestowed upon him when he was captured. One of the first things we did was to dress him in some of Add's clothes, and I well remember how funny Tim looked in his new outfit. The poor Mexican boy seemed literally scared to death and did not know which way to turn or what to do next. Mother did all she could to put him at ease and to help him feel that we were his friends, but for awhile he seemed dazed by his new surroundings and whatever he did was done mechanically. If Mother pointed to a chair, for example, he seated himself gingerly and awkwardly upon it. Apparently all he wanted to do was to look across the creek and stare at the large hills in the distance.

Mother knew that the best way to get him settled and contented was to give him some work to do, so she put him to washing the dishes. While he was doing this, she noticed him picking up the meat and bread left on the plates and carefully stowing these scraps away in his pockets. She wondered what his purpose could be, but in an instant the reason flashed into her mind. The poor boy had starved so much that he could not bear to throw away any food, and he was storing up what he found against some future time when he might need it. Mother tried to make him understand that we had plenty of food and that there was no need to save it so carefully, but she could not make him understand. Finally she had to scrape the food off the plates herself in order to get the scraps for our dogs.

Timio stayed with us as a member of our family — a sort of adopted child, in fact — until he was twenty-one. Then Father gave him a horse, bridle, and saddle, together with an outfit of clothing, and set him up in the world. But Timio did not want to leave us, and Father employed him, paying him the same wages he would have paid to any other employee who did the same work. He stayed with us even after he got married. He eventually died, in February, 1925, a faithful and honest man, as well as a good citizen. How different it might have been with him had not Father rescued him from the Indian captors!

He often talked of how he was captured as a small boy herding sheep at Aguas Legunas, Old Mexico. He believed that all of his family had been killed by the Indians, for he had afterwards seen them wearing clothing that had belonged to his mother and sister.

He always remained terribly afraid of Indians, and even after he came to live with us, he would hide whenever he heard that the Indians had broken out from their reservation. The poor boy feared that he might fall into their hands again, and made to resume the hard life of a captive. There was a large scar across his forehead which evidenced the many heavy loads the Indians had made him carry on his back, so heavy that the head strap had cut deep enough into the flesh to make that scar.

The taking of these prisoners was a means of ending the Indian trouble for awhile. The commanding officer of the Fort induced the squaw of Old La Paz to leave her children at the Fort while she herself went to find the old chief and give him a message from the white man to the effect that the white men wanted him to come in and make peace and live as friends. Mounted on a good government mule and loaded with all kinds of provisions and all sorts of presents, beads, red calico, and the like, for the other wife of La Paz (and I think she took along a nice suit of clothes for the chief himself), the squaw started on her journey.

But it was not an easy matter for even one of his wives to find the wary old chief. After being away for ten or fifteen days she returned with the report that she could not find him. A little later she went out a second time and was gone for thirty days. Then she came back bringing a little Indian pony with an Indian saddle and blankets. This time she gave out the story that she had been on a long and difficult journey, her purpose evidently being to create an impression that the chief and his bucks were a long way from the Fort and so to deter the soldiers from going out after them.

Finally her negotiations with the old chief were successful and La Paz and a number of his warriors came to the Fort for a peace talk. Captain McKibbin sent down for Father to come, and on his return he told us how the officers had given the Indians a fine supper, with plenty of roast beef, of which they were very fond. Along with the beef was an abundance of light bread. The other item on the bill of fare was strong coffee with lots of sugar but no milk. Captain McKibbin talked peace strongly, telling the Indians how he had saved their squaws and children and trying to make them feel that the Government wanted them to settle down peaceably on the reservation. When the Captain had finished his speech, Old La Paz arose and pointing toward Father, said, "Yah, Yah, there is the man save my squaw and children." Father's kindness was remembered — in fact it was never forgotten. Thereafter they were on the friendliest terms with Father and all the rest of us, and were not inclined to molest our cattle. We did afterwards have some troubles, as I shall tell subsequently, but these cases were the work of small parties of Indians who went marauding on their own hook, independent of the tribe as a whole, and without any sanction from Old La Paz.

Eventually the other chief, Cadette, also came in, but in his case it took much longer and much more persuasion to get him to surrender. Both of these famous old chiefs are now dead. La Paz died of old age on the Mescalero Reservation. Cadette got shot in a drunken row, supposedly by old Juan Cajo [Cojo], the Apache interpreter; but the old chief lived long enough after being wounded to cut off Cojo's head. He was actually able to sever it from the body and set it up on a pole in the road. Then the old chief stumbled a few yards further and dropped dead.* Even in his last moments Cadette showed that savage cruelty which was always his characteristic and which made him a terror to southeastern New Mexico for so long.

───────

*There are other versions of this story.

PART II

Reign of the Six Shooter

II

The Lincoln County Ring

FOR YEARS LINCOLN COUNTY was dominated by a group designated as The Ring. At the center of this ring was the powerful and influential firm of L.G. Murphy & Co. Financial stringency forced this firm to reorganize several times and in each instance it took a different name, owing to the appearance of a new partner. Thus it was successively known as Fritz & Murphy, L.G. Murphy & Co., Murphy, Dolan & Co., and finally as J.J. Dolan & Co. I shall call it by its early name, L.G. Murphy & Co.

Major Lawrence G. Murphy and Colonel Emil C. Fritz founded the firm. Both had come into the country in Civil War times with what is known in New Mexico history as the California Column. They had secured the post trader's store at Fort Stanton, and when we came into the country, were prosperous from proceeds of the big Government contracts they had obtained. But in 1873 the commanding officer at the fort became disgusted with the way they were defrauding the Government and ordered them to leave the fort. When they refused to do so, the officer sent a party of nine soldiers to their store and ejected them from the military reservation.

Major Murphy and Colonel Fritz moved their business to Lincoln, where for some time previously they had been conducting a small branch business which they called the "Placita Store." They had kept Alec Duval in charge of the business which was in a small, two-story adobe house on the north side of the street. When Major

Murphy and Colonel Fritz brought the stock of goods from Fort Stanton and combined it with what they already had in Lincoln, it became evident that they needed a much larger building. They put up a large, two-story adobe which, when completed in 1873, was certainly the most imposing and pretentious business building in the county.

Major Murphy, as I remember him, was a slender, sandy "complected" man, a little above average height. Although he had been a soldier he always dressed carefully and expensively in the best of broadcloth suits. He was what we called a "city man"; that is, he was fastidious about his looks and dress, and not inclined to manual labor. His manner was affable and he was very popular, having many friends not only in Lincoln County but in Santa Fe as well. The rumors were that he was well educated and had at one time planned entering the priesthood of the Catholic Church. As all Irish seem to be, he was quick tempered and likely to explode when things did not suit him. He had a softer heart, however, than some of the others in the firm, and in more than one instance was generous in aiding those in need of money. He was a dreamer and planner rather than a practical man capable of executing his schemes. He was just entering middle age but his habit of drinking heavily was beginning to affect his health and appearance.

His partner, Colonel Emil Fritz, was very unlike him. Fritz was energetic and businesslike. It was largely because of his business ability that the store prospered as it did. I remember what an impression Colonel Fritz' deep voice and German accent made on me when I first saw him. He had come from Stuttgart, Germany, reportedly from a prominent and wealthy family, and died there during a visit with his father in 1874.

Upon the death of Colonel Fritz, Major Murphy reorganized the firm and renamed it Murphy, Dolan & Co. He took into the business James J. Dolan, a former clerk who was reported to have been a drummer boy in the Army, mustered out at Fort Stanton.

From the beginning Jimmie Dolan had been suspected of using practices that were dark and devious. He seemed gifted in concocting and carrying through crooked and underhanded deals, usually getting someone else to do the dirty work and take the consequences. If compelled to do it himself he cleverly concealed his actions. He was suspected of complicity in many discreditable occurrences in Lincoln but proving his participation was difficult.

In 1872 a native boy, Heraldo, was killed at Lincoln and it was suspected that Dolan was the murderer; it was believed that Murphy's money and influence got Dolan out of that scrape. It was alleged that he had killed another native in order to keep him from stirring up a row with George Peppin, who was one of Murphy's henchmen. Peppin was allegedly carrying on an affair with the Mexican's wife and when it seemed that the irate husband was about to shoot Peppin, the latter went to his friends, Murphy and Dolan, with an account of his danger. Dolan, so the story went, volunteered to get rid of the husband, and did so by shooting him during a pretended quarrel in a cowshed.*

Apparently it was Dolan who was behind most of the nefarious occurrences of the Lincoln County War. Murphy by that time was so besotted with liquor he was almost a negative quantity in the trouble. Dolan, though physically small — about five feet, three inches in height — was aggressive and unscrupulous. He had dark, small eyes, dark skin that well suited the Mephistophelian role he usually played.

After the death of Murphy in the fall of 1878 the firm, now J.J. Dolan & Co., had a new member, John H. Riley, an ex-soldier who had been employed by the firm much as Dolan had previously been. He was a hot-headed Irishman, always ready to fight, and figured in many of the shooting scrapes of that time. I do not know that he killed anyone but at Fort Stanton he shot Juan Patron who, though seriously wounded, recovered.

The company had begun to deal in cattle and it was Riley who handled that part of the business. During the Lincoln County War, Riley left the country but returned for a short time. Later he married and lived at Las Cruces before moving to Colorado.

The firm of L.G. Murphy & Co. did a very large and profitable business. Either directly or indirectly it not only supplied the whole of Lincoln County with the necessities of life, but it held the population in what was approximately peonage. It sold merchandise at extremely high prices which the owners attributed to the expense of having merchandise hauled by teams from Santa Fe or Las Vegas, although much of it was owing to exorbitant charges. Green coffee

---

*These charges made by Mrs. Klasner lack substantiation.

sold from fifty cents to a dollar a pound; thread was twenty-five cents a spool; saleratus (soda) fifty cents a pound; and loaf sugar fifty cents a pound. The cheap grade of sugar was fifty cents, and the cheap, black, navy tobacco was fifty or more.

The people had to have necessities and could get them nowhere else; consequently the company had accounts with almost every person who came into the county, and the outcome was usually an indebtedness surprising to the customer who brought his product for sale. He paid in hay or cattle, and often found himself in debt before delivering his product for his year's work. If he lacked sufficient funds to balance his account the firm foreclosed on his personal property or even his land. If a note were taken in settlement of an account it bore a high rate of interest, 12 percent or more.

The most lucrative part of the business consisted of Government contracts held by the firm. In the beginning the contract was for furnishing corn to the soldiers at Fort Stanton. L.G. Murphy & Co. bought seed corn and sold it to the people, thus promoting the cultivation of that grain. When the crop was harvested they took all brought to them and gave credit on the accounts. The usual procedure was for the farmer to take his corn to the Fort and have it weighed on Government scales. The firm allowed its customers a cent or two less per pound than they received from the Government, alleging this was a commission to which it was entitled. If a customer did not like the terms he was not forced to accept them, but he had no other market, so what could he do? Hence the firm had a double profit, one on the goods sold and another on the price paid.

The same plan was used in the handling of hay. The people cut the tall grass growing in the lowlands and also the fine gramma grass on the flats. They loaded it on ox wagons, took it to the Fort and disposed of it much as they did their corn, and had no alternative.

When the Apaches were placed on the reservation this firm secured the flour contract, and its handling of this became a scandal that the governor investigated. The "establishment" bought the wheat and sent it to the Casey mill for grinding. We were equipped to grind graham flour and it was this that the firm supplied, though the contract specified a better grade.

The firm also padded the rolls in regard to the number of Mescaleros they were supplying, showing a count of more than 1200 when there were only about 900. That, too, gave Murphy a nice margin of profit.

The firm had contracts for supplying beef both to the Fort and to the Indians. At first it bought the cattle from herds passing through. By the time a herd reached Lincoln some cattle would be so exhausted that they were worth little and the company bought them at a very low price and placed them on its ranch near Carrizozo. Since there were no fences they could not put the animals near the Fort because the half-starved Indians might have stolen them; also, the unfenced fields would have been overrun by the cattle. On the ranch the cattle were still subject to raid by Indians, and also from Mexican cattle thieves in the vicinity of Manzano, Chilili, and Tularosa.

In 1877 the firm picked out a ranch in the Pecos country, near Seven Rivers, where there was less danger from Indian and Mexican marauders. Because it took more cattle to fill their contracts than they owned, it was said that they frequently stole from the Chisum range. It was then that the firm adopted the arrow brand [that of the Apache reservation later] which could easily be burned into the long rail used by John Chisum.

Though many stories were current in regard to the devious methods of Murphy no proof has been produced that they made moonshine on an extensive scale in a cave near Fort Stanton. Those who supplied grain for the project did not discuss it because they were well paid for delivering it. The firm sought the good will of officers of the Fort and of powerful citizens of the Territory by entertaining in the form of dinners and poker parties. Drinking was a necessary adjunct to the conviviality of such social gatherings and the firm considered it good business to procure whiskey by another route than the long, slow, and dangerous one of having it transported through the hostile Mescalero country. Besides, there was Major Murphy's need to be supplied.

A large cave about three miles below Fort Stanton in the steep foothills of the mountains was selected for the distillery. A more suitable one could hardly have been devised. The cave was thought to run back into the high mountains and even to have an exit on the north side of the Capitans.

If smoke, the tell-tale sign of a still, were seen, the superstitious and ignorant natives attributed it to volcanic origin.

To shorten the process of making liquor the firm had the corn cracked. This was done at ours, the only grist mill in the county. Down to our mill came several of the big wagons which Major Murphy had had built especially for his hauling and freighting. They were loaded with quantities of corn that kept the mill operating day and night to crush.

The procedure aroused Mother's curiosity. Learning that the corn, instead of being ground, was merely cracked, she made inquiries. Father no doubt had surmised the purpose of the process but he explained, jokingly, that the Fort was going into the chicken business and needed feed. At first Mother accepted the explanation but later suspected the real purpose and objected to the continuation of the profitable proceeding.

Distilling was not the only contraband activity allegedly carried on in the cave. During 1868 and '69 it was associated with a gang engaged in counterfeiting, the bogus money being easily passed in the vicinity of the Mexican border. The cave afforded a safe place for its very profitable manufacture.

Tom Cooper was believed to be a counterfeiter. I remember him well. When he attempted to pass a counterfeit ten-dollar bill he went into a little store and bought a bandanna. He offered the bill in exchange and received $9.50 in legal tender. When the bill was found to be counterfeit it was Murphy & Co. that came to his rescue. This experience alarmed the people and the gang left the country.

Only those who have experienced it can realize the extent to which Murphy & Co. dominated the country and controlled its people, economy, and politics. The establishment put into office whatever men would serve them best. They controlled the District Judge, Warren H. Bristol. They handled the governor, S. B. Axtell, as well as the much more powerful politicians in Santa Fe. They had great influence with the officers at Fort Stanton and could secure favors from them.

All Lincoln County was cowed and intimidated by them. To oppose them was to court disaster. If the Murphy Company could not run a man out of the country it would bring about his death at the hands of the henchmen. A few discovered a means of evening the score by renting a ranch upon which it had foreclosed and running up as big an account as Murphy & Co. would permit. Then they would sell the crops to another rancher and skip. That meant that the establishment, too, had its problems.

To escape Murphy's clutches, Billy Gill rented one of his ranches and established a very good blacksmith shop on it. When his account with the firm exceeded what the management considered reasonable, payment was demanded. Gill refused to pay and Murphy & Co. undertook to collect by attaching the expensive tools owned by Gill. He reported that they'd been stolen but his story was not accepted. Nevertheless the firm was unable to take them.

While hunting for stray cattle in Chávez Canyon, my brother Will found some expensive tools of the type Gill had lost. Father investigated and decided that they'd been hidden there, but that they were not his property. Gill was accustomed to passing through the canyon when he hauled wood. Perhaps he recovered his property.

We never asked.

12

The Harrell War

A GOOD DEAL has been written about the Harrell War, as it was usually called, which took place in Lincoln County in 1873, but every account I have seen is full of inaccuracies and distortions. As we knew the Harrells from the time they came into New Mexico until they left, and as one of the so-called battles of the war was fought on our place, I believe I can come nearer giving the real facts of that trouble than anyone else. That at least is to be my endeavor in this chapter. Of one thing I am certain: the Harrells themselves were not the bloodthirsty ones of the crowd. The terrible deeds that make up the incidents of the war were done not by them but by their followers, among whom were some very desperate men.

The Harrells had become involved in a feud with the Higgenses in Lampasas, Texas, and had decided to leave there, so packed up their families and started for New Mexico. Along with the Harrells came a number of associates, who were all more or less desperate fellows. In the entire party there were about twenty men, five of the Harrell brothers and about fifteen others. It is true that several in the Harrell crowd were wanted for killings back in Texas, but these were killings that were more generally approved of than condemned under the code of the time.

This party of Texans settled up on the Ruidoso at what is now the Frank Coe place. At that time the place was owned by Frank Reicken [Regan] and Heiskell Jones, who sold to the Harrells. Of course, there were some in the Harrell crowd that did not settle at all — the stragglers and renegades that clustered about the band, and it was not long before their recklessness brought the whole party into a bloody feud with the native element of the population in that section of the country.

One day Ben Harrell went over to Lincoln and got to drinking with two of the Americans living there, Jack Gillam [Lewis J. Gylam] and Dave Warner. When well liquored up, they became noisy and apparently determined to cause trouble of some sort. A Mexican deputy sheriff, Juan Martínez, thought it advisable to disarm them, and made an attempt to do so. It so happened that this Mexican and Dave Warner were bitter enemies, a fact which made the situation more complicated than usual. Another complication was the fact that Jack Gylam was the sheriff of the county. When the Mexican deputy made the demand to disarm, Gylam said to Dave Warner, who seemed about to comply with the order, "I'm sheriff. Don't surrender. You don't have to surrender."

Dave Warner thereupon changed his mind about obeying the deputy's demand. Seized with an impulse to settle the old score between him and the Mexican, he pulled his six-shooter from its holster. Martínez, the Mexican, noting the movement, drew his at almost the same time. They fired simultaneously, and Dave Warner fell dead inside the dance hall, at the door of which the row occurred, and the Mexican deputy fell outside.

This killing of Martínez aroused the Mexican element of Lincoln to a high degree, and they got after both Gylam and Ben Harrell. No one knows just how it was done, but the Mexicans managed to kill both men. Their bodies were found next morning lying in the road about a quarter of a mile from the dance hall. Some claimed that the two men ran that far pursued by the incensed Mexicans; others thought the Mexicans killed them in the vicinity of the dance hall and dragged their bodies to the spot where they were found. However that may be, the spirit in which these Mexicans sought to avenge the death of one of their number is clearly enough exhibited in the story current at the time to the effect that in order to get a large diamond ring worn by Ben Harrell, some of the Mexicans cut off both finger and ring after he was killed.

The three killings naturally fomented bad blood between the surviving members of the Harrell party and the Mexican element in that section. The result was a race war, in which the Harrells seemed bent on ruthlessly exterminating the Mexicans, and the Mexicans determined to retaliate as much as was in their power. The Harrells gave clear indication of their mood and purpose in the next incident of the war, which occurred a few days later.

One night while the Mexicans were having a *baile* in the old dance hall at Lincoln, a group of the Harrell crowd broke in and shot it up. Four of the Mexican men were killed and one of the women wounded in the knee. The names of those killed were Juan Padilla, Ysdro Patrón, David Balisán, and José Candelario. The woman who was wounded was Apolonia García.

The Mexicans of course made a strong effort at retaliation for such a wanton attack. They first swore out warrants for the persons who composed the Harrell party and, armed with these, some went over into the Ruidoso country and tried to arrest those that were supposed to have made the attack. The Mexicans, however, were not absolutely sure just which of the Harrells had been implicated in the shooting up of the dance hall; and so, when they tried to make arrests, none of the Harrells would submit to arrest unless the Mexicans could make a positive identification. But this was impossible, because the shooting had all been under cover of darkness.

From such beginnings grew the further troubles between the Texans and the Mexicans. Some American friends of the Mexicans took a hand in the matter. Ham Mills, who had succeeded Gylam as sheriff, gathered a posse and went over into the Ruidoso country to see what he could accomplish in behalf of the Mexicans. He managed to surround the Harrell place with his posse, but that started shooting between the two crowds. The skirmishing went on for a day but no one was killed on either side. The only casualties were some stock that were wounded. Finally, seeing that it was impossible to get the Harrells to give up, Ham Mills withdrew his posse and took it back to Lincoln.

For a few weeks there was a lull in the fighting, and the Harrells decided to take advantage of this cessation of hostilities to get their women and children into a place of safety. It occurred to them that my father, being a fellow Texan, might be willing to help by letting them leave their women and children at our place. They brought them down and asked Father's permission to leave them there. Although Father disapproved of the actions of the men in their troubles with the Mexicans, he did not think he could refuse to give women and children protection; so he permitted them to stay in the mill. As well as I can remember, the women and children stayed about ten days at our place.

About the same time the Heiskell Jones family came to our place seeking refuge; along with them was Frank Reagan, who had been in partnership with Heiskell Jones. After they sold their ranch on the Ruidoso to the Harrells, they moved over to Lincoln where Mrs. Jones started a hotel. The Harrells made her hotel their stopping place when they came to Lincoln, and when the trouble first broke out between the Harrells and the Mexicans, they continued to do so.

The Mexicans did not like the idea of the Joneses allowing the Harrells to come to their hotel to eat, and they got pretty mad at the Joneses. The Joneses thought the best thing to do was to go to a place with a more friendly atmosphere, and came to our place. Father, for the sake of old friendship, gladly allowed them to establish themselves in the house of a renter.

After leaving their women and children at our place, the Harrell men went back to the Ruidoso and tried to go on with their farming. But it was so dangerous for them to appear in the fields that they finally realized the hopelessness of trying to farm while the Mexicans were so inflamed against them, so quit trying to make a crop. After discussion among themselves as to the best course to follow, they decided to take their families still further away, and selected Roswell as a safe location. A further part of their determination was to come back and wreak vengeance on the Mexican population at Lincoln. To tell the truth, they contemplated nothing short of a complete massacre of the Mexicans at Lincoln.

With such a program decided upon, they turned up at our ranch on their way to Roswell and gathered up their women and children. Although I was only a child, I remember quite well waking up that night about ten or eleven o'clock to find our house and yard filled with a number of fierce-looking men, all heavily armed. In particular do I recall a big, tall fellow, known as Jack Grunton who was standing by the fireplace talking to Mother. He was trying to hold her attention, but she was furtively watching as much as she could, both what was going on inside and outside the house. This was because Father had gone out among the men outside and Mother was concerned about his safety. She knew that Father and the Harrells were supposed to be on friendly terms, but she knew how easy it was for trouble to rise, even between friends, when they were flushed with excitement and whiskey. Someone among the formidable visitors might fly off the handle and stir up a row.

When I looked into the front room, I could see Tom Harrell sitting on Frank Reagan's bed and endeavoring earnestly to persuade him to get up and come outside so they could discuss some business connected with the ranch. But the request was of no avail. Reagan pulled the covers over his head and said positively, "No." Sleeping on the floor of the front room were six soldiers from Fort Stanton, whom Father had deemed it wise to secure as a guard in those troublesome times. I noticed Tom Harrell look at those men when he found that Frank Reagan would not get up and come outside with him, seeming to count them as if to make sure how many there were. Then he went outside and joined the crowd in the yard.

At the time there flashed into my mind the suspicion that Tom Harrell had some evil design on Frank Reagan, and the next morning my fear found confirmation. Living in the mill were two of our men, Jerry Hocradle and Frank McCubbin, and the next morning when we were all talking over the incident of the night before, they told how some of the Harrell men had come over to the mill and called them out. When they came, Tom Harrell said to Jerry Hocradle, "Do you know where Frank Reagan is?" "Yes," replied Hocradle, "he's sleeping in the house." Then Tom Harrell said, "You go tell him there is a man out here that wants to see him on business that is very important. But be sure you don't tell who it is." Jerry Hocradle did not suspect anything wrong just then and started to do what Tom Harrell had asked him to do. But as he walked over to the house, he noticed that there were two men, heavily armed, standing on either side of the mill door, and that there were two more, likewise heavily armed, at each of the four corners of the building, so concluded that their desire for Frank Reagan was not altogether a friendly one. He delivered the message of Tom Harrell and added, "But you better stay where you are; you're not safe."

This warning was what probably saved Frank Reagan's life that night. Harrell must have realized the uselessness of starting trouble in the room where there were six United States soldiers sleeping. What the Harrells had against Frank Reagan that made them want to kill him, I have never been able to discover. But it is certain that if Jerry Hocradle had not given a warning, Reagan might have become a victim of the murderous impulse that had overtaken the Harrells.

It was on this same trip down to Roswell that some of the Harrell crowd went to the house of Joe Haskins and killed him in a brutal manner simply because he was married to a Mexican woman. Haskins was a good, hard-working young man who had married a Mexican girl who had been reared by the mother-in-law of Steve Stanley and Ham Mills. The old lady had adopted her when she was a small girl and had trained her in the ways of industry and thrift, especially in housekeeping, making her a very suitable girl for a young man like Joe Haskins to marry. They had moved down to the lower end of our land and were living in one of the houses down on our Section 16. They were good neighbors, and no one seemed to have anything against either of this young couple.

When the Harrell crowd reached Picacho they went to the house of the four American families living there — those of the brothers Rainbolt and the brothers Akers, and demanded food. Mrs. Jim Rainbolt happened to be over at Mrs. Lib Rainbolt's house and the two women, assisted by their daughters, went to work cooking breakfast as rapidly as they could in the fireplace. While the preparation of breakfast was going on, a small sandy-complexioned man known as "Little Hart" [Edward Hart] who was with the Harrells became impatient about his breakfast and pointing to a house visible across the river, inquired if Americans lived in it, adding that as he saw smoke coming out the chimney, it might be a good place to go to get something to eat, since there were so many to be fed at the Rainbolt's.

Lib Rainbolt replied, "Yes, an American lives there, but he is married to a Mexican." "Well," said Little Hart in a casual tone of voice, "we'll just go over there and kill the fellow for that." Turning to his comrades he inquired if any wanted to go with him. Two offered, and mounting their horses the three rode rapidly over to the Haskins' house. When they reached the door, they called out "Hello!" and Haskins, who had just got up came to the door and stepped outside to talk to his visitors. He had hardly put his feet beyond the door when Little Hart shot him down, right under the eyes of his wife who was looking through the door to see who it was that had come. It was as brutal a killing as was ever done in Lincoln County. Neither Little Hart nor his two companions had ever before seen Haskins, and they had no personal grudge against him. They shot him simply because they had developed a blood lust to kill all Mexicans and as many as possible of Americans who had allied themselves with the Mexicans by marriage or any other way.

This journey of the Harrells to Roswell was marked by another killing, this time one of their number, Ben Turner, a brother-in-law of the Harrells. Shortly after leaving Picacho, Ben Turner left the party and rode over to a Mexican house a short distance from the road to see about some corn he had traded for before the feud began. When he reached the house, some of the women who had lived there came to the door and claimed that they knew nothing about the transaction. Ben Turner inquired if any of the men were about. The women assured him that none of them were at home. Seeing that it was useless to pursue the matter further, Ben Turner wheeled his horse and started to rejoin the Harrell party.

But he had not got far from the house when someone fired at him from ambush and killed him. It was always said that it was Martin Chávez who did this killing, but it was never known positively that this was the case. All that could be said with certainty would be that some Mexican having heard of the coming of the Harrells had accordingly seen a favorable chance to shoot Ben Turner and had taken advantage of it. I remember that my father, together with Major Hunter who happened to be at our house, went down and brought Ben Turner's body to Picacho. They placed it for the time being in an empty house there, then buried it the next day. The rest of the Harrells had not been inclined to stay in the vicinity and look after the body of their comrade.

On this same trip to Roswell there were five other killings. When the Harrell party was about fifteen miles from Roswell, it met six ox teams, five of which were driven by Mexicans, while the remaining one was driven by an American, George Kimbrell, who was married to a native woman. The Harrells immediately began shooting and killed all five Mexicans. George Kimbrell somehow managed to come out of this affair with his life, but no one ever clearly understood why, since he had a Mexican wife, he did not meet a fate similar to that of Joe Haskins. Some have said that he made the Harrells believe that he was just an American who happened to be traveling with the Mexicans, while others claimed that Kimbrell hid in his wagon under blankets and so escaped notice by the Harrells. However it may be, it is quite certain that George Kimbrell had a close call that day.

After this slaughter of Mexicans, the Harrells continued on their way to Roswell. Undoubtedly they would have killed others during that journey had not most of the Mexicans living on the river received warning somehow that the dreaded *Tejanos* were coming, and promptly betook themselves to secure hiding places.

After reaching Roswell the Harrells spent several days trying to formulate plans for going back to Lincoln and exterminating the population. But as the leading spirits could not agree as to the best plan of attack upon the town, they dropped the idea and decided to return to Texas. Some of the Harrell crowd attempted a final piece of lawlessness that resulted in the bodies of four of them finding graves in the soil of New Mexico. Van Smith, who conducted the store and hotel at Roswell, was a sporting man who kept the finest race horses that could be procured. Zack Crumpton and three others in the Harrell crowd cast covetous eyes on a fine racing mare belonging to Smith, and laid plans to raid Smith's corral and take her. Smith somehow got wind of their purpose and locked his little mare up in his house, where she was secure from all horse thieves.

Finding themselves balked by Smith's precaution, Zack Crumpton and his associates determined to get even with him by stealing the rest of his horses. Activated more by a spirit of revenge than a desire to obtain valuable horses, they proceeded to break into Smith's adobe corral, using the means generally employed. Pulling a horse-hide rope back and forth like a saw across one side of the corral, they made a gash from top to bottom. Then they moved their sawing apparatus to another point in the wall and cut a similar gash. It was then an easy matter to knock out the adobes between the two cuts making an opening wide enough for one horse to pass through.

The next morning when Van Smith discovered what had happened, he lost no time gathering a party of his friends and starting after the horse thieves. His party came upon them a little before daybreak of the second day when all were asleep. Van Smith and his companions showed no mercy, killing all four then and there and burying their bodies.

This was the last trouble caused by any of the Harrells in Lincoln County. Soon after this they went back to Texas, and their going was certainly a good riddance for New Mexico. But even with them out of the Territory, Van Smith did not feel that his life was safe in Roswell. It was likely enough that some of the friends of Zack Crumpton's crowd would return and try to even the score with him, so he left the area, going first to Las Vegas, then to Santa Fe, and never afterwards had much to do with Roswell.

In closing this account of the Harrell War, I shall tell what became of the seven Harrell brothers. I knew only five of them, but in order of ages were Bill, John, Sam, Tom, Hart, Ben, and Merrett. A striking fact about the group was that they all came to violent deaths except possibly Sam. Ben was killed in the beginning of the war and five of the others met violent deaths later.

13

The Casey Store and Its Clerks

SHORTLY AFTER THE HARRELL WAR SUBSIDED, Father determined
to enlarge the store at our ranch. Since about 1870 he had kept on
hand a small stock of goods to supply the needs of his renters and
of our immediate neighbors; but now he planned to go into the
business of running a store in a regular way and on a larger scale
than before. He thought there was a good opportunity for a store
at our place since the only stores in the country then were at
Lincoln, Roswell, and Seven Rivers.

Another cause for Father's deciding to go into the store business on this impressive scale was that he had on hand some money
needing to be invested. He had just returned from a trip to Arizona
where he had sold his cattle, receiving a rather large sum for them.
A. P. Harding and Peter Robertson, prominent cattlemen of Texas,
and both particular friends of Father, were delivering a large herd of
cattle to fulfill a Government contract. They came by our ranch and
Father took advantage of the opportunity to throw in with these
friends in the hope of selling his own cattle for something like the
same good price the herd of Harding and Robertson would bring.

But on the way to Arizona, Harding and Robertson made
Father a good offer for his cattle, and he sold to them.

As one condition of the sale was that Father was to continue
with his cattle in order to help look after them, he remained with
Harding and Robertson until they reached Tucson. Then, when all

the cattle had been disposed of, Father started to return to New Mexico. He came back by Santa Fe and used the money received for his cattle to buy a large and complete stock of goods from Speigelberg Brothers and Staab, the well-known wholesale firm that in those times conducted such an extensive business all through the Southwest.

Father at once began preparation to start the store. Needing a suitable building, he chose the old two-room adobe which we had used for a dwelling when we first came to the ranch. By knocking out the partition in the middle, he made it into one long room, large enough to serve as a store. One of the things I remember distinctly about the overhauling of the old building was the making of the door and window shutters. Dowlin's Mill on the Ruidoso was the nearest source of supply for the lumber, and it then had to be hauled forty-five miles with ox wagon down to our place over one of the worst imaginable mountain roads. The lumber was rough and full of knots, and every inch of it had to be dressed by hand before it was in shape to be used.

The carpenter was secured from Fort Stanton, and he had a hard enough time working with such lumber, but he made a good job of it, as shown by this description of the door. It was made of two thicknesses of boards laid straight, while the second, or facing part, was of two-inch boards tongued and grooved and laid slantingly. The result was a door sturdy and picturesque. The reason it was made four inches thick was to make it a real protection, and indeed it needed to be that in those days. I remember how the old door looked years afterwards. There was many a bullet hole in it where some cowboy had tried his .45 on it as a target. The window shutters were made equally as strong as the door, and were just as important in giving proper security to the stock of goods.

The store, of course, handled general merchandise, which in those times consisted of dry goods, groceries, hardware, and whiskey. Having whiskey as a part of the stock of a store excited no comment; in fact it was the usual and ordinary thing. The whiskey, in barrels, had as much a place in the stock of goods as did a sack of flour or a keg of nails, for that was a time in which almost every person took a drink, the only noticeable difference between most people on this score being that some drank more constantly and heavily than others.

Sometimes a group of cowboys bringing a herd of cattle through from Texas could become so dry from the long trip across the Staked Plains and up the Pecos that when they reached a source of supply, such as was Father's store, they could not refrain from partaking too freely, with the result that generally they felt an irresistible impulse to draw their pistols and shoot in a frolicsome way at whatever might be around. There also were in the country some men so addicted to liquor that it might almost be said they were never entirely sober. But the number of such drunkards was so small as to be almost negligible. While drinking whiskey was common enough in those times, drunkenness was by no means the prevalent condition of the old timers.

While on the topic, I might add that some men went on terrible drunks periodically, but the general impression was that these served as a sort of safeguard for the man's physical and, perhaps, moral well-being. The common saying was, "He's been on a big drunk and vomited up some of the damn meanness he had in him, and now he'll be extra good for a spell." And so it usually was; these fellows really would behave in a very exemplary manner for from three to six months. I suppose the truth was that they needed a good emetic to remove biliousness or some other obstruction to their well-being.

But to continue about the store and give some description of the stock of goods actually on hand, it will be interesting to know what were the necessities of life the people expected to have supplied by a store like ours. We usually kept on hand three kinds of woolen goods — alpaca, merino, and delaine. These were the materials out of which the women chiefly made their heavier dresses. In cotton goods we generally carried calico, lawn, and domestic, both bleached and unbleached. Of the unbleached domestic usually called by the Mexican designation, *manta,* we carried two grades, a very thin and coarse quality which was used largely by the natives for shirts and drawers in the summer, and a heavier and stronger kind that was generally made into sacks for corn and other grains. In our stock of dry goods were always piles of shawls, for the natives used them altogether as an outer garment, for protection from the cold. The women would buy heavy woolen shawls for winter and lighter ones of merino for summer, while the men would buy and use blankets. Overcoats, either for men or women, were virtually unknown at that time.

Some of the other articles always kept on hand were stockings, both woolen and cotton, and ribbons which were especially popular with the natives for sashes and hair ribbons. We had also lots of cheap ginghams and cotton checks, which were in demand for dresses and aprons. I remember also a brown soft goods, the name of which I have forgotten, which I always liked for my skirts. It would not tear easily, and I could easily walk or ride through weeds and undergrowth without my skirt's suffering any disaster. It may be noticed that in the enumeration of our stock of dry goods I have made no mention of silks or satins; these, in those days, were conspicuous by their absence.

The stock of hardware was rather extensive, consisting mainly of tools needed in farming and of household necessities. We carried the old style iron hoe — big and heavy enough to kill a man — pickaxes, grubbing hoes, adzes, spades, and shovels, and two kinds of axes, the common and the broadax.

There were plows and two kinds of harness, chain and leather. We also kept a good supply of old-style iron nails, horse shoes, and the nails for them, taps and bolts, together with hammers and hatchets and saws. We also had tin plates and cups, with iron knives and forks. We often had to supply men going out on the range with what they needed for camping, so also kept on hand frying pans, Dutch ovens, and the like.

In the line of groceries there always were large quantities of sugar, several kinds of brown sugar as well as white. Of the brown there were two grades, the ordinary and a yellow sugar called "YC" which was said to be the purest made. The white sugar we kept both in granulated form and in cubes, the latter being preferred by campers because if the packages spilled the contents could easily be picked up. Coffee was always in demand and we always had a large supply of it. Sperm candles were sold in large quantities as they were the only means of lighting at night. Coal oil was unknown at first, and when people did learn of it, the price was too great for common use. We did not need to keep lard and tallow, because the people had their own sources of supply in their hogs and cattle. There always was an abundance of dried apples and peaches, and we kept a small quantity of canned goods such as sardines, oysters, peaches, plums, and pears.

Patronage grew rapidly until Father was selling to all the nearby ranchmen and natives. In addition there was always a good deal of transient trade, both herders who were driving cattle through and soldiers who were passing by on scouting expeditions. From even as far away as the Pecos, Seven Rivers, and the Beckwith ranch, people came to Father's store, finding it more convenient to buy from the "Casey Store" than from the Murphy store at Lincoln. Father's store was eighteen or twenty miles nearer, and even when people from the lower part of the county had to go to Lincoln on other business such as taxes, court matters, and the like, they often would wait to make their purchases of needed supplies until they reached Father's store on their way home. This reduced the distances they would have to haul a heavy load; also Father's popularity, always strong among the people of the Seven Rivers section, had much to do with securing this trade. Everybody knew that the honesty and fairness of his dealings were in marked contrast to those of his main rival, L.G. Murphy & Co. But this did not tend to make the "establishment" in Lincoln appreciate him.

Another competitor, Van Smith's store at Roswell, was not popular in the country, either, because its owner was a sporting man and his life too fast for the more circumspect citizens of the lower part of the county.

Father was much too busy with his various other interests to give the store much personal attention; he always had a clerk, especially to look after the store. He tried to pick a man with enough education and intelligence to assume the double role of clerk and schoolmaster for the children. Most of the clerks we had were from the drifting class of men, those of good education and better antecedents who were knocking about from pillar to post, as the old saying was in the West, for some cause or other. They generally stayed only a short time with us, and then the wanderlust or some other cause took them elsewhere. In 1872 and 1874 we had as clerk M. Ashmun Upson, whom everybody called Uncle Ash; in the latter part of 1873, a man by the name of Howard as well as one by the name of Campbell; in the year 1874, we had Abneth McCabe; in 1875 Ash Upson again with us; in 1876, we had a man by the name of Turner, and in 1877, there was John Brown.

Howard found it altogether too lonely so did not stay long. He was a fine bookkeeper, although not good as a teacher. John Brown did not stay long, either, for he was there at the time we all had smallpox. He was a "lunger," and at the prospect of smallpox he got scared and left. Abneth McCabe was with us only about a year as clerk and teacher. However, he remained in the country and proved himself in difficulties a true friend of the family, as I show in other portions of this book.

The children were too young to have much to do about the store, but sometimes we helped in selling of small things such as candy and canned goods. I usually made myself useful as interpreter when the natives came into the store. Most of the clerks knew little if any Spanish, and as I had learned early to speak it readily, I often facilitated transactions by serving as intermediary between the clerks and native customers. The store business always had a great fascination for me, and when I was somewhat older, I interested myself in learning all I could about business methods. I learned the prices of different goods and how to mark them in such a way as to show both the original cost as well as the retail prices. I also became familiar with making entries in the various ledgers and account books that had to be kept, for the business was conducted on a credit basis. I also learned how to draw up a bill of sale, a power of attorney, a note of hand, and a due bill, possessing as I did a wonderfully retentive memory. I had learned all these forms by heart by the time I was twelve years old, and was able to write any of them either in Spanish or English.

Most of the transient trade, the cowboys and the soldiers, paid cash for what they got from the store. But all resident customers traded for what they wanted. They would bring their corn, wheat, beans, oats, and barley and give it in exchange for what they needed from the store. Father was able to use all the grain that came to him in this way. The Government insisted that the Army horses be fed on corn, and as there was a great deal of scouting going on all the time by the soldiers — either in pursuit of the Indians or cattle thieves — Father needed to keep on hand a large stock of corn. I recall that he kept a good deal of it at Diego Salcido's place at Redepente, and that he would have it hauled down to Cottonwood, Peñasco, Seven Rivers, and even out into Dark Canyon, when the soldiers were on scouting expeditions that took them as far away as those places. We got nine cents a pound for this corn.

The store helped add much to our prosperity. Father knew that it was likely to increase the envy and enmity that the powerful L.G. Murphy & Co. were prone to feel toward any competitor, and he was very careful never to trespass on any of their lucrative Fort Stanton contracts. He felt, however, that he was entitled to a fair share of the patronage of the resident and transient trade, and especially that which was in his vicinity.

Live and let live was his policy, but it did not suffice to protect him from the sinister machinations of L.G. Murphy & Co. who would stand no rivals, even if they had to take the life of a rival.

14

Ash Upson: Rolling Stone of the West

HIS NAME WAS MARSHALL ASHMUN UPSON but he was called Uncle Ash Upson, or simply Uncle Ash. He played such a major part in my young life as my first and most stimulating school master and also in the early development of Lincoln County that I feel that it is imperative to devote a chapter to the qualities of this remarkable man. He came to our place first in 1872 and in this way. Father went to Fort Stanton shortly before his store was to be opened, met Ash Upson, and engaged him to come to our ranch to clerk in the trading post and to teach what was commonly called the Casey school.

Uncle Ash was an old newspaper man who had drifted into the West and had been knocking about in various parts of it for fifteen years. When he was living in the East he had held important positions on several leading newspapers, one of which was *The Cincinnati Inquirer,* but he was in the throes of a wanderlust that kept him moving from one place to another. In 1870 he was in Santa Fe, and in 1871, in Las Vegas working for *The Mail.* From Las Vegas he came to Lincoln, the reason being best given in an extract from one of his letters, several of which were later published by his niece, Mrs. A. J. Muzzy of Bristol, Connecticut, in one of the Carlsbad, New Mexico, papers.

In a letter dated "Casey's Mill, Lincoln Co., N. M., Jan. 1st,

Marshall Ashmun Upson
was a roving newspaperman
who taught school to many
Lincoln County youngsters and
lingered pleasantly in pioneer
memories as "Uncle Ash."

Courtesy of Ola C. Jones

1872, he tells of his leaving Las Vegas and going to Lincoln as follows:

I was offered a printing office worth $3000 if I would publish a Republican paper. I refused it with scorn. "My offenses are rank and smell to heaven" but with all my faults there is no price for me. . . . I made enough out of the Las Vegas office to buy me a horse, saddle, and bridle. A friend asked me to come to the little town of Lincoln, and go into business with him. He represented that the sutlers at Fort Bliss, Unions and Lombard would give him a stock of goods on commission. So I came.

However, the story I always heard about Uncle Ash's presence in Lincoln was somewhat different from his version. It was said that he had come to Lincoln expecting to start a newspaper in that town, which was then supposed to be most certainly on the road to becoming a metropolis. A partner in the enterprise by the name of Alec Duvall [Duval] had also come to Lincoln. But the paper had never had an existence, the local accounts being that neither of the partners could remain sober long enough to get it on its feet. However, the two accounts are not inconsistent for in those times a man's occupation or profession was likely to be a mingling of several activities, and it is altogether likely that Uncle Ash may have intended to combine merchandising and publishing.

I remember distinctly how Uncle Ash looked when he appeared at our ranch. He was a small, frail-looking man obviously not in good health, even for his years — I think he was about forty-five. His features were far from attractive, his complexion being sallow and his face badly pitted from smallpox. His nose had been broken and was almost flat. Uncle Ash used to joke about it, calling it "an unfortunate nasal necessity," but boasting that "it blew as sonorously as of yore." But the man soon showed such endearing qualities that we forgot the lack of what he, himself, with his turn for high-sounding language, might have called "personal pulchritude."

Uncle Ash's impressions of us and the ranch on the Hondo I am able to give by another extract from one of his letters:

I went down with S. to Placita (newly named Lincoln) stayed a few days, met an old Texan, Robert Casey, who lives some twenty-five miles below the Fort. The valley is pretty well settled with American rancheros, and most of them are married to Mexican women. Casey is the wealthiest of them all. Has the only grist mill in the valley, over 6000 acres of land under cultivation, hundreds of head of stock, — horses, cattle, mules, burros, sheep, hogs, fowls — and last but not least, a splendid American wife and seven fine, healthy, handsome, well-behaved children. He is one of Nature's noblemen. No education, but a gentleman by intuition — it is no credit to him — he can't help it. His wife is a lady for the same reason. His children are pleasant, no quarrels, no bad language, and they, like their parents, are very handsome.

I met a great many of the rancheros at the Placita, and was astonished to find how many of them I knew. Casey insisted on my going home with him for a week or two. I went, or rather, came. I found the children untaught; got stuck after little Lillie, eight years old, commenced teaching her letters. The old lady jumped on me and Casey, too, and declared that I could not leave the ranch until all her children who were old enough (five) could read and write, no matter what it cost; Casey took his wife's part — and what could your old uncle do? I knew, and I did it.

The next morning a comfortable room in the spacious house was fitted up, books and slates and all the requisites were procured from Fort Stanton, and I was duly installed as the proper agent to lick the Casey cubs into educational contour! The fame of your uncle's great store of knowledge went forth into all the land. Casey's house was besieged by neighbors from every direction with their progeny in their hands, seeking for them the hidden mysteries of A, B, C. Hardly any of the neighbors' children can speak English. One old Mexican woman brought a child that could not talk at all, to learn to read. What could I do?

Casey is going to Chihuahua in the spring and insists on my staying here until May and then going with him. Now, darn it! Quit your laughing. I have as good a right to teach school as you have! . . . . You can't guess how well we live here. A large family, lots of peons (Mexican laborers). They kill a steer or a hog, or a sheep, or a half dozen chickens every two or three days. Sweet milk, butter milk, whey, fresh eggs, butter, broiled chicken, fresh fish, wild duck! Oh, there's no use talking, I can't do justice to the subject. Great, nice clean mattress *(colchon)* a foot thick. Fishing tackle, shot-gun, and rifle. A choice of twenty horses to ride. Deer in the mountains, antelope on the plains, duck on the river, and fish in it. Why should I not be happy?

I think Uncle Ash really was happy during his stay with us and I am sure that we all grew very fond of him.

In another of his letters written March 8th, 1872, Uncle Ash gave to his Connecticut relatives some other details regarding the Caseys, especially the children he was teaching.

Mr. Casey has lived in Texas nearly all his life, and has been in this valley going on four years. The ranch was considerably improved when he bought it, having been left on account of Indians. Casey is an old Indian fighter. The Apaches fear him as the devil abhors holy water. He has lost some stock, but not lately. He lost $3000 worth at one time (in 1869).

A better teacher, I am sure, never lived. He was patience personified and did most of his teaching orally. In fact that was about the only way it could be done for our facilities in the way of textbooks were very limited. Such as we had were procured through the post trader's store at Fort Stanton. But books were not a necessity to a teacher like Uncle Ash. He delighted in explaining causes and effects and to use as the basis of his teaching even the homeliest object. I remember his once putting before us a steaming teakettle, and with that as a starting point carrying us along into an explanation of clouds, vapor, and rain.

No matter how busy he was through the day at the store he never suffered our lessons to fall into the background. Each day he saw that we had done the day's work and recited upon it before he went to bed, even though the school sessions had to be extended into the night.

Our school was the end room on the east in a building having three rooms in a row. Father had this one fixed up for a schoolroom, and we always afterward spoke of it as the schoolroom, even though it had long before served its day for such use, and had become devoted to other uses. Even at that time it was not unreservedly devoted to school uses, being used also for general storage. There is where we kept the spare bed which was brought into use when company came. Once when Father had a chance to buy 50 one-hundred-pound sacks of flour at a Government sale at Fort Stanton for the low price of fifty cents a hundred, he stored it in the school-room until he could sell it at a higher price. Some of the surplus stock for the store also found a place in this room.

The equipment for the room, was of course, homemade. The carpenter, a man by the name of White, made a long desk with a sloping lid. Under it there was room for the equipment of the three older children. My brothers, Add and Will, preempted the end seats and left me the middle. The younger children had simply small benches or stools. He also made us a blackboard by merely taking some lumber, planing it smooth, and painting it black. Uncle Ash had his table and chair near the center of the room. On the former were his books, paper, ink, and rulers.

Our books were McGuffey's Reader, Webster's Blue-back Speller, Ray's Arithmetic, and Monteith's Geography. Uncle Ash made our copy books for us himself by folding several sheets of paper to the middle and sewing them together. The copy he wrote at the head of the page, and we wrote our imitations of it on the lines below. For doing sums (as we designated our arithmetic work) we used the old-fashioned slate and slate pencil, which the present hygenic generation has rejected.

Ordinarily we were well behaved. Uncle Ash's biggest problem was protecting sacks of sugar stored in the schoolroom. By placing them on top of the flour and keeping the mouths of the sacks securely tied he could prevent our eating it. As a rule he went fishing on Saturdays and extended the sugar additional protection by locking the door and giving Mother the key. The flour sacks, I may add, were useful in other ways. I can remember how I liked to climb upon them and sit comfortably while studying my lessons. Up there, I could lean back against one of the sacks, while on our benches I could not, for they were without backs and often I got very weary sitting on them.

Uncle Ash insisted upon our being thorough in our work, and extremely careful as to details, even minor ones. With him anything worth doing was worth doing well. All my life I have benefitted from his exacting my conformity to his standards. Our only assignments in composition were letters which were to be mailed. Uncle Ash demanded excellence not only in the writing but even in the folding of the paper and the placing of the stamp on the envelopes. We used paper about the size in vogue today and in order to fold it suitably for the envelope Uncle Ash trained us rigidly in doubling the paper in the middle so that the two corners coincided, and then in putting one forefinger on the two points to turn it over and fold one-third, and then the remaining third back. In this process the corners must be even and the edges tightly creased. Once this procedure was mastered the letter looked better for it.

He was equally exacting as to the stamp. No slovenliness or eccentricity was tolerated. His training was ineffaceable and today, after the passage of many years, I find myself folding a letter and placing a stamp as carefully as though it were to be inspected by Uncle Ash.

As he states in the letter quoted, some of the families in the neighborhood sent children to our school. Father was glad to have them but he felt that they should pay a small tuition to augment Uncle Ash's income. He began with the five Caseys, Ham Mills' little daughter, and Matilde Clene. Gradually the number increased until he had a half dozen who were not of our family.

In one of his letters Ash Upson speaks of an interesting experiment on his part in what would today be termed adult education.

My pupils are very good in their behavior, with the exception of the children of larger growth. I have seven men, heads of families, who only require sufficient education to keep their own accounts! Casey has a mill and has accounts with the neighbors for many miles around. The trade here is all traffic — there is little money in circulation. Corn, wheat, oats, horses, cattle, sheep, hogs, etc. are pretty much considered legal tender. So there are interminable accounts, and as very few of these Texans, Californians, etc. can figure at all, their original modes of keeping accounts are interesting and astonishing.

One six-foot-three genius, of Southern proclivities, has been in the habit of keeping fractions of *fanagas* (measures of 2¼ bushels, Mexican) with little dots of a pen or pencil. He complains that although it does very well in cold weather yet the advent of flies or other insects most aggravatingly interfere with his bookkeeping; and he is determined to use figures in the future exclusively, doubting the ability of any insect to counterfeit his formation of them. I share his doubts, for I cannot do it myself.

Casey, who is a very intelligent man, uses more original methods of keeping accounts, or did so before I came here. They are all getting so they can tell how much 4 fanagas or 400 will come to at $6.50 per *fanaga* and put it on their books in proper form. I rather like it. I started in to correct one of my lambs — Ham Mills, a six-footer who has killed three white men and innumerable Indians in his time — with a ferrule. He laughed, held out his hand, took his medicine pretty hard, and then had the temerity to seize his preceptor, take away his weapon, turn him across his knee, and remind him of juvenile days, by inflicting a good spanking.

The other lambs interfered; there was a general scuffle, benches, tables, and chairs upset, my bed broken down, books and papers strewn over the floor, and at the *finale*, Casey and I stood over him with the ferrule, belaboring him most unmercifully — my lambs are good natured and full of fun, but they are mighty rough!

With him the important thing in teaching was to start with the known and the familiar and to lead our minds out to an understanding of the unknown and remote. I remember that he led us to an understanding of a vacuum by starting with the explanation of how the housefly is able to walk on the ceiling by having attached to his feet an apparatus by which he creates a vacuum.

He believed also in making us observe things about us. He had us watching the variations in time of the sunrise, and led us to discover for ourselves facts that would not have been very interesting had we read them.

Uncle Ash was very fond of jokes. I recall that he had difficulty with the individual spelling of Old Judge Kimbrell, who was the justice of the peace in our neighborhood. In the oath attached to a legal paper which the Judge had drawn up there were several glaring blunders in spelling. Ash brought the paper to the schoolroom and exhibited the mistakes to us. The next time the Judge came to the ranch we met him with the pleasing news that Uncle Ash criticized his spelling. Kimbrell, who had no idea how poor his spelling was, "jumped" Uncle Ash: "Now, if you'd make fun of my writing I wouldn't have said a word, because I realize that it is bad. But I want you to know that I always stood at the head of the class in spelling." Uncle Ash looked at the Judge quizzically and replied, "Well, Judge, you might have done that, but you have surely degenerated. You spelled 'God' the other day with a little 'j' in that oath you drew up." The Judge laughed and admitted the charge.

He was an energetic soul, always busy about something. His activity sometimes was not in lines generally termed worthwhile, but to him it was satisfying. While we were studying in the schoolroom he sometimes played solitaire, of which he was very fond. He spent much of his time writing letters. The neighbors frequently called on him for that service, for few of them could write.

He seemed to enjoy raising chickens, and while he was with us he put in nearly all his spare time looking after the two or three hundred young chickens he had. Though he was successful with them there was occasionally a disastrous attack by a skunk that managed to burrow its way into the chicken house where there were a number of hens with their broods. It made a terrible killing and Uncle Ash grieved as though one of the children had died.

A simple, kindly spirit — that was Uncle Ash. He seemed to have lost ambition and was content to drift with wind and tide. "Viva este día, y mañana cuidado por mañana" (Live today and tomorrow looks out for tomorrow), he used to say, and I think that represented his outlook. Yet he sometimes expressed the futility of being a rolling stone. In a letter he wrote to his sister about her son he said, "I do not censure Bertie for disliking the irksomeness of a shop, but dear sister, if he has a penchant for wandering, you should strangle it. I know what I might have been and what I might have had if I had but settled and remained *industriously* in any of the localities my erratic disposition prompted me to desert. Give my love to Bertie, and tell him to ride his impulses with a rough bit."

After two or three terms of school he left us and went to Roswell. His urge to roam took him to Las Cruces and Silver City. Then he returned to us for a few months and was very helpful in settling the estate after Father's death. Again he went to Roswell and became a sort of right-hand man to Pat Garrett in his irrigation projects and land deals. Uncle Ash could always pick up a livelihood, because he was almost in a class with the fabulous Jack-of-all-trades. If not newspaper work, it might be serving as clerk in a store or acting as postmaster, being a justice of the peace, or a notary public, or even a teacher. Being one of the few truly educated men in the area, he was in demand for all sorts of services and was really the intellectual handyman for the country.

When Pat Garrett ran for sheriff in Chávez County and was defeated he got disgusted and decided to remove to Uvalde, Texas, and Uncle Ash elected to go with him. It was at Garrett's in Uvalde County, Texas, that Uncle Ash died in 1895.

The Rolling Stone of the West had at last come to a standstill.

15

Murder Most Foul & The Law's Vengeance

DISSATISFACTION WITH THE GENERAL CONTROL of politics in Lincoln County by the Murphy ring reached a crisis in the summer of 1875. By that time there were a good many more Americans in the country than before, and they were eager to do something to break the grip Murphy and his followers had on the county. A sort of general agreement was reached among the Americans that at the political convention to be held sometime in the summer a strong effort would be made to put some good men into the various county offices. As the county was altogether Democratic, there was no likelihood of a ticket made up of Republicans being brought forward. The whole success of the scheme to down the Murphy aggregation depended upon the Democratic convention's being induced to put forth nominees who were not under the Murphy control.

The day before the convention was to meet, Colonel Mickey Cronin, an ex-Army officer who had settled in Lincoln, came down to our house and spent the night. The object of his visit was to persuade Father to go to Lincoln and attend the convention. He explained to Father that his presence was especially desired because of his prominence and influence in the county. At first Father tried to beg off from going. Mother, too, was strongly opposed to the idea. They both felt that the efforts to shake the grip of the Murphy ring would be fraught with some danger to those who were responsible for the move or who participated prominently in it. Father was disinclined to incur any enmity from the Murphy crowd, for he well knew the ruthlessness of their methods in getting even with those against whom they held a grudge. But Colonel Cronin was insistent, and finally Father consented to go with him.

Early the next morning they set out for Lincoln, accompanied by the young man, Edmond Welch, who was then the clerk in our store. Father hoped to return the same day for he did not want Mother to have to assume the extra care of the store which she would have to do in the absence of Father and Edmond Welch. When Father said good-bye to Mother, he told her that he would start back home from Lincoln as early as possible in the afternoon.

The convention met on Sunday, August 2nd. It may seem somewhat strange that a Sunday should be selected for such a meeting, but there was no preaching whatever anywhere in the whole county, and farmers would be able to come to the county seat without losing a workday. That, of course, was important.

After Father left, we children went on to our nearest neighbors, the Lloyd's, expecting to spend the greater part of the day. We had a hilarious time playing with their son, Dick Lloyd who, although older than we, did not hesitate about entering into our games. But about the middle of the afternoon a dark shadow was cast over our merriment. Edmond Welch rode up, his horse showing plainly that he had been ridden hard, and the young man himself evidently under the greatest excitement. He brought the dreadful news that Father had been shot that afternoon in Lincoln about 2 o'clock, and was very badly wounded. Young as we were, we had heard of killings so frequently that we were inclined to take them as everyday events, but this time when it was our own dear father who was the victim, we felt differently about it.

Edmond did not stay to give us further particulars, but hurried on to carry the terrible news to Mother. Mrs. Lloyd realized that we should get home at once, and having a wagon hitched up she took us as rapidly as she could over the mile that intervened between the Lloyd place and ours.

When we reached home we found Mother all ready to start for Lincoln. She had had the best team on the place hitched to the hack, and had got herself ready for the trip. She told us that she did not think it best for us to go, as we could not do anything, and that we were to stay at home until she came back. Mrs. Lloyd agreed to stay at our house and look after us, and Mother felt sure we would be well taken care of. Mother afterward told me that she had made Edmond Welch drive the team in a high 'lope every foot of the way, when the road was free enough from rocks to make such rapid driving safe. She covered the distance to Lincoln in a remarkably short time and I am sure she risked her own safety more than once in her determination to get to Father's side as soon as possible.

When she arrived she found that friends had taken Father into Steve Stanley's house, and had done everything that could be done to make him comfortable and to save his life if that were possible.

William Wilson, who had done the shooting, was under arrest, although there had been such a strong feeling against him among Father's friends for the cowardly way he had done the shooting that he had narrowly escaped being lynched. Milder counsel, however, prevailed, and he was left in the hands of the law. Father's friends were reconciled to this course, because men of the Army who were in town that day declared that Wilson would most certainly be in safekeeping until the next term of court. This seemed to guarantee that Wilson would be held until his trial, although everyone knew that if he were placed in the jail at Lincoln he would in all likelihood make his escape.

Major Clendenin, Captain Randlett, and Captain Fechet, also stationed at the Fort, were warm personal friends of Father. They also appreciated the service he had rendered to the Army both while in it as a soldier and afterwards as a guide in the Indian campaigns. For these two reasons they were very active in securing the arrest and safekeeping of Wilson. Captain Fechet himself took the prisoner up to the Fort and saw to it that he was kept there under extra strong guard.

As we afterwards learned the particulars regarding that dreadful Sunday afternoon, what had happened was about as follows: The Murphy ring had been defeated in the convention by a large majority. The session in the morning had been a stormy one, and Major Murphy and his associate, Jimmie Dolan, had been greatly angered at the turn of events. They attributed their defeat to the fact that Father had thrown his influence against them. The convention adjourned with them both very furious and very loud in their declarations that they would win in the ensuing election, come what might.

The convention broke up about noon, and everyone went over to the hotel to eat. Father asked Welch to go with him to the Wortley Hotel and have dinner, and as they walked toward it, they happened to meet Wilson. Wilson had been working for Father up to a short time previous, and Father greeted him cordially and invited him to go along and have dinner with them. Wilson accepted the invitation, and the three, Father, Welch, and Wilson, ate dinner together at the hotel. When they had finished their meal Father paid the bill for all three. I am positive that these details are correct, for I learned them from Edmond Welch.

At the close of the meal, Wilson left the company of Father and Welch. Shortly afterwards Murphy and Dolan got hold of him and offered him $500 if he would waylay and kill Father. They included in their proposal a guarantee that he would not be punished if he were arrested. They claimed they held sway in the county and could manipulate the sheriff and the court. They even armed Wilson out of their store and then instructed him as to where to conceal himself so as to accomplish his dastardly undertaking.

Not in the least suspecting danger of that sort, Father had gone ahead getting ready to start home. He had somehow lost track of Edmond Welch, and in searching for him, he went to the Murphy store, which was the great gathering place in the town. Not finding him there, Father started down the street to look in other places. Wilson had by that time stationed himself in concealment at a little house a few hundred yards east of the Murphy store. When he saw Father approaching, he deliberately waited until Father had come within fifteen or twenty paces, and then fired his rifle. The bullet struck Father in the hip, inflicting a severe wound but not bad enough to cause Father to fall to the ground. Father, of course, had his pistol, but he did not draw it even after he had been shot. His impulse was evidently to take shelter behind the walls of a vacant house that was close at hand, and this done, to prepare to defend himself.

But Wilson had not completed his murderous work. No sooner did he perceive that Father was attempting to get in the shelter of the east end of this house than he went around to the west end of it.

Consequently he and Father met face to face back of this house. Wilson did not hesitate to fire again, this time sending the bullet into Father's face near the corner of his mouth.

The shooting quickly brought many people to the scene. Some of Father's friends picked him up from where he had fallen and carried him into the Steve Stanley house. Dr. Carballo, post surgeon at the Fort, happened to be in town that day and at once gave Father medical aid. His efforts to save Father's life were unavailing. Father lingered all night and the next morning, but died about two o'clock the next afternoon. The wound in his face made it impossible for him to speak but he remained conscious to the last moments of his life, and knew clearly that Mother was with him. She stayed right at his side all the time, for if she left but for a moment, Father became restless until she got back to him.

The next day the body was brought down to our place and buried the same day in our family graveyard. I remember the funeral very distinctly. There was a multitude of people present, more than I had ever before seen together. What particularly impressed me was the number of Americans who came. I did not know there were so many in the whole country, but the news of what had happened at Lincoln had spread quickly and all who heard it had come, some from a great distance. The burial rites were simple, as they perforce had to be. There was no priest available, and the religious part of the service was conducted by Major Murphy, whose previous education for the priesthood seemed to give him more of a right to officiate in such matters than anyone else in the county.

At the time Mother knew nothing of the part he had played in bringing about the killing of Father. Father, as I have said, was unable to tell Mother anything of the motives he might have believed were behind Wilson's action. In fact, the connection Murphy had with the killing did not come out until months later. At the time of the funeral, no one dared to suggest a suspicion that Murphy was the instigator of Wilson's crime. Major Murphy had clearly chosen as agent a former employee of Father's and had coached him to put forth as the reason for the killing that Father had tried to beat him out of some wages that were due him. If Mother had in the least suspected Major Murphy of having a hand in the deed, she would never have permitted him to profane the occasion with his presence.

As so much was made in the newspaper accounts of a quarrel

in the morning between Father and Wilson over a few dollars in wages I feel it needful to tell something about the relations between Father and Wilson when the latter was working at our place, and also how he came to leave. Wilson just dropped in at our place, and applied to Father for work. As there was need for hands just then, Father put him to work first on the farm. A little later, Father took him along with some other men to our Feliz place and started building a stock house and a corral. When they completed this work, Father sent Wilson back to our home place with the ox wagon that had been over on the Feliz. Father and the other men remained on the Feliz, and during their stay, the Mes* crowd came and stole all the horses they had with them, leaving them afoot. This delayed the return of Father and the others longer than they had expected.

In the meantime Wilson, after his return to our place, made the acquaintance of an old man by the name of Harper who was working for a few weeks at the Lloyd place while resting his team — a fine pair of black mules — before going on to California. No sooner did the acquaintance develop than Wilson became fired with the idea of going to California with Harper and he told Mother that he would like to be paid off immediately so he could start. Mother told him that this would not be possible until Father returned from the Feliz, and she encouraged him to expect Father's return shortly. Wilson seemed entirely satisfied about the situation and continued on at our place. He told us he was not in as much of a hurry to leave as he thought he was because Harper, who had left the Lloyds, was going to remain in Lincoln until Wilson was ready to go along with him. All the time Wilson seemed in the best of humor toward Mother and the rest of us.

He did not work for us during this time, for he considered that his agreement with Father had terminated when he got back to our place from the Feliz. He simply stayed on and spent most of his time getting his traps ready for the journey to California. As he was not especially busy, he talked rather freely to us about himself. According to his story, he was from New York State and had been in jail several times. He even went so far as to claim he had spent some time in the penitentiary at Sing Sing. To hear him tell it, he was most certainly a hard criminal and seemingly very proud of the fact; but

---

*Four brothers and their followers whose livelihood was said to be stealing.

I have no way of knowing whether or not he was telling the truth. Vicious men of his stamp often tried to give, after coming West, the impression that they were very bad men of the sort described in the language of the time as "wild and wooly and hard to curry." That may have been what Wilson was trying to do in all his big talking.

A few days later Father arrived. I remember that he reached the placc about two o'clock in the morning after a particularly arduous journey. Before he went to sleep Mother told him that Wilson wanted to be paid off and allowed to leave. Father said, "All right. Tell the clerk in the store to settle with Wilson and pay him all that is coming to him. Have him do this first thing in the morning."

The next morning Wilson got up early and came into the kitchen. Seeing that the fire had not been made, he got kindling and wood and started one. All the time he talked volubly about how anxious he was to do all he could before leaving us, and he was very expressive of his appreciation of all that we had done for him while he stayed with us. Mother told him that Father had given instructions that his wages were to be paid, and Wilson went over to the store to see the clerk about the matter. He came back and said he would like to have a chance to say good-bye to Father, but when Mother told him that Father was very tired and was sleeping late that morning, Wilson said, "Mrs. Casey, I wouldn't have you wake him up for anything in the world."

Under such circumstances Wilson left us and went to Lincoln. He hung around there a week or two but he did not get to go with Harper to California. It seems Harper had decided to go on without waiting for Wilson. I often wondered if somebody did not put Harper wise to the sort of man Wilson was and if Harper did not suspect him for some sinister motive in seeking to associate himself with Harper. One would not have to go farther than Harper's fine span of mules to find an inducement that would have appealed strongly to a man of Wilson's stamp. He would realize that there would be many a spot on the long journey to California where by killing Harper he could equip himself with that valuable pair of mules.

The trial of Wilson came up in the October term of District Court. Mother went to Lincoln and remained there during the entire time consumed in the trial; she did not, however, think it advisable for all the children to go, but since the baby was too young to be left at home, Mother took me along to look after him. By that time Mother understood that the Murphy ring had brought about Father's death and she was determined to thwart any of their plans to let the murderer go free. She could not do much actively, but her presence at the trial would be a mute but powerful reminder to the friends of Father and to those conducting the prosecution that Wilson ought to be given the full penalty of the law.

Undoubtedly the plan was for Wilson either to be cleared or to escape before or after the trial. The Murphy ring so generally had things their own way in Lincoln County they felt certain of carrying out their scheme in this instance. One day while we were in Lincoln Captain Fechet came to where we were staying in some rooms Mother had rented, for she would not go to the Wortley Hotel as it belonged to the Murphy ring. He called for Mother, and when she asked him to come in, he declined, saying he did not have time. Then he explained he had just come to assure her that the officers at Fort Stanton who had known Father had vowed they would stand by her, and were determined to bring about the assassin's receiving the utmost severity of the law. He then disclosed that an emissary of the Murphy crowd had just presented to him the proposal that he turn Wilson over to them and let them lynch him so as to save the necessity of a trial, claiming that such a step had Mother's sanction. Captain Fechet gave her this advice, "Mrs. Casey, if I were you, I wouldn't believe a single one of that crowd of dirty scoundrels. Don't trust them at all, for they'll do anything on God's earth to turn Wilson free. Now I have come to learn from you how you feel about this thing. Do you want Wilson turned over to them — and I'm sure that means he'll be allowed to escape — or do you want him carefully guarded and tried according to the law?" Mother's answer was positive and definite; I remember it word for word: "My God! Captain, no! I know nothing in the world about having Wilson lynched. I want the law to take its course. I am sure he will get full justice and I want that above all else for the sake of my children."

Captain Fechet replied, "You are exactly right, Mrs. Casey, and we'll bring the murderer to justice. I left him in charge of my sergeant and eight men, and gave them orders to shoot the first man who tried to approach the prisoner. You need not be uneasy about a mob's taking him away from me. If they do so, they'll have to kill me and my nine soldiers as well. We intend to see him convicted and hung by law, and I'm sure Major Clendenin, the commanding officer, will support me in this statement to the extent of using every soldier in Fort Stanton, if necessary."

I recall distinctly how Captain Fechet looked as he stood in the doorway talking to Mother in this determined manner. He was of medium height, rather heavy set, wearing over his shirt a heavy outer shirt of blue flannel, which was then a part of the uniform. This was a double-breasted affair, and thrust into the bosom of his shirt were two formidable .45's, their handles sticking out on each side. Mother, noticing the pistols, remarked, "Be careful, Captain, the pistols might fall out and go off accidentally and hurt you." "Don't worry on that score, Mrs. Casey," he answered, "you just take care of yourself and your children. Your husband is gone, but we were his friends. Now we're your friends, and we'll stand by you through thick and thin. I'm ready for them if they try to interrupt the processes of justice; and I mean business." With that he left us and returned to where he had left the prisoner.

In those days the sessions of court were held in the oblong adobe building just east of the Catholic Church in Lincoln. This old building has seen much of the lights and shadows of life in Lincoln. I do not know who built it, but in the early days it was used as a dance hall. It was here that the baile was going on the time the Harrell crowd shot it up, killing four men and wounding a woman. It was really the first courthouse of Lincoln County, and court sessions as well as other public gatherings were held in it.

In early October the grand jury, of which Major William Brady was foreman, returned a true bill against Wilson for murder and also one against Charles Myrick, who was keeping the Wortley Hotel at the time, as accessory to the crime. The indictment of Myrick, however, did not amount to much, as he had left the country and could not be found. At least that was what was said, although it was generally understood that he had simply gone out to Arizona. Wilson's defense was conducted by two of the ablest lawyers in the country, S. B. Newcomb and W. L. Rynerson, both from Mesilla. The fact that such men as these were employed to defend Wilson certainly lent color to the view that the Murphy crowd were interested in protecting him. These two attorneys handled the case expertly. No sooner had Wilson pleaded not guilty than his lawyers moved for a continuance on the ground that Myrick and another material witness, a soldier by the name of Felvy, were absent and could not be found at that time.

The prosecution in charge of the District Attorney, John D. Bail of Mesilla, was assisted by Col. A. J. Fountain, whom Mother had employed for that purpose. These were able to resist successfully the motion for continuance, and Judge Bristol proceeded with the trial of the case. The selection of a jury occupied a day or two, and when finally empaneled it consisted of the following: Juan Andreas Silva, Anzelmo Pacheco, José Chávez Sánchez, Pablo Pinto, Pedro Annalla, Tranquilino Montoya, Francisco Sánchez, Augustín Torres, Juan Lucero, Francisco Romero, Luceros and Ramón Montoya. The taking of testimony and the arguments by the lawyers required only a day or two more. When the case was finally placed in the hands of the jury, they very promptly brought in the verdict of guilty. As I have always heard it, the jury was out only about fifteen minutes, the first ballot showing that all were for conviction of first degree murder.

Although the trial had progressed rapidly, it had not been devoid of excitement. Certain incidents seemed to show that efforts were still being made to bring about Wilson's escape. One day Captain Fechet, personally guarding Wilson in the courtroom, happened to notice that Wilson was sitting in a suspicious way. His handcuffed hands were held down between his knees, while at the same time there was a slight movement of the shoulders. Captain Fechet jumped up from where he was sitting and rushed over to the prisoner. Pointing his pistol at him, the Captain shouted, "Wilson, what're you trying to do? If you make another move you're a dead man!" An investigation showed that Wilson had nearly succeeded in working his handcuffs off. Then Captain Fechet exclaimed angrily, "Whose work is this, I'd like to know? Mr. Sheriff, get your key and tighten those handcuffs up good and tight on the prisoner; also do the same for his leg shackles."

Thereafter Captain Fechet redoubled precautions, giving the soldiers directly on guard orders that they should never for an instant take their eyes off the prisoner. This could not be termed an unnecessary precaution because it was evident that the Murphy crowd would try any scheme to free Wilson and make good their promise of immunity. When the trial ended and Wilson had been sentenced by Judge Bristol to be hanged on Friday the 11th of November, Captain

Fechet immediately took Wilson back to Fort Stanton for safekeeping until the date of the execution.

Wilson's friends, however, made every effort to save him from the noose. His lawyers tried to secure a new trial, but did not succeed in doing so. The Murphy crowd laid siege to Governor Axtell in an effort to get him to commute the sentence, and the Governor did go so far as to issue a reprieve until December 18th on the ground that he desired additional time to consider the case. Whether he might in the end have commuted the sentence, it is impossible to say, but as it was, Colonel Fountain effectually checkmated the other side. In a letter to Mother dated January 25th, 1876, he refers to what steps he took, saying, "I have seen a letter from Wilson in which he denounced me very bitterly for 'hounding him to death' as he calls it. My conscience is very easy on that point, however. I had a long talk with the Governor in regard to the case. He (the Governor) had been informed that Mr. Casey had been killed in a street fight with Wilson and that it was not a murder. The Governor seemed inclined to grant Wilson a longer reprieve; and I disabused his mind and gave him a correct history of the affair, and he concluded to let justice take her course."

When the day for the hanging came around, Wilson was brought down to Lincoln from the Fort under guard of three companies of soldiers. The Murphy ring threats about preventing the hanging by some means or other induced Major Clendenin to run no risks. The ring was in a tight place; either they must make good their promise of release or Wilson would make good his threat to tell how he had been employed to do the killing. Captain Fechet guarded Wilson right up to the scaffold, but in order for the hanging to be legal he had to turn him over to the sheriff, who at that time was Captain Saturnino Baca. On the scaffold, besides the sheriff and the prisoner, were Father Lamy, of Manzana, and Major Murphy. Just why and how Major Murphy came to be there, it is hard to say; but his general prominence in everything that was done at Lincoln made it easy for him to be allowed to be on the scaffold. His purpose there can readily be guessed by those who knew the character of the man and the sort of schemer he was.

When everything was ready for the trap to be sprung, Wilson took the opportunity given him to say something, to turn to Major Murphy and say bitterly, "Major, you know you are the cause of this. You promised to save me, but . . . " Before he could say more, Major Murphy kicked the trigger that sprung the trap door, and Wilson's body shot down through it until the rope was taut. After hanging a few minutes, someone examined the body and pronounced the man dead. Then the sheriff and his helpers cut the body down and placed it in a coffin which was in readiness. There was some delay about removing the coffin from the place of execution, and while it was there a Mexican woman noticed that the lid was not screwed down, and her curiosity made her raise the lid enough to look in. No sooner had she done so than she screamed at the top of her voice, "For God's sake! The dead has come to life!"

This startling news brought others to the place, and a further examination showed that Wilson was not dead, for the movements of his chest in breathing slowly could be detected even by the eye. To those who knew the situation, it was evident that here was evidence of Murphy trickery. The plan evidently had been to have Wilson taken down as though dead and then have the body spirited away before the coffin was placed in the grave. But the curiosity of a Mexican woman had brought confusion to this well-laid scheme.

Many people were exasperated at this attempt at a ruse, and there was a strong demand that Wilson should be hanged again. Major Murphy, however, intervened with the argument that having once been legally hanged, Wilson could not be executed a second time. Naturally his henchmen supported him in that position and seemed ready to try to make the other side accept it, too, at the point of pistols and rifles. But Captain Fechet promptly took the wind out of their sails by simply saying to the companies of soldiers, which were drawn up around the scaffold, "Ready!" And before he could complete the command, the Murphyites had thought better of their determination to use force of arms. Then Captain Fechet said to the crowd, briefly but pointedly, "I am here to see the law carried out. I propose to keep the peace and allow no mob violence."

While all this had been going on, several of Father's friends had procured a rope and were ready to see that the hanging was completed. They tied the rope around Wilson's neck, while the body was still in the coffin, and then threw the free end of the rope over the crossbeam at the top of the scaffold. While some lifted the limp body of Wilson from the coffin, five men took hold of the other end of the rope and dragged Wilson up until his body was swung by the neck entirely suspended in air. Then they held it in this position until entirely satisfied he was dead past all possible mistakes in the matter.

Feeling against the Murphy crowd was so strong among the friends of Father that there was talk of going further and lynching either Murphy or Dolan, or both. But the soldiers prevented any such outburst of lawlessness. Major Clendenin, Captain Fechet, and Captain Randlett addressed the wrought-up crowd, and counseled them to quiet down and conduct themselves peaceably, now that the law had been vindicated and Wilson executed. Neither group felt like becoming the aggressor, and so the danger of a fight, which probably would have been bloodier than any Lincoln saw in later times, was averted. The murder of Robert Casey was avenged in what was the first legal hanging in Lincoln County, and what was also one of the gruesome executions which might be termed a twice-told tale.

16

Abneth McCabe: A Friend in Need

IT IS DIFFICULT to convey the distress and apprehension that came upon our household following the killing of Father. We felt that our prop had been taken away and everything might collapse. But as I think back, there arises the image of one who in that trying time proved himself a true friend. This was Abneth McCabe who served about a year in the combination capacity of store clerk and school teacher at our place.

Uncle Mac, as we called him, was a Virginian who first came to Lampasas, Texas, and from there into New Mexico. It was in 1874 that Father hired him for the dual role. He had a good education and was altogether an honorable and sensible man. As I remember him, he was somewhat old when he came to our place, but this may simply be an exaggeration of my childish mind.

After working for us about a year, Uncle Mac went to work for Uncle John Chisum at the Bosque Grande ranch. He looked after the store there, but he was also the "chief cook and bottle washer," as he would have expressed it. When Father was killed, Uncle Mac came at once to our place and for several weeks helped Mother and the rest of us attend to various important matters concerned with the settlement of the estate. About the first of October, Uncle Mac had to return to Bosque Grande, but in his absence he wrote, especially to Mother, sensible advice mingled with encouragement to carry on; and to different ones of us children, advice about conduct and studies and other appropriate matters.

Several of Uncle Mac's letters I have treasured through the years, particularly because they remind me of the kindly interest and the friendly helpfulness he gave to us all, but they should appeal to others because they present many interesting sidelights on men and events of those times. Uncle Mac was what might be called a good letter writer; he somehow was able to make his letters more than bare summaries of happenings and to infuse them with his personality.

The first one was written shortly after he had left us. His concern for Mother is the most marked feature, but the letter also reveals the fact that Uncle John Chisum wanted to assure the widow of his old friend that he was ready to be of whatever service might be needed. He had already done that in coming to our rescue.

Bosque Grande, N. M.
Oct. 6th, 1875

Mrs. E. E. Casey,

Dear Friend:
When I arrived home I found a letter from Mr. Chisum requesting me to come and help tally the cattle. I have just returned to Bosque and have only a few minutes to write. I will fix your accounts this week. Be certain to see the officers and try to sell all the corn you can even if you have to haul it two hundred miles, for it is cash. Mr. Chisum says he does not charge you a cent for my time and that he will befriend and advise you whenever you call upon him. If anything serious should ever happen, send down and I will come up immediately. Do try and take care of yourself, for you have too much at stake to break down now, and there is no use of your worrying yourself so much.
Tell Lillie and Tricks I will write to them next mail, for I have not time now. My love to them, and Will and Add. Kiss Mollie and Stonewall for me. Let me hear from you once in a while and tell me how you are getting on.

Your friend,
A. McCabe.

The second letter to Mother was written a day later, when he had time to interest a reliable young man by the name of George Clark in going to see Mother about employment. The message about our horses that Jimmie McDaniel sends relates to some which had been stolen and which after being recovered had been left at Shedd's ranch in San Augustin Pass. The letter concludes with a reference to the indefatigable industry of Mother in making buckskin gloves.

Bosque Grande, N. M.
Oct. 7th, 1875

Mrs. Eveline E. Casey,

Dear Friend:
Mr. George Clark, the bearer of this note, comes up to see if he can hire to you to take care of your cattle. I recommend Mr. Clark to you as a

The widow of Robert Casey (left) carried on difficult frontier existence in New Mexico with the help of her family. Shown several years after their father's death are Lily (standing), John, and Ellen Casey Moore.

sober, industrious young man, one who will do for you what he agrees to do and will look out for your interests. He has always given satisfaction wherever employed, had money, and is no "bummer."

Mr. Clark is riding a horse of Jimmie McDaniels. Jimmie says you can take the horse and use him just as your own and as long as you wish for nothing; but if you and Clark cannot agree you must let Clark ride the horse back to Bosque, and he will send him to you. Jimmie says if Reed does not get your horses, he will go after them as soon as he can. By whom did you send the cartridges to Jimmie McD.? He has never received them.

I hope you are all right once more — in good health and nerves steady. But do not run the sewing machine all night, if you have buckskin. I would tell you how many pairs of gloves I have sold, but am afraid "Gloverville" would become excited and never the let sewing machine rest day or night, and it is very necessary that Stonewall should sleep some. I will write to Lily and Tricks by Clark. My regards to Will and Add. Kiss Stonewall and Mollie for me.

I have had no time to attend to accounts. Been crowded ever since I got home but will go at it today or tomorrow. Write whenever you think necessary.

Your friend,
A. McCabe.

The third letter to Mother illustrates that Uncle Mac preserved even in the rough life of our section a good deal of the formality characteristic of the Virginian, for he evidently felt the proper thing was to equip George Brown with at least the semblance of a note of introduction to present as credentials.

Bosque Grande, N. M.
Oct. 29th, 1875

Mrs. E. E. Casey,

Dear Friend:
Mr. Chisum sends Mr. George Brown up to attend to business for him and wishes Mr. Brown to stop at your house. You will find Mr. Brown a gentleman and will not be much in your way. Mr. Chisum will pay you whatever is right for Mr. Brown's board. I am very busy and no time to write. Will write by mail a long letter to Lily and Tricks.

Your friend,
A. McCabe.

P.S. Anything Mr. Brown wants let him have it. He might need a little money, if so let him have it. I will return it immediately.

Yours,
A. McCabe.

The fourth letter is to my sister Ellen, and is a good example of the way Uncle Mac could step down to the level of our childish minds and give us good, sensible advice. To the modern generation, his ideas about the conduct of children and of girls in particular may seem old fashioned, but I am inclined to think he was nearly right in his views as the proper course to adopt.

Bosque Grande, N. M.
Nov. 5, 1875

Miss Ellen E. Casey,

Dear Tricks:

I was glad to receive your letter and to see that you are determined to learn to write. You have no idea how fast you will learn, if you will only try. You have been prompt in writing. I will tell Mr. Brown not to whip you, but to give you a green pup — or perhaps you want a blue pup — anyway you shall have a pup for being such a good little girl.

Mr. P. H. Chisum was bragging to me what smart little girls you and Lily were; said that you made on the machine five sacks in five minutes and talked to him all the time, and that Lily got him a meal of the best kind, before he thought the stove was hot. Now that is the way I like to hear people talk about my little girls. It is a great deal better than to hear them say, "Why them girls? They are no account. They can't sew; they can't cook. They are not fit for anything but to dress up and giggle." Now, whenever the boys and old bachelors come around, just make that sewing machine sing and the stove roar, and when they are not about, study your books; and you will have more cowboys and old, bald-headed toothless, old bachelors running around Casey's ranch than there are mosquitoes on the Pecos.

The main thing now is to learn to read and write and cipher, which you can do if you will mind Mr. Brown and study; and if you don't, your mother must give you some "quirt tea" — that is a fine remedy for little girls when they will not learn. It brightens up their ideas amazingly. When I was a boy going to school, I would brag mightily if I did not get but one whipping a week, and I tell you the old fashioned school teachers when they did whip, made you dance juba for sure. The whippings I used to get at school! And if I told at home about getting whipped, Pa would give me another and say, "No telling tales out of school." Now, I don't believe in much whipping, but children should be taught to mind, even if it is necessary to whip a little.

Will and Mr. Clark were here last week, but there were so many here and I had to cook and see to everything, that I did not have time to talk to them much. They helped me cook and wash up the dishes. My "father-in-law", H. M. Beckwith was here at the same time, and you know I had to fly around like a bug with a mashed head. I never saw any one improve as Will has. He is a real business man and talks business as though he were an old man. Your mother need not be uneasy about him whenever she sends him off on business, for he will certainly attend to it and that in the right way.

You must answer this letter soon and when you write, take pains, write plain, and try to spell all of your words correctly. I want you to improve fast so you can write to all of your relatives in Texas. My love to all the family.

Your friend,
A. McCabe.

The next and rather long letter is especially interesting because of the references to people and happenings at Bosque Grande, the first Chisum ranch on the Pecos River. It is addressed to Johnny

Brown, the young man whom he had vouched for and who had become one of Mother's employees. He mentions Lawyer McSween's having been down to Bosque Grande, as well as Colonel Hunter of St. Louis, who bought cattle frequently from Uncle John, and Contractor Curtis, who represented the Government. The references to McSween having killed a buffalo is an interesting point, for his friends claimed the reason he did not do more shooting in the Lincoln County War was because he was totally inept in the use of firearms! Uncle Mac had evidently sensed Mother's dissatisfaction with McSween's handling of certain business matters she had committed into his care as her attorney. The reference to the uncertainty the children in Lincoln might feel regarding their paternity is a glimpse of the disgust a man of the fine type of Uncle Mac would feel at certain conditions in the country. I shall quote him more positively on this point farther on.

Bosque Grande, N. M.
Nov. 24th, 1875

Johnny Brown,

Dear Sir:

Yours containing Miller's account has been received. I was glad to hear from you and from the tone of your letter you seem to be satisfied and enjoying yourself in your new neighborhood. It would be a great pleasure for me to come up and spend a few days with you and I will do so as soon as Mr. Pitzer Chisum comes up from the lower part of the range, which will be about the last of next week. He is down about Good Bend with a branding outfit and is coming up the Pecos.

Mr. John Chisum has gone to Arizona by way of Vegas and Santa Fe. He will take the stage at Santa Fe and send his buggy and horses back by the Honorable Judge McSween, Mrs. Casey's particular *friend* (?). The lawyer was with us over a week. Mr. Chisum had him employed in fixing up some papers and accounts which he wished placed in the hands of some one to collect; and as no other lawyer would come to Bosque for such little accounts, he had to get McSween, and if McSween does not collect anything, he gets no pay — that is the sum and substance of his big fees.

There are a great many buffalo on the Pecos all around Bosque. I went out the other day and killed one and it was very fat. Tell Add and Willie to come down and take a buffalo hunt. Billy Maxwell and some Mexicans are here from Fort Sumner hunting buffalo. They stay with me of a night and go out to hunt in the day. I will go out with them in the morning. Send me one hundred needle gun cartridges by the buck-board if I do not come up. I would like for Add, Lily, and Tricks all to come down and have a chase after buffalo. It is a fine sport if you have a good horse. The lawyer killed a buffalo and now he thinks he is a second Kit Carson.

Col. Hunter and Contractor Curtis have been to Bosque. Old John kept a man here to cook, and I dressed up and "cut" the gent all the time they were here. Any stranger would have taken me for boss; now cook and all are gone and I am nothing but a *peon*. Billy Maxwell and his Mexican help me cook. I like this kind of life — there is some *variety* (?) in it, especially the cooking. I never saw but one person that was as fond (?) of cooking as I am, and that is Lily Casey. I believe she had rather cook than eat.

I have Mr. Chisum's account drawn off and he said it was all right; so the books are all right except the hands' accounts, and when I come up we can settle with them. I am in hopes you settled with Peters and took his note, as he passed up. If Mrs. Casey has his note, it is all right. All those accounts should be bonded if not paid when presented; that will stop all difficulties and disputing accounts, if they are pushed on.

I understand through McKittrick that George and Kelly Hoag's mine has played out or "petered" and that Kelly is sick at old man H. Jones [Heiskell]. Very good place to be sick at for Mrs. Jones is a fine nurse.

As to the queer noise Mrs. Casey heard in a room at the plaza, I am not the cause of it nor do I know of any one who has claims on me for clothing or wrappers of any kind. From what I know of the ladies of Lincoln I would suppose it would be very difficult for them to tell who ought to send clothes, that is, if the father was the only one who should be the sender. The "machachitos" would go naked a long time before they could point to the right one.

Mr. Johnson* from H. M. Beckwith's stayed with me last night. Our girls are all well and will be here on their way to Santa Fe in a few days. I will draw with you and give you the first draw. My regards to Mrs. Casey and the family.

Your, etc.,
A. McCabe.

Where is the pistol?

Uncle Mac enjoyed joking about sometimes wearing Uncle John's $750 watch. He and Uncle John were about the same size and on special occasions, such as when he would a-courting go, Uncle Mac would don Uncle John's clothes. He especially like wearing Uncle John's expensive broadcloth suit which had been purchased on one of his visits to New York, and to complete the costume, Uncle Mac got unbounded amusement out of presenting himself to his lady friends in his borrowed deluxe clothing. He never sought, however, to disguise the fact that these fine feathers were borrowed; he rather considered it a huge joke to disclose the fact. This letter also indicates the time when Uncle John moved his headquarters from Bosque Grande to South Spring River.

Bosque Grande, N. M.
Feby. 1st, 1876

Miss Lily Casey,

Dear Lily,
    You "dog-gone little devil," you are so busy or mad that you cannot write to your old correspondent. I looked for a letter from you by last mail,

---

*Captain William Johnson, Beckwith's son-in-law.

as you did not write to me by Mr. Chisum. I do not know what you and I will do about the robbers' taking Mr. Chisum's gold watch and chain. I cannot wear it any more, and when you become Mrs. Chisum, you will not have any watch. We are both out of luck but there is no telling what may turn up yet. Mr. Chisum may get another watch and then we will be all right.

Col. Hunter and Mr. Chisum have decided to move me and the store down from here to South Spring River ranch where Beaver Smith now lives. I will be a ranchman, merchant, and attendant to the fine heifers that were brought from Kentucky, about 25, if they all live. If Beaver Smith leaves, I will have to attend to the farm, but I am in hopes Beaver will stay and run the farm. I am going to have a garden, anyway. I want to raise some nice vegetables and melons, so when my friends come to see me, I can treat them with the very best the country affords — milk, butter, eggs, and vegetables.

Won't you all come to see me? I am thinking about trying to get some one to become Mrs. McCabe; and if there were not so many little fool boys flying around you, I think I would ask you. But I do not like to be kicked in my old age. I will wait and see if some of them don't get killed, and then I will try.

If your mother does not want Negro Clark I would like to get him to live with me this year. Tell him to come down to see me, that is, if your mother does not want him, and I will wait and see if some of them don't get killed, and then I will try.

We will commence moving the goods from here next week, and I will be very busy until we get through. But I will try and write you every mail until I get you in a good humor. I wrote for garden seed this mail. I am going to plant sweet potatoes and everything that is good. I hope your whole family will come to see me sometime this years. My love to all the family. Scratch your mad fit out of you and write to an old friend.

A. McCabe.

Uncle Mac did not stay long at South Spring River. In the last letter I have, written to Mother in the late spring, he realized the drift of events and did not hesitate to express general disgust at the situation. His statement about wishing to leave the country may be lacking in delicacy, but it indicates the feeling many men of Abneth McCabe's caliber had toward this trend. The last paragraph gives an interesting sidelight on the famine-like conditions that prevailed when provisions would run low and wagon trains from Las Vegas would not come through on time with new supplies.

South Spring River Ranch, N.M.
May 24, 1876

Mrs. E. E. Casey,

Dear Friend,

Yours came to the ranch whilst I was up on the range after milk cows, and that is the reason why I did not write to you last mail in regard to the corn.

The corn received by Brown at Repente and Bosque, was 9,194 pounds. Enclosed you will find a rough statement that I made out at Diego Salcido's house the morning we were there of all the corn coming to you from the parties at these places, and you are credited on the books by that number of pounds received by Brown. James Reynolds on the 30th of December received of you 685 pounds of corn.

I have examined all the receipts and books and find no other statements of corn received by other parties from you. No one else ever reported corn received from you. I supposed you had it all down on your books, for I know that the men were getting corn from you when they passed and perhaps it is months afterwards before I see them.

I have been looking for the children down for some time. The boys are eating up all my vegetables, and I will raise nothing but onions, beans, cabbage, and corn. I am very sorry to hear of your troubles and hope that you will get out of them without anything serious happening. I am getting tired of the way things are conducted in this country and think I will leave next year. It is no use trying to make an honest living in a country where you are respected whilst living and mourned for when dead, provided you steal, kill, and run a "blister."

I received the hose and am very thankful. My milk cows off of the range are very bronco and don't give much milk; I am out of everything to eat except cornbread and beef — no coffee and but little milk. How is the grub question with you? I would like to make a raid on Ash's chickens. I cannot tell when the goods and supplies will get here. Mr. Chisum ordered them before we went to court and no news from them yet. I have just received a note from John S. Chisum asking if I wished to lock up the store and come on to the range and eat fat beef. I think I shall go if he does not come down with Teague who had gone to see him. My regards to all the children and Ash.

Yours, et.,
A. McCabe.

I have dwelt at some length on Abneth McCabe because he represents the better sort of old-timer. He never got into any of the troubles then besetting Lincoln County that were to bring about even worse conditions in the next year or two. In contrast were a great many rough characters in the Southwest of all sorts and descriptions. Yet when I recall such men as Uncle Mac, Uncle Ash Upson, and Uncle John Chisum and his several brothers, I feel compelled to say that God never made better men than these old-timers. Rough though they may have been in dress, coarse and unrefined though they may have been in some of their habits and actions, yet it was environment that forced such characteristics upon them, and they well deserve the grand old name of gentlemen.

Let me close these recollections of Uncle Mac with a few words about his subsequent history. In 1877 he came again to our place and helped us at a critical time in our fortunes. When we were ultimately forced by conditions in Lincoln County to go into Texas for a time, Uncle Mac accompanied us on that trip, but he did not care to return to New Mexico. He located himself again at Lampasas, Texas, and we lost track of him thereafter, although we always held him dearly in our hearts. Of course, while he was with us, he always received wages for his work, but his service and his faithfulness were of a quality above price. It was friendship and loving service he gave us, two commodities not to be bought with coin of the realm.

17

Happenings on the Feliz

FATHER DISCOVERED the Feliz country when he acted as guide for Lieutenant Yeaton. The land was well watered and admirably suited for grazing, and Father was determined to acquire it for a stock ranch as soon as the danger from Indians was reduced. He took up about ten miles along the headwaters and built substantial improvements. Later he moved his stock there where they remained for several years. After his death Mother continued the operations. When the Lincoln County War broke out and Dick Smith was killed at the Beckwith place, District Attorney Rynerson and Uncle John Chisum advised her to take her boys and cattle to Texas. This she did, leaving Old Man Turner to care for the ranches and buildings. By this and similar arrangements she was able to hold possession until 1881 — eleven years the Caseys had owned that property.

* * *

(The following account of the persecution of Mrs. Casey by the Dolan crowd and of their finally "jumping" her claim was checked and typed by Colonel Fulton, early collaborator with Mrs. Klasner, but were omitted in his final draft. Since other pioneer families told substantially the same stories, this version is being included.)

It was in the fall of 1877, I think, that Mother must have sent the boys and me, together with four or five men, over to our stock ranch on the Feliz to gather the cattle and take them down to my uncle's in Menard County, Texas. When we reached the Feliz a rain set in that lasted a week and delayed our departure.

When we finally got off we followed Feliz Canyon to Lower Peñasco, now called Dayton, and on down the Pecos. We were traveling with two wagons drawn by oxen and driving about 800 head of cattle. We continued past Red Bluff and were fifteen or twenty miles across the Texas line I think, although the line was in dispute, when we saw a mob of men descending upon us. Headed by Dick Brewer, there were at least fifteen men, most of whom were Mexicans. They evidently had been following us, waiting for us to cross the Texas line where we naturally would relax our watchfulness. Mother and McCabe had cautioned my brothers about keeping the wagons and cattle together, but feeling that danger was past they had let the cattle get ahead of the wagons. Consequently the Brewer party overtook the wagons first. I was driving one and Bob Stewart the other when we were stopped. Sequio Sánchez stepped in front of the steers that were drawing my wagon and held his gun on me while another Mexican did the same to Bob, and ordered us to overtake the cattle.

When my brothers and their men saw the mob approaching they rode back to meet it, not suspecting unfriendly intentions, although anyone was suspicious of a band of men, even a small one.

When our men and Brewer's met, Brewer demanded a portion of the cattle, which he said were the property of Tunstall and McSween. After some heated discussion, about all my brothers could do was to let Brewer take about 400 head. We decided to leave the cattle we still had at some point in the vicinity while some of us went back to our ranch. [They were left at Pope's Crossing with Ramer and Nash.]

When we told Mother what had occurred, she hurried us to Lincoln to see her lawyer, McSween. It so happened that Brewer, having taken our stolen cattle back to the Feliz ranch, had reached Lincoln ahead of us and reported the incident to Tunstall and McSween. I do not know what his story was but next day, just after Mother reached home, Brewer and pretty much the same crowd came to our ranch and threw their guns down on my two brothers, saying they would have to accompany them back to Lincoln. The boys wanted to know what it was all about, but Brewer would say only, "You'll have to go to Lincoln with us and find out." They never showed any warrant, but simply took the boys by force of arms.

Of course Mother would not submit to such treatment of her sons. When the mail hack passed our place on the way to Roswell, Mother got on, in hopes of overtaking Uncle John Chisum who had passed our house earlier that day on his way to his Spring River ranch. She felt he was the only person who would have any influence with McSween. She was fortunate in catching up with Uncle John, who returned with her to Lincoln and used his influence to get Add and Will released. As they brought the boys back to our ranch, Uncle John advised Mother to send the boys to Texas to keep them out of trouble. He explained that serious trouble was developing in this part of the country and the boys probably would be drawn into it, possibly get killed or kill someone else, and would in all likelihood have to skip the country. At first Mother was reluctant because she did not see how she could run the ranch without them. But when other influential persons such as Colonel Rynerson gave similar advice, she realized it was the only prudent course. Other friends stressed the advantages of taking her children where they could have better schooling. This all made sense to Mother and she started preparations at once to pick up the remaining cattle and proceed to Texas.

Our journey from Pope's Crossing to Fort Concho, Texas, was made exciting by the fact we were in the wake of a band of marauding Indians. While we were held up at Pope's Crossing waiting for the river to subside, a band of about ten Mescaleros escaped from the Agency and began a raiding expedition. Although they camped about three miles below us for several days, they did not molest us — possibly because our horses were poor and not very desirable, but more probably because the Indians knew who we were and felt on friendly terms with us.

But they did cause a great deal of trouble for the people in that section, and we saw frequent evidence of their having passed ahead of us. We camped one night near Grand Falls at a cattle ranch belonging to a widow who had put a man named Charlie Snow in charge of it. As Snow related it, he and his men had a brush with these Indians one dark, foggy morning, a stiff one in which one Indian charged near enough to take close shots at Snow, luckily not well aimed. The men all thought this very daring Indian looked more like a squaw than a buck, and the story soon spread of this squaw and her notable bravery. Snow thought she may have been among those wounded. Blood found on the ground when the fog cleared indicated there may have been several.

We went on through Castle Canyon [Gap] and reached China Ponds where we heard further stories of Indian depredations, including the theft of all the horses from a group of buffalo hunters camped there. Nothing had happened as yet when we reached Mustang Ponds, but the next night Indians stole all the horses from the buffalo hunters camped there. As Pete Baze afterwards told us, a sortie of these buffalo hunters tracked the Indians and also noticed the one who was supposed to be a squaw and found her the most recklessly brave of the whole lot. [It is possible that this was Lozen, or Losa, sister of Victorio, renowned for her fighting ability. The Indians at Mescalero think it was she.] The Indians' last camp was at Mr. Baze's on Dove Creek, about sixteen miles from Fort Concho, considered the deadline beyond which the Indians would not venture.

After my return to New Mexico two years later, some Mescalero women came to our Hondo Ranch and I took this chance to ask about the party of which we had heard so much in Texas. They were very evasive, saying indifferently that they were just *paseando,* or visiting. They also were noncommittal about their depredations or whether there was a squaw of the Joan of Arc type among them.

But they admitted they recognized us at Pope's Crossing and that was why they did not harm us except to kill one of our steers and jerk the meat. They even knew how many men, women, and children were in our outfit. These Indians could get passes from the Indian Agent to camp on the river and trade with the ranchers. They brought dressed deer and antelope hides which Mother bought to make buckskin gloves and pants. They also brought buffalo robes and mescal made from the sotol plant (a species of the yucca) and Tishwino [tiswin, a drink made of fermented corn].

It was while we were in Texas that we children received our most advanced education, a privilege that was of lifelong service to us.

Ownership of the cattle taken by Brewer was still unsettled when Mother returned from Texas. She found they had been left in the care of "Dutch Charlie" Kruling, and it was understood he had moved them to the Copeland ranch near Stanton. When she visited the headwaters of the Feliz she discovered that all the improvements had been destroyed and the horses she had brought back from Texas had been stolen. Although she was now afoot, she managed to take a lot of hogs out to the Feliz to keep alive her claim to the tract. I was not with her at the time, but my sister and little brother have told me what a time they had getting these hogs over the twenty-five miles that lay between home and the Feliz. One of the horses she was using was wild, the other balky, and the boy she had with them was of little use. They had sideboards on the wagon to keep the hogs from jumping out. In spite of having the hog's feet tied, one did get a sideboard loose and escape. And of all the trouble they had catching him and getting him back in the wagon! They put one end of a sideboard on the ground and the other on the wagon gate, retied the hog and slid him up into the wagon, all the time being afraid he would bite.

Mother put a renter on the Feliz land, but he was killed in cold blood by a noted desperado who had come to Lincoln after a career of lawlessness in other parts of the territory. Political influence was used to keep the murderer from being prosecuted. Thereafter, Mother was afraid to make much further effort to keep it.

There was a one-room adobe left up near the head of the spring and in 1880, after I had come back from Texas, Mother sent my brothers Add and Johnny and my sister Ellen and me, together with three men, out to the Feliz to make some other repairs and improvements. When we got there we found that cattle owned by Dolan and a nephew of Col. Emil Fritz had been put on the place, thereby "jumping" it. Mother employed Col. A. J. Fountain to protect her rights, but he was unable to overcome political power stacked against him.

*   *   *

Up to this time Mother had maintained full possession of the ranch and had done everything required by law to perfect *bona fide* right, for a squatter's right was all that could be acquired. It was, and still is, the best right by law and was all that could be done legally until the land was surveyed and opened for entry.

At this time Dolan was under indictment for the murder of Chapman, a one-armed lawyer. Dolan had married Lina Fritz who died when her baby was two weeks old, thus gaining the sympathy of many people in the community.

By 1881, Mother realized the futility of trying to manage alone so rented all her land and ranches to Bob Olinger, who informed

Dolan he would now have to deal with a man rather than a poor crippled invalid. This stopped Dolan and Fritz until Olinger was murdered, when Mother was again left old, crippled, and sick.

This Feliz country played a large part in the life of our family. Though only twenty-five miles from our home place it was, as the Irish express it, "the back of beyond." Frequently news came of strange occurrences, and it is of some of these that I shall write.

Our main source of information was our men who worked there, or occasionally Will brought news of what occurred. One of the reasons Father sent our cattle to the Feliz was to get them so far away that Will's attention would not be diverted from going to school. He had a liking for handling cattle, and as long as there were any about the place, it was next to impossible to get him to give attention to his books. Father's scheme worked for a while, then Will managed to be sent there also during vacations. As he was still just a boy he was under the oversight of an older man who served as foreman. Father ordered this man to let him know immediately if anything unusual occurred; and this led to our being informed as to occurrences.

Will, although very young, participated in many episodes. I remember his coming home with a report of an Indian scare. While riding alone cutting sign, he saw three Indians in the distance. They rapidly came close and Will started toward camp. They signaled him to stop but Will let his horse out and made a run. The Indians tried to cut him off from crossing the river and reaching camp, but Will beat them to the crossing and made good his get-away. When he reached camp and told of his experience the foreman, Tom Bostic, decided it would be best to get out. That night they saddled up and came to the ranch.

In 1874 Will took part in a skirmish with the Apaches. A bunch of renegades had been causing a good deal of trouble in that part of the county, and Will went with some others to cut sign, finding that the Indians had gone to the Peñasco. Men living over there got together to retaliate on the Indians and Will joined them. They got some of the Indians' horses, and Will was given a bald-faced roan. He turned out to be one of the best horses I'd ever seen, and at the risk of disagreeing I must tell something of him. Father liked him so well that he used him for his saddle horse and said he would be willing to bet anyone a hundred dollars he could ride him from sunup to sundown and make the trip from our place to the Beckwith ranch, going by the cottonwoods — a distance of a hundred miles. Father maintained the horse would have endurance to make it. The horse was stolen from him by the Mes gang but when we were in Texas in 1878 we recovered him in peculiar fashion. Will happened to be at Fort McKavett and saw the horse in the hands of somebody there. He was sure it was our horse, and he took steps to replevin him.

After the skirmish of which I have spoken, Father had instructed Will to set off for our place with Marcos Baca to bring a report of the Indian fight. They planned to make the trip by night and took the most direct route, a distance of twenty-five miles. The Indians were on the lookout and waylaid them in a little arroyo; they fired six shots but missed. Will and Marcos wheeled and went back to camp; then they went by the Peñasco and made their way home.

The men Father had on the Feliz met with dangers other than Indians. One I recall vividly from having heard it told frequently is that of George Hindman and a grizzly bear. Father had been working on the Feliz with Will and several men; among them was George Hindman. The latter had gone into partnership with Sam Bass and they were renting from Father. They planted corn because Father needed all he could get to feed his horses.

There were many bears in the timber, and they gave Hindman and Bass much trouble. They not only ate the corn but broke the stalks down. Also they would frequently break down the banks crossing the irrigation ditches and let the water run over the corn land, thus causing a great deal of damage to the crop. There was one bear in particular who had the habit of coming down regularly to make a meal of corn and do as much damage as possible. Hindman concluded the only way to get the troublesome fellow would be to go after him at daylight. Armed with his Winchester and six-shooter, he went to the field one morning and picked up a hot trail almost at once. When he came upon the huge grizzly, breaking and tearing down corn, he shot at the animal and hit him. But the effect was only to enrage the old fellow. He charged Hindman, and though the latter fired a second shot, it did not stop the animal. He came directly to Hindman and slapped the Winchester from his hands.

Quick as a flash Hindman jerked his six-shooter and fired. That did not stop him either, and he grabbed Hindman's hand with his teeth and started to chew it. But Hindman's shots were taking effect and he was bleeding like a stuck pig. When too weak to chew he would groan, walk a few steps, lie down, and watch Hindman closely. Then he came back and tried to work on Hindman's arms, legs, and shoulders. He even tried to drag the man off by taking hold of his leg, but Hindman was too heavy. The bear next proceeded to dig a hole by Hindman and put him into it. He probably intended feeding off him. When the sick bear lay down Hindman tried to get his rifle, but his hand was wounded so badly he could not use it. He put his hat on the muzzle, and stuck the gun upright to tell anyone who might be hunting him that something was wrong.

When Hindman did not return, his partner, Sam Bass, started to look for him. He found Hindman with the bear still guarding him. Hindman yelled, "He's a monster, Sam — badly wounded but fighting. Don't try it alone; get help." The cowboys, horseback, and the Mexicans in a wagon, with two Negroes afoot came to Hindman's rescue. They could hear the bear groaning but could not see him. They fired into the tules but accomplished little but to cause the animal to get up and slink away.

They picked up Hindman and took him to the house to dress his wounds. The only doctor in the county was at Fort Stanton and they started a man with Hindman. They also sent a runner ahead to ask the doctor to meet his patient on the road.

The others discovered the bear lying quietly in some tules; at his first sight of a man he lunged at him. Losing him he went after a mulatto, George Washington, and he, too, lost no time running. Washington, it was said, pulled both boots off in the mud while running to climb a tree. From his perch above the bear he said, "Oh, Lordy, I's a goner!"

The other men were shooting and the animal went further into the tules. The men followed regardless of the fierce charges the bear made at times. Some dropped their guns and pistols and at one time the men said there were two rifles and three six-shooters dropped in their trying to escape. When he made a dive at Will and Tom Bostic the latter dropped his gun. Will shot the animal in a fore paw and broke it, but he went on, using three feet. Bostic recovered his gun as Will turned to run. There was a hole of water ahead, too wide to jump, but with the bear at his heels he had little choice.

Meanwhile, others who had recovered their weapons came to Will's rescue. The bear went down the river and took refuge under a bluff. The men climbed to the top and rolled stones on him until he quit moving.

The perils of the Feliz were not limited to Indians and animals. Shortly before Father's death we lost our horses there to the notorious Mes gang. They said they did not intend to get our horses, only those of some men who happened to be staying at our camp for the night, but they took our horses along with the others. The four Mes brothers, Juan, José, Paz, and Juanito, lived at La Boquilla, a little Mexican village above Missouri Bottom, and their only means of livelihood was stealing horses, cattle, or anything of value. Some of the people there were good citizens, but not the Mes brothers. They pretended to be farmers but subsisted so far as meat was concerned on Chisum cattle.

In the summer of 1873 Uncle Pitzer Chisum and two of the young men working for him, Jimmie McDaniels and Jesse Evans, found the trail of men who had been stealing the Chisum cattle and followed it right up to Boquilla. These three men were bold enough to go into the village, throw their guns down on those they found there, and force the Mexicans to permit them to search their houses. But they were unable to find any trace of the stolen animals, for the people of Boquilla had already converted the cattle into beef and hidden it in an underground room or cellar, the only entrance to which was a tunnel.

The Mes brothers resented the search and openly made threats about waylaying and killing Jesse Evans and Jimmie McDaniels as well as any Chisums they might happen to find. News of the threats reached Evans and McDaniels, and being footloose they decided to leave the Chisums and go elsewhere. I remember their staying all night at our place on their way up to Bosque Grande. They told us they were headed for Arizona but expected to return when the Mes brothers quieted down.

They planned to reach our stock ranch on the Feliz the following night, and to get to Blazer's mill, on the Mescalero Reservation the next night, then on to Arizona. The long detour over the Feliz country was made in order to keep away from the villages and travel in the hills, thereby keeping secret their departure.

Carefully planned though it was, the trip did not work out as the boys expected. Either their Mexican enemies at Bosque Grande passed on the information to the Mes brothers or they, themselves, were watching the two. Paz Mes and his two uncles, Jesús and Matilde, followed them to our place on the Feliz, slipped up and stole every horse in the valley, including ours. The Feliz was so remote from other settlements that there had been little stealing over there; consequently people did not take precautions as they did elsewhere, just turned their horses loose at night to graze. That made it easy for the Mexicans to get a good haul — five horses of Father's, four from Evans and McDaniels, as well as three from Bass.

With the aid of his men Father "cut for sign" afoot and picked up the trail which led over one of the steepest mountains in the country, the intentions of the Mexicans being to make it appear that Indians had got the horses. Father did not go with the pursuing party, but sent Tom Bostic with Evans and McDaniels. Sam Bass also went. They eventually came upon the Mexicans at Palo Chino just this side of Shedd's ranch near San Augustin Pass, killed all of them while they were asleep, and succeeded in getting back the horses. These tender-footed horses gave out as they got back to Shedd's ranch, so were left there to rest before being brought back to the Hondo. But this was never done, for shortly afterwards the horses were re-stolen and never recovered.

The country at that time was full of both American and Mexican cattle rustlers and horse thieves. The ranges of the larger cattlemen like the Chisums were constantly preyed upon by the smaller cowmen, who sought to build up their herds in this way, and by others who wanted an easy way to supply meat for themselves and their friends. Along with stealing went mavericking and brand burning. There can be no disputing the fact that some of the citizens of southeastern New Mexico, who in later years became most highly respected, got their start fifty or more years ago by rustling.

Up to this time Jesse Evans and Jimmie McDaniels had been working for John Chisum and both were considered good, hard-working boys. I know that Father regarded them as good young men, especially Jimmie McDaniels, of whom he was very fond. I do not believe that Jimmie ever killed anyone, nor do I think he was guilty of rustling. In regard to Jesse Evans I cannot make my statement so favorable. He came under the influence of the Murphy and Dolan crowd, and served their crooked purposes in several ways. But on his own initiative he managed to get into other troubles. In the early stages of his career in Lincoln County, I believe he robbed a store over at Las Cruces and was arrested for stealing horses from Dick Brewer's place, which belonged to Tunstall. He was put in jail at Lincoln — which in 1877 was simply an underground room or cellar — along with his associates, Tom Hill, Frank Baker, and George Davis. But with the aid of their powerful friends, Murphy and Dolan, they managed to effect an escape. Because of Tunstall's resisting their getting bond, Jesse Evans and Tom Hill cherished an implacable hate against Tunstall and were perhaps more directly responsible for his murder than any other persons. Jesse Evans remained in the country during the early part of the Lincoln County War, but as indictments were out for him, he felt he would be more secure elsewhere. He did, however, come back afterwards, but he never stayed long. The end of his career in this section I have told in the chapter recounting the aftermath of the Lincoln County war.

Sam Bass was a refugee in New Mexico. I believe the robbery of the U.P. train was his first exploit as a bandit, and it was shortly after this that he came into New Mexico. The usual statement is that he hid out in the Panhandle, but as a matter of fact he was up on our Feliz place. Father, not knowing anything about him when he turned up at our place and asked for land to farm, sent him to the upper ranch. Father supplied him with milk cows and saw that he had all needed facilities for farming. But Sam Bass requited this kindness in a strange way.

The cows got into a field of corn Sam had planted and he vented his anger on the poor creatures by killing them. Will heard that he had done this and, thinking he ought to investigate, took Father's range boss, George Clark, with him to Sam's place. They learned from Bass' wife that he had gone over to the Freeman and Matthews place on the Peñasco, so headed over there. Sam was evidently on the lookout and suspicious that he might be taken to task for shooting the cows. From behind the cabin of Freeman and Matthews, he caught sight of Will and George and fired his rifle through an opening in the log wall. The bullet struck Will's horse in the chest and wounded the animal. Both Will and George wheeled and started on a run toward our house on the Feliz.

The next day they came over to our Hondo ranch and reported. As this was after Father's death, it devolved upon Mother to take steps to have Sam Bass brought to justice. She went to Lincoln and swore out a complaint, and a warrant was issued. But when the officer got out to Sam Bass' place he found that his man had skipped. The next grand jury took up the matter, and returned an indictment, but Bass was never found and brought back to Lincoln County. This incident brought to light some things in his past, and it was said in our section that there was an indictment for murder against him in Texas. I could readily believe that such might have been the case.

We younger children heard so much about the Feliz country from Will's reports that we were eager to go there. It must have been in 1876 that I made my first trip into that section. I remember more vividly a second trip made in 1877 by my sister Ellen and me and our brothers, Add and Will. Especially vivid is Add's adventure with the Indians. On reaching the place we found the men busy building a large picket corral. Add could be of very little help at that job, so he and a Mexican boy were detailed to ride sign for an indication of cattle having been driven off. On this day the two boys took a lunch, as they expected to ride too far to get back in time for dinner. At noon they stopped to eat, taking the bridles off the horses and putting ropes on them so they could be staked out. Lunch eaten, the two boys wandered over to some high bluffs in the vicinity, just out of curiosity to look down from the top and see how high the bluffs were. Reaching the top, the two boys got down on their knees and crawled very carefully to the edge, and peeped over. Imagine their astonishment to see, far down at the bottom, five Indians camped and cooking their dinner. Add always said he was almost paralyzed with fear and realized fully the helplessness of their situation should the Indians discover them, for their rifles were back where the horses were. The Mexican, however, was certainly not paralyzed with fear. He started back for the horses on a dead run, begging Add "Por Dios" to hurry. When they reached the horses, there was a quick untieing of ropes, and equally quick bridling and mounting, and then the two boys started their horses on a dead run.

They were not lucky enough, however, to get away unobserved by the Indians. The boys were a long way from the bluffs when the Indians happened to catch sight of them and tried their favorite trick of cutting the two boys off from the only crossing in that locality. But the boys had such a good start that they succeeded in beating the Indians to the crossing. When the boys came back and told what had happened, the men thought it best to guard our horses very securely that night, but the Indians did not put in an appearance. The next day the men went out to where the Indians had been camped, only two miles from the house, and found plenty of Indian sign but no Apaches.

It was on this trip to the Feliz that I took a notion to go up on a little hill in front of the house and stake a claim or homestead. My location included the head of the river down to the bluffs, and to indicate it was my claim, I gathered some rocks and built what we called a "monument." That pile of rocks still stands there, but alas for my hopes, the Lincoln County War came on soon after, and we had to take our cattle to Texas to save them and keep the boys out of trouble.

Mother went over in 1879, taking with her old Dan Dyer who was working for her, my sister Ellen, and my baby brother Johnny, then about four years old. While Mother was working in the garden which she had planted earlier, Johnny went to sleep on a pallet on the ground, and Mother told Ellen to watch him. Ellen tired of this and wandered down to the creek to gather wild grapes. She became so absorbed in this that she forgot Johnny. An hour or two later she came back and found the little fellow gone. Thoroughly alarmed, her first thought was that a bear had got him. She rushed to the head of the river where Mother was working and told her what she feared. Mother was almost distracted, her first thought being that her child had fallen into the water and drowned. She ran to a deep pool near and looking in saw a root which she took to be Johnny. Despite the fact that she could not swim, she plunged into the water. She almost drowned in this futile effort, but she was frantic to save the baby, if that were possible, or to bring back his body.

In the meantime she had sent Ellen to the house to tell Old

Man Dyer to come at once on his horse. He came quickly and hunted thoroughly on the north side of the stream, the side the child had been left on. Having no success, he crossed to the south side and rode up into the hills, continuing his search. He had gone over a mile when he caught sight of a little figure in the distance. He knew it must be Johnny, and rode rapidly to the child. But a change had come over Johnny; it must have been something like what happens when domesticated animals get back to their native heath. If we may say of such that they have become wild, I think that is what we might say of little Johnny.

For ten or fifteen minutes he would not permit Old Man Dyer to come near him. When the old man tried to approach him, he would run further away and scream as if frightened to death. Dyer pleaded and begged but all in vain. Then he thought of some candy he had in his pocket, and used that to overcome Johnny's wildness. He finally got the little fellow to come to him and then it was easy enough to pick him up and ride back to where Mother was waiting. I have often thought how narrow an escape it was for Mother from losing her child. It was nearly sundown when Old Man Dyer rescued him, and I am sure that had he remained among the hills during the night we would never have found him.

18

Plagues and Pestilences

THE YEARS 1876 and 1877 were indelibly impressed upon the people of southeastern New Mexico because of two things: a succession of insect plagues, and the terrible epidemic of black smallpox that ravaged the country.

It seemed as though insects were attempting to take the country. In 1876 came grasshoppers — hordes of them. Crops disappeared as they advanced; wheat, oats, barley, corn, and vegetables were ruined. Even the leaves and bark of the trees were devoured by the voracious insects. We did not suffer so much from their ravages as some of the neighbors because just before the advance guard reached our place there came a terrific windstorm — almost a tornado — lasting for three days, and the grasshoppers were unable to withstand it. When they invaded a place it was no uncommon sight to see the roof, the doors, and the windows of a house literally covered with countless thousands of the loathsome things. There were enough of them to strip a field in a short time of everything but stalks. They even peeled fence posts and boards.

The people had scarcely got their fields and gardens replanted before cabbage lice made their appearance, covering the leaves of the plants and sucking the juice from them. There seemed to be no effective means of destroying them. We tried to kill them by sprinkling ashes on the plants; others used lime water but this method was slow and tedious. So the cabbage was destroyed and it seemed as though the people must go next.

Then along came the fleas! Where the millions came from nobody knew, but they were there, and they made life a burden. Nobody could sleep at night nor find peace by day. They chewed viciously on both people and animals, and seemed to move constantly.

My first acquaintance with them was made while I tried to nap on a rug, but their bites kept me awake. I found small black specks on me and went to Mother. She took one look and said, "Lily, where have you been? You've been playing with the dog and got fleas from them." Mother found the rug full of the things and hung it on the fence. She washed the walls and floor with strong lye water and soapsuds as strong as she could stand it. The fleas had spread through the house, and seemed to have taken possession of all outdoors as well. We had no other disinfectant than lye soap, and it had little effect, so we were afflicted with fleas until a freeze occurred.

This was followed by an epidemic of smallpox. It was the type known as black smallpox and much more infectious and harder to control than the ordinary kind. Little could be done to stop the scourge and it swept unchecked throughout the country. It was so prevalent that crops had to be neglected for people were compelled to nurse the ill and bury the dead. The Mexicans accepted the epidemic as a chastisement sent by the Almighty and refused to believe that it could be controlled by human means. Could a puny creature like man, they argued, stop a malady sent by God to punish the wicked? This argument was accepted by many, including officers at the Fort; and people quoted Scripture to prove their contention. Had not God visited plagues upon the Egyptians because of their ill treatment of the Israelites?

One who has not seen a case of black smallpox cannot believe its loathsomeness. Flesh rots to a mass of putrid corruption which affects eyes, nose, or any other part of the body, and becomes a mass of pus. If the disease breaks out in the mouth and throat the patient suffers intense pain. The entire body burns and itches and the slightest movement intensifies the suffering.

Vaccination was a new idea to almost all the inhabitants of this country and attempts made at using it even by doctors (there was one at the Fort) were crude and ineffective. People had to become their own physicians. Old Man Clene at the Junction advocated vaccination. He went to Fort Stanton, procured a scab which the doctor there assured him was taken from a child who had recovered. It had been removed from the patient by use of a silver instrument as silver was thought to be safer than other metals. He prepared the vaccine by putting a fragment from the scab into a cup of water and letting it soak. The scab was far too precious to be risked in its entirety. Then he scratched the skin of the upper arm till he drew a very little bit of blood, for more would wash away the vaccine. He let drops of the preparation fall on the chafed skin and sent the patient into the sunshine to let the spot dry thoroughly before a sleeve was placed upon it.

Mother sent me to Clene's to get some of the scab and learn how to apply it. When I returned with both the preventive and the knowledge of its application she had me practice first on the arm of one of the employees who volunteered to undergo the ordeal. I was reluctant to attempt the task but when I saw not only one but several brawny men, supposedly afraid of nothing, flinch and show fear I was highly amused. I knew that not one of them would have flinched from the use of a six-shooter if it were necessary. One man became so pale that Mother thought he was going to faint.

Few of the Mexicans would submit to the use of the vaccine; instead they helped spread the disease by accepting it as another of the plagues and ignoring ordinary precautions. I have known of a whole family going to visit relatives, some of whom were bedfast with black smallpox. If one died of the disease the whole community flocked to the wake regardless of the fact that others of the family might be ill at the time. In a few days there was usually a report of numerous new cases. Because some adults had been victims previously, they were usually immune; it was the children who succumbed. I believe the mortality among them was as high as fifty per cent. Those who survived were apt to be lifelong defectives, deafness and blindness being common sequels to black smallpox. Those who recovered showed evidence of the ordeal in pitted faces, for it was almost impossible to avoid scratching off scabs, so intense was the burning and itching.

The first news we had of the presence of black smallpox came from El Paso. The epidemic reached Tularosa and from there spread to the Ruidoso, finally radiating over all the southeastern part of the Territory. It raged for many months and possibly three-fourths of the population suffered from it. The summer was unusually hot, and it was essentially a hot-weather disease; but the coming of winter seemed to check it. Treatment of patients was crude, and as few could have a doctor the victims relied upon the care of relatives and friends. Remedies, too, were few and crude. Patients were poulticed with leaves from a plant called *lengua de vaca* (cow tongue) which grew in the water and along the banks of ditches and streams. Wheat bran, too, was used for poultices which were applied as hot as the patient could endure them.

Despite our precautions our family suffered greatly from small-pox. Vaccination "took" only in the case of our baby brother. We thought ourselves immune because of my ministrations, but we took the disease. To attend to the settlement of Father's estate Mother was compelled to make several trips to Lincoln. When she returned from one with headache and a pain in her chest we were alarmed. That night she went to bed early and asked me to bring her some coal oil (kerosene) which she used extensively for various illnesses. She rubbed it on her skin, including her scalp, then told me to give the children their supper and put them to bed.

The next morning Mother's body was covered with pustules. We learned that the use of kerosene had been a mistake, for her scalp became a solid scab. To treat the skin it was necessary to cut her long black hair as close as possible. Her breasts were a solid blister as were her hands and arms, and her body swelled to twice its normal size and turned black. For twenty-five days she lay in bed, attended by myself and successive neighbor women.

She was not a docile patient, for she had her own ideas as to what should be done for her, and required those about her to adopt her methods. I remember that when the sores on her hands began "to ripen" she wanted them opened. That the Mexican women refused to do, but her demands were met in a very repulsive manner. Because we were working day and night not only with Mother but others who were ill, mice invaded the house. We had no time to attempt to eradicate them and they ran over the floors and even on the beds. When Mother was suffering terribly from her hands and arms she raised them above her head, and the pustules were bitten by mice. Perhaps she was delirious; at least she did not call us, and she said that the opening of the pustules afforded great relief.

She demanded that I bathe her. Accustomed as I was to obeying without question I brought from the yard our large brass wash pot and filled it with warm water. Under Mother's directions I put a spoonful of concentrated lye and a bar of soap in it. She managed to bathe herself by dipping a cloth into the water and sponging her body. For two more days this was repeated and her body got so raw that the slightest movement was agonizing. She asked that oil be applied to relieve her suffering, and I used a feather for the process. It was necessary to turn her in a sheet for she could not be lifted in any other way.

Thirteen days after Mother went to bed, Will came down with the disease. Though she had tried to keep all the children but me out of the room, Will had begged to have his bed put close to hers, and she, probably too weak to remonstrate, had permitted it. Ellen, Add, and my baby sister became ill; and last, I took it. All of us were put in Mother's room which served as the pest house, all except Add who preferred staying in an adjoining room. Not one of us could do one thing for the other.

If Abneth McCabe had not stayed with us I am sure all would have died. Mexican women in the neighborhood did the housework and nursing. Cresencia, wife of Timito, had had smallpox and helped Petra care for us. When Jim Johnson, foreman on our ranch on the Rio Feliz, heard of our plight he left a Mexican in charge of the cattle, came here, and installed himself as cook. Tom Cochran, the field boss at the home place, cared for the stock and did the milking. But Uncle Mac, good Samaritan as he was, was head nurse and manager of all.

When my youngest sister, four years of age, died not one of the family could get out of bed, so it fell to Uncle Mac and the good neighbors to bury her in the little cemetery on the ranch in which there were already six bodies. (Two were white men who had been waylaid and killed by Indians in 1866.) In 1872, three of Mother's children, Johnny,* aged five, Kathleen Belle, three, and Mollie Florence, one, had died within twenty-four hours and were buried in one grave. Doctor Styer, of Fort Stanton, diagnosed their sickness as diphtheria. Mollie Kathleen was the seventh buried in our grave-yard.

Nursing six of us must have been a terrible ordeal for Uncle Mac, for patients are restless and troublesome. Ellen, half delirious,

---

*The Casey family so loved Johnny that when their last child, a son, was born, they named him Johnny, also.

begged to be plunged into the irrigation ditch near the house. Several times Uncle Mac found her trying to get out of the house to the water.

Hallucinations seem to accompany the disease. Will had always been a good child who talked to the younger children of Heaven and angels. His interest in them was intensified during the illness; he told of angels, indescribably beautiful, coming to lead him to Heaven, and even taking his hands to compel him to come with them.

Add's visions were of a different type. He loved horses and saw two of his favorites entangled in a rope which Jim Johnson, ranch foreman, had let fall. The horses' feet were tied and Johnson was spurring and whipping them in an effort to release them. For days he begged that if he died those horses might be led to his grave and shot so that never again could they be abused.

My problem was centipedes. To me they were horrible and in my delirium masses of them crawled over my hands. For three nights I begged that they be taken off me.

Uncle John Chisum also had smallpox. Upon learning that a bunch of his cattle had been stolen and driven to El Paso, he followed in an attempt to recover them. He took with him Jim Highsaw, an employee highly skilled in the use of a six-shooter, and as brave a man as ever lived. In El Paso they found that the brands on the animals as well as the jinglebob* had been skillfully transformed. The ear mark had been changed into an underslope, and the long rail to an arrow. Yet they succeeded in recovering most of the stolen cattle.

In his zeal to get a certain yearling which he had seen taken into an adobe house, Uncle John entered and found the animal "hog-tied" under a high bedstead. While searching other rooms he found seven children bedfast with smallpox. Though he realized the danger of exposure, he took no precautionary measures against contracting the disease.

On his way home with the cattle he stopped on the Delaware River, a small, clear stream flowing southward from the Guadalupes where his cowboys under Uncle Pitzer were rounding up and branding the calves and getting the beef cattle together preparatory to starting them to market. A few days after reaching this camp Uncle

---

*An ear mark made by splitting the ear longitudinally, so the outer half hangs down.

John developed a high fever and aches, which he at first attributed to the hard trip he had made. His cowboys, however, recognized the symptoms and were able to convince him that he was taking the smallpox.

As a first move, Uncle John's faithful Negro servant and horse wrangler, Frank Chisum (so-called because he had been a slave before the Negroes were freed), was dispatched to Fort Stanton, nearly two hundred miles distant, for medicine. Frank was ordered to make as quick a trip as possible and he carried out his orders by covering the round trip in four days. This was a remarkable record and to accomplish it he rode night and day.

A tent was used for a sick room and isolation ward. Two cowboys, Benito Juárez and Juan Álvarez, who had had smallpox, were installed as nurses. Uncle Pitzer wished to do everything possible for his brother, but never having had the disease, thought it best not to risk exposure. The expressions, "good care" and "having everything he needed" are ironic when this took place more than 200 miles from a doctor, and about sixty from a store from which the necessities of life could be procured.

Uncle John's devoted cowboys would have risked their lives to help him. Their ministrations were reinforced by his iron constitution, and he pulled through the attack. During his illness his inveterate sense of humor was not diminished. I've heard Uncle John laugh over his seeking relief from the monotony and suffering by observing the differences in his nurses. One, who was elderly, often reminded the patient that he would be badly pitted provided he recovered. Uncle John, with the usual perversity of the ill, often demanded things he should not have had and the younger man was inclined to indulge him. Uncle John demanded foods forbidden him and with the connivance of the young man, sometimes got them. He insisted that outwitting the elder contributed to his recovery.

At one time it seemed as his illness might prove fatal. During one of the heavy rains common during the summer, water overran Uncle John's camp bed before his nurses could rescue him. They got another bed and transferred him to it, but were greatly alarmed lest the cold bath might cause a backset. Instead of doing so it might even have been beneficial. Uncle John thought so and used to tell how soothing the cold water was to his tortured body.

When he was able to be up he had to undergo several days of

isolation before danger of contagion was over and he could return to South Spring Ranch for convalescing. He thought the time lost by the illness well spent for he seemed to have almost a new body.

Though his face was badly pockmarked, the pitting was not deep. He treated the disfigurement jocularly and often said to the ladies and girls that though he had lost some of his good looks he still retained his winning ways. In time the pits faded to a great extent and were scarcely noticeable.

19

Echoes of the Lincoln County War

WHEN UNCLE MAC HELPED MOTHER take her five children and a small herd of cattle to Texas, they headed down the Pecos to Seven Rivers where we stayed with the Jones family about three weeks. This was where we first met Billy the Kid. He was not known by that name at the time but was Billy Bonney to us. Later I heard him referred to as "the Kid." He asked Mother if he might go to Texas with us but she refused to take him. Mother had reason to be suspicious of him. She had a very fine mare named Dallas, one Add had seen and taken a fancy to. Mother traded McCullum, the owner, a pair of steers for the mare and got a bill of sale for the animal.

When Bonney saw this mare among our horses he offered to trade the horse he was riding for her. He told Add that he must repossess the mare, admitting he had "taken" her from Mariana Barela near Las Cruces. Though he undoubtedly had stolen her he did not use that word. He added that Jesse Evans, recently returned from Las Cruces, had brought word from Barela that the Kid was to return the animal and *pronto*. If this were not done Barela would come for her and the Kid, also.

Mother asked that Billy talk the matter over with her because she felt sure that the horse he wanted to trade for the mare had been stolen from John Chisum. It was Uncle John's policy never to sell a horse having his brand, so she asked the Kid, "How dare you offer to sell me a stolen horse?" Unabashed the boy replied, "Sure, Mrs.

Casey, the mare you have is stolen." Mother was surprised and asked how he dared to make such a statement. Nonchalantly the Kid replied, "I should know. I stole her myself."

Mother told the boy that she purchased the animal from a reliable man and that she had a bill of sale for her. She added that if anyone took her that she would have recourse to the law to be paid. Then, realizing the boy's hazardous position she said, "My God, Billy! I can't take a Chisum horse. The boys and I would be arrested and put in jail."

Both of my brothers urged Mother to take him to Texas with us but she refused. Then he left for the Murphy-Blake Spring where Billy Morton was in charge. Upon returning he told Will that Morton had given him a terrible "bawling out" for some trivial offense and that he intended getting even with him. Again he broached the subject of accompanying us, and again Mother courteously refused.

The small herd traveled slowly and not until February, 1878, did we reach the home of my aunt near Menard even though Mother had disposed of what was left of the herd at Fort Concho. There was no school at Menard so she sent Will, Add, and me to Fort Mason under Uncle Mac's supervision. He consulted Colonel [Rid] Hunter, an old friend of Father's, who advised that we remain there. Then Uncle Mac returned to Menard to help Mother return to New Mexico with Ellen and Johnnie. The older boys stayed only until fall before returning to the ranch. Mother insisted that I remain there to attend school but kept in touch with me through letters. One she wrote March 14th, 1878, told of the terrible happenings in Lincoln County. But Uncle Mac's letter gives much more detailed information:

I landed here from Santa Fe on Monday, the 19th; found all well, Grey, his wife, and three hundred children, more or less, in the house; Johnny rather bossing the crowd. Grey had planted twenty acres of corn and tends to plant more. Mr. McCurran is here trying to fix the mill. He is helping Grey to plant, and Grey will help him about the mill. Your mother started with Timio down to Paxton's camp on the Pecos by way of the Feliz after the work oxen we left there on the way to Texas. She will be gone about twelve days. I expect to start for Santa Fe in four or five days. There is no wheat sowed on the ranch. Longworthy has sowed about four acres in wheat on the Price ranch and planted about the same in corn. He is an old fraud, fit for nothing but lying. Turner is driving the buckboard from Vincente, Dow's ranch, to Roswell. Kline, George Kimbrell, and Francisco Romero are all farming at the same old place and had nothing to do with the fight. Martin Chávez is peddling on a small scale for Montana. All your Mexican friends are well and as big old hypocrites as ever.

The goat herd is at old Francisco Romero's and the same herders are herding them. "Add, how'd you like to herd goats?" "Dry up, Mac, I'm a student now." The Coe boys are farming on the Hughes ranch for Lola Wise. Marcos, Ysidro, and Manuel are at Analla's ranch. José Chávez' boys and girls are getting on as usual. Joe Storms, ragged, half-starved, and lousy, is attending to everyone's business but his own. Timio is farming on his ranch. Clene is feeding his poor old hogs with weeds and cursing the county and everybody in it. C. Fritz, wife, Emil, Linoa, Clara, and all the children are well, attending to their own business and trying to make a living. The *chosa* Mexicans are doing nothing but living on the wind. Mrs. Brady and children are at the old place; Juan José and some other Mexicans are farming on her ranch.

Ellis and family are all well. Mrs. Bolton and the girls are getting on in the same old way. Juan Patron has got nothing and is doing nothing but a little writing in the clerk's office. Montana has a good stock of goods brought from Santa Fe. Captain Baca and family are at the old place. Gray Wilkinson is no magistrate but as grand an old rascal as ever.

At this point McCabe's letter begins to deal with the Lincoln County War. First references are to the cold-blooded killing of the young Englishman, John H. Tunstall, on February 16th by members of the sheriff's posse under Billy Matthews that went to his ranch to attach some cattle:

Tunstall's father has appointed Weidermann [Robert A. Widenmann] to take charge of everything belonging to his son at his death. Weidermann has opened the store and moved the cattle from the Feliz to John Copeland's ranch above Fort Stanton. McSween is down on the Pecos on Chisum's ranch afraid for his life. Mrs. McSween is in the Plaza. Steve Stanley's wife, mother-in-law, Ham Mills, his brother, and brother's family are all gone to Pecos. Murphy, Dolan, and Jim Longwell are in Santa Fe and intend to stay there until the fight is over.

Now for the war news. If you and Add received the papers I sent you from Santa Fe and the letter I wrote to Will, you are posted to the fighting up to the killing of McNab* [Macnab] and the wounding of Ab Sanders at or near Charley Fritz' and the wounding of Dutch Charley (from Seven Rivers) at the Plaza. For fear you have not I will give a synopsis of the killed and wounded, and who by. First Tunstall was killed by Morton, Baker, and Evans, they trying to arrest him and his party. Morton and Baker, together with McCloskey, were killed by Dick Brewer and party near Capitan Mountains. Tom Hill was killed and Jesse Evans badly wounded in the right wrist and arm by a sheep man from Arizona whom they were trying to rob near Tulerosa. Brady and George Hindman were killed in the streets of Lincoln by men hid in the corral behind the new store of McSween and Tunstall, shot in the back as they were passing. John Middleton, Weidermann, a Negro, George Washington, and another Negro, Little Henry, "the Kid," and a man called French were seen to come out of the corral after the firing. All must have shot. At the same time a stray shot from the corral hit old Gray Wilkinson and made it uncomfortable for him to sit down for some time. Had it killed him, the loss to the county would have been small.

Dick Brewer, John Middleton, Doc Skurlock,* Charlie Bowdre, George and Frank Coe, "the Kid," Wait, McNab, and seven more whom I do not know, attacked a man by the name of Roberts at Blazer's house. Roberts wounded John Middleton in the lungs, George Coe in the hand, Charley* Bowdre in the side. Roberts was shot in the bowels by Shurlock. After he was wounded he crawled into the house and barred the door with a mattress. Brewer told Doctor Blazer if he did not bring Roberts out of the house, he would burn it down. Blazer said, "You may kill me; you may burn my house down; but I will not drive Roberts out, for he is wounded." Brewer went down to the mill, got behind a saw-log, and shot into the door at Roberts. Roberts took deliberate aim at Brewer and shot him right through the head. Brewer's men went off and left him, dead on the field, too cowardly to take his body off and give it decent burial. Roberts died the next day. Roberts had been in the country but a short time, and had done nothing, only he was herding Dolan and Riley's cattle at the Agency. He was not within thirty miles of where Tunstall was killed.

Court coming on soon after the killing of Brewer and Roberts everything was quiet for ten or fifteen days, though both sides were employing the most desperate characters they could find to aid them in the fight. Dolan and Murphy moved all their goods, books, and papers up to the Fort, leaving a man by the name of Easton [David Easton] in charge of the house. Both then went to Santa Fe. McNab was elected as captain of the McSween party after Brewer was killed, and he sent word to the men on the Pecos that he and his crowd were going to clean out all the men on the Pecos, commencing at Beckwith's house. This caused the Pecos men, and Paxton, Pearce, Powell, Bob and John Beckwith, Johnson, Perry, Dick Lloyd, Sam Cochran, Dutch Charley, Wallace and Bob Olinger, and enough others to make twenty-five men (I do not know them all) start up to Lincoln Plaza to fight it out, if they had to fight, or to settle it without a fight if they could.

They passed your mother's, but did not stop long. At Fritz' home some stopped to get their horses shod; others went to the house to get something to eat. Just as they arrived they saw McNab, Al [Ab] Saunders, and Frank Coe come in from the Plaza. They concealed themselves, and let Coe and Saunders pass as they were in front, and halted McNab when he came up. All three started to run; McNab was killed; Coe's mare was killed and he himself taken prisoner. Al Saunders was badly wounded in the ankle and hip, and his horse killed. Ab is now in the hospital at Stanton. The Pecos men would have . . . . [illegible]. I am afraid Ab Saunders will die. Dutch Charley can go about. I talked with them two hours. Jesse Evans is about the hospital every morning to have his wound dressed. He will soon be well.

All the Mexicans inquire about you, Add, and Will. They say they are glad the boys are not here, for they might be killed. Tricks sends love to you.

---

*The correct spelling of proper names is difficult to establish. In quoting handwritten letters the name of one man may be spelled several ways. The correct spelling of McNab is known to be Macnab; Skurlock is spelled Scurlock (Joseph G., "Doc") in Colonel Fulton's history of this period; and in one letter, McCabe spells Bowdre's first name both Charlie and Charley.

Johnny grows fast and has a great time with Gray's children. Old Tom is walking around as dignified as a preacher. Excuse paper. I left my valise at Fort Stanton and Tricks has nothing but book papers.

As I have indicated Mother was at the ranch while the greater part of this happened. Though she tried to be neutral it was hard. The location of our ranch caused both sides to put up with her as men went back and forth on expeditions and forays. Both sides annoyed her by searching the house and premises for someone hiding.

On one occasion there was some shooting at the place. The Murphy-Dolan crowd had managed to chase the McSween men away from San Patricio. A running fight ensued and both sides came down through the field shooting. The McSweens got away by turning west through Casey Canyon and making their way to the Chisum ranch. The Murphy-Dolan crowd gave up the chase when the McSween contingent left, and turned back to Lincoln. En route they stopped for dinner at our house.

Mother told of another occasion when Billy the Kid stopped for breakfast. In a fight the preceding day he had lost his horse, saddle, and bridle, but had somehow picked up a little pony. Mother fed him, not through choice but because she did not want to antagonize the McSween side.

From her point of view the Lincoln County War was a three-sided affair. There were two factions in Lincoln, the Murphy-Dolan and the McSween; and there was a third group from the lower Pecos valley whom McCabe termed the Pecos men. Many of the latter were good and honorable people who became involved in the difficulties through being summoned to serve on different posses. Some of them were with the ones who killed Tunstall; and Macnab, leader of the McSween party after the death of Brewer, sent a threatening letter to the ones in the Pecos group, of which Marion Turner was the leader.

When he and his men stopped at our place for meals Mother extended the same hospitality as she did to others. She regarded the Pecos group as friends, and doubtless the knowledge that she had their support prevented her suffering from the others.

Another letter from McCabe described the later occurrences of the conflict. In it he described the three-day fight which terminated in the burning of the McSween home and the killing of McSween and others as they ran from the flames invading the last room of the building. Among those who lost their lives was Robert Beckwith, son of Hugh Beckwith on the Pecos.

He told also of the terrible tragedy that occurred at the Beckwith ranch. The father was greatly distressed not only by Bob's death, but also by the subsequent killing of his younger son John.

The Kid gave my brother, Add, an explanation of his relations with Tunstall which I believe to be true. Jesse Evans, George Davis, Frank Baker, and Tom Hill were suspected of stealing some horses belonging to Tunstall and McSween. Many believed the Kid to have been with them. Among the horses taken on the Rio Ruidoso was a pair of fine ones, light gray — almost white — that Tunstall drove to his buckboard. The loss of his favorite team caused Tunstall to get Sheriff Brady to go down into the Seven Rivers country and arrest the entire group. I am uncertain whether the Kid was put in jail with the others, but it was reported that a group of his friends effected his release. Andy Boyle and Dick Lloyd were said to have led the rescue party. At any rate the stealing caused Tunstall to become interested in the Kid whom he hoped to induce to turn state's evidence against the others, so the Englishman employed him at the ranch.

How much work the Kid did for Tunstall I do not know but he was not addicted to regular work. From what I learned at Seven Rivers I judged him to be "harum-scarum," and his subsequent career seemed to substantiate my opinion. I did not consider him to be the hero that legends have made of him. He undoubtedly did take desperate chances from which there was no escape except by shooting. Having done that he disappeared for awhile. Once I heard him say, "He who fights and runs away will live to fight another day."

McCabe's letter indicates that public opinion condemned the Kid and his companions for leaving the body of Dick Brewer at Blazer's Mill. Their action seemed to indicate disorderly retreat animated by fear.

The Kid was as active and graceful as a cat. At Seven Rivers he practiced continually with pistol or rifle, often riding at a run and dodging behind the side of his mount to fire, as the Apaches did. He was very proud of his ability to pick up a handkerchief or other object from the ground while riding at a run.

Jesse Evans, at one time a close friend of the Kid's, was an outlaw, though the Kid eclipsed him in popular notice. I met Jesse Evans in 1873 when he was one of a group of Chisum's former cowboys who went to the farm near ours owned by Uncle John, to keep tab on the Indians' horses. They wished to regain some of the mounts stolen from the Jinglebob on the Pecos. Uncle John had lost so many he was handicapped in branding and rounding up his herds, so was forced to let some of his cowboys go; they had nothing to do but get revenge on the Apaches.

In this group was Jesse Evans, with his invariable companion, Jimmie McDaniels. I recall among them also Marlon Turner, Frank Baker, and Joe Hardy. Jesse Evans was a low, heavy-set dark-skinned young man. He seemed to be jolly, good-natured, and far from bloodthirsty. He probably did some rustling but I do not know of his having killed anyone, though he was known to have participated in the Lincoln County War. He was also with the notorious Graham boys in the robberies at both Forts Stockton and Davis, where he was captured.

Because Frank Baker was suspected of having a part in the killing of Tunstall I must say that I think that rumor a misrepresentation. I knew him a long time. He was from a good family in Syracuse, New York. Shortly after we came to the Hondo, Frank Baker, who was working for Uncle John Chisum, came through with a herd of cattle en route to San Carlos, Arizona, and stopped at our place. When on my way to the store, I met a cowboy who noticed a cheap ring I was wearing and said, "Little girl, let me see that." I handed it to him with the expectation that he would return it; instead he put it on his little finger and said he would keep it. He had been drinking and scarcely knew what he was doing. I ran toward the house crying; I was only about nine years old.

Frank Baker asked why I was crying and I told him, adding that I was afraid I would not get my ring back. Frank said, "Don't cry, Little Girl; I'll get it for you." Later in the day he brought the ring which he had taken from the sleeping man's finger. He asked for a bucket of water and I watched him pour it slowly over the head of the man who had taken the ring.

I knew, too, that Uncle John thought well of Baker. I never heard of his having stolen anything or killed anybody. Perhaps after he went to work for the Murphy-Dolan crowd he suffered the corruption of character that characterized that outfit. But so long as he was with Uncle John he conformed to Uncle John's standards which prohibited stealing or killing.

The killing of Sheriff [William] Brady and of Hindman was a shock to the citizens who had remained neutral until that time; it alienated many who had been inclined to be in sympathy with the McSween party. Brady was a good, well-meaning man who probably had faults but none that justified his being shot down like a dog in the streets of Lincoln. It is true that he and Major Murphy were friends and it is also true that they tried to implicate him in their dishonest schemes; but Brady tried to avoid trouble. That is probably why he sent Billy Matthews to the Tunstall ranch instead of accompanying the posse.

The news of Hindman's death, too, was distressing because he had worked for Mother, and I knew him well. He had come from Texas in 1875 with a herd of cattle owned by a Mr. Jordan and others bound for Arizona. They stopped at our place a week or so to rest the herd and the men. Hindman disliked summer weather and dreaded the heat of Arizona. He also had heard of depredations by the Apaches there, so decided to stay and work for Father. Bill Humphreys, part owner, was with the herd and he abused George Hindman for quitting them during the drive. Hindman declared he had not agreed as to how long he would work, and in anger he jerked his pistol. He and Humphreys fired simultaneously, and Humphreys got a scalp wound from a bullet that penetrated his hat. Humphreys' bullet struck the cylinder of Hindman's pistol and battered it so that it would not revolve.

Humphreys fell and Hindman, out of ammunition, started to run. He jumped down a ten-foot bank into the river and out on the opposite bank, ran across a meadow, and dashed up to our house. The bullet that struck his pistol had split into several pieces, some of which imbedded themselves in his hand. Mother said, "Come in under shelter. You're wounded and unarmed." She told me to bring a pan of water and when I came with it I helped her dress Hindman's hand.

As soon as Bill Humphreys regained consciousness, his brother John rode to their father. The old man jumped on his horse and started to the aid of Bill. By the time he reached his son, Hindman was halfway across the meadow. The old man jerked his gun and commenced shooting at Hindman. He charged Hindman, then turned his horse and rode toward his son's body. He repeated these tactics several times and lost his chance of killing George.

Because the bullets came toward our house Mother was alarmed and sent a man to tell Humphreys that he might hit one of the children. Humphreys replied, via the messenger, that if she did not run Hindman out of her house he would come over and get him if he had to burn the house in doing so. Hindman heard the threat and said, "Now, Mrs. Casey, I don't want you to have any trouble on my account. I'll just get out and hit for the hills." There was no further trouble.

When Father got home that evening he rode over to see Old Man Humphreys. The son who had fallen was not badly hurt and Humphreys agreed to pay Hindman and let him go, but did not keep that promise when Hindman followed the herd in an attempt to collect his wages. He returned and worked for us a long time. He was a good, quiet, inoffensive person and I do not recall of one instance in which he got into trouble. I regard his being shot from ambush by a cowardly aggregation concealed behind a corral wall at Lincoln as a dastardly act.

Charlie Bowdre was another of the participants in the Lincoln County War whom I well know. He worked for us for awhile on our Feliz place, and seemed a very friendly, good sort of fellow. When the Lincoln County War began, he joined the McSween side and was in all the fighting. I do not think he was ever charged with killing anyone directly except Buckshot Roberts. When the War came to an end, he went with Billy the Kid and was a member of his gang of cattle thieves. Bowdre never seemed satisfied with this sort of life and was always on the point of pulling away from his associates. He never, however, succeeded in doing so and was killed by Sheriff Pat Garrett when the Kid's gang was trapped in the rock house at Stinking Spring. I have heard it said that Bowdre would never steal stock from a woman or from a little cattleman, although he was entirely willing to steal from some big cattleman. I have myself heard him justify such a course by the argument that the big men had too much, more than they could use in their natural lives. Why, then, should not a poor devil like himself get a little from them when in need?

I also knew Tom O'Follard [O'Folliard], another conspicuous member of the McSween fighting forces. He also was a member of the Kid's gang, and was killed at Fort Sumner by Garrett's posse a short time before Bowdre was shot. What I remember most vividly about O'Folliard was his coming to our house when he and Len Daniels (whose name was really Dan Lemons) were being taken under arrest to Lincoln by Bob Olinger. The two men had just been caught, and Bob Olinger and his two companions, Buck [W. H.] Guyse and Dave Peverhouse, spent the night at our place, with the two prisoners. A few days later O'Folliard appeared again at our place, this time as an escaped prisoner. One morning about daylight, we heard a knock on our kitchen door. When Mother opened it, there stood a man with handcuffs on his wrists and shackles on his ankles. He had managed to get the chain of the shackles cut in two, but had been unable to remove the rings that were around his ankles. It was Tom O'Folliard who, after escaping from jail, had managed to get down as far as our place. He said he was hungry and asked Mother if she could give him something to eat, especially some hot coffee.

Mother invited him in and told him to sit on a box in the corner of the kitchen while she fixed him a good breakfast which included all the hot coffee he could drink. Then Mother told him some strangers, about whom she knew nothing, were staying at her place for the night and consequently he should not linger about the house but should get out in the hills where he could rest until night. I remember as if it were yesterday watching him strike out for the hills on a long trot just as day was breaking. That was the last time I ever saw him, and I never did hear how he managed to get out of the country and rejoin the Kid's band.

20

Aftermath

ALTHOUGH THE LINCOLN COUNTY WAR reached its climax in the three days' fight, July 16–19, 1878, at Lincoln in which Alexander A. McSween, Robert Beckwith, and several others were killed, the troubles in the county did not come to an end for several months. This aftermath of the war during the fall was in some respects more terrible than the war itself. A number of the participants on both sides apparently cast aside inhibitions and resorted to high-handed crimes. What had been done during the Harrell War or during the Lincoln County War paled into insignificance in comparison with the ruffianism that became rampant in Lincoln County.

A number involved in the lawless deeds banded themselves into an organization known as The Rustlers, but were more accurately described by the name the Mexicans bestowed upon them, *Vivo Diablos* (Live Devils). The membership was made of both the Murphy and the McSween sides in the Lincoln County War, together with others later drawn into the country by the opportunities afforded for the gratification of their proclivities. The organization went so far as to have its distinctive regalia — large white hats with a conspicuous band of blue ribbon about two inches wide.

Sam Collins, its first leader, was from Mason County, Texas, the area in which we had lived before coming to New Mexico, and we were acquainted both with him and his real name, Caleb Hall. The band was never very large — usually not more than nine members — but they could do enough devilment for two or three times that number. They moved through the whole section, stealing and robbing whenever they found anything they wanted, and not stickling at murder or worse crimes if it were to their advantage. They preyed principally upon the poor Mexicans, taking their jewels or anything else of value. They made a point of taking all the guns in the houses they entered provided they were worth taking. If they were worthless the Rustlers broke them.

Our place was never molested by this crowd because of Collins. We always treated him well, and in return he prevented his men from offending Mother, even though she were alone when they came.

News spread among the ranchers up the Ruidoso that Sam Collins and his gang were coming, and John Newcomb's Mexican wife made preparations for getting rid of the troublesome gang. She was a large woman and what her people call a *natrix* (witch doctor). She prepared some kind of poison which she put into the coffee she served the gang when it stopped at her place and demanded a meal. Sam had the Texan's habit of drinking at least one cup of coffee before eating. None of his men took coffee at that time. He got more of the poison into his stomach then did the others who had just been served the beverage when he realized that he had been poisoned.

To get revenge for the treachery he tried to draw his six-shooter but fainted. The others jumped up, left their coffee scarcely touched, and rushed to their leader's aid. They accused Mrs. Newcomb of having poisoned Collins and threatened to kill her if she did not give him an antidote. Whether or not the tea she administered aided his recovery they did not know, but he regained consciousness and was able to ride away. John Newcomb's wife disappeared and thus avoided being killed. Perhaps the fact that they had previously decided to leave Ruidoso for Seven Rivers had something to do with her escaping punishment.

This experience frightened the band and as soon as they could they rode to the Pecos. They stopped at the Junction [Hondo] where there lived an elderly man, José Chávez y Sánchez. He was of the better class of Mexicans — he was part French, was fairly well educated for that time, and was refined and progressive. He had one of the best houses in the country where he lived in patriarchal style with his four sons and their families about him, cultivating their fertile land efficiently.

His sons were harvesting the lush gramma grass upon which fine horses were grazing, when the Rustlers rode to the mowing machine upon which one son was riding and ordered the young man to take the harness off the horses and turn them over. The boy replied, "Señores, the horses are not for sale. They belong to my father. Please see him." The outlaws opened fire on the entire group, saying, "We have no time for talk. Take that!"

Desiderio Chávez, aged sixteen, was killed. Lorencio Lucero, an inoffensive neighbor, and Clito Chávez also fell. A fourth was wounded, but not severely. Had the father and two other sons been present, they, too, might have been injured for not one of the men expected an attack or was armed. This was especially brutal and wanton in view of the fact that Chávez was one of few that had succeeded in remaining neutral and taking no part in the Lincoln County War.

It was argued that the father had been considered a friend of Major Murphy and it was believed that at one time Jimmie Dolan had found refuge in the Chávez home. It is possible that some of the Rustlers sought revenge, but it is more probable that the act was motivated by the blood lust of reckless men who knew that neither military nor civil authorities had power to cope with the situation.

Among those indicted for murder were Nelson, John Gunter, Gus Gildea, Thomas Selman, Charlie Snow, Reese Gobles, and V. C. Whittaker. Sam Collins, still ill, was not present.

On this trip they stole what was left of our cattle of the KC brand. They had changed hands so frequently during the past year that they had caused successive owners much annoyance. Under the order issued by Governor Wallace empowering John Newcomb to act as cattle collector for Lincoln County and take all the cattle whose ownership might be uncertain, the KC cattle were placed in the hands of Dutch Martin.

The Rustlers headed for Rocky Arroyo where the cattle could be hidden. They could hardly have selected a better spot, for it was secluded and in the range of the Jones boys, Heiskell's sons, whom people trusted because of their honesty.

Shortly after they got there with the cattle, John Selman, a member of the band, killed one of the others, (Edward [Little]) Hart. It seemed unlikely that Collins would recover, and Selman was an aspirant for his position. So was Hart. While dinner was being cooked Selman got the drop on Hart and shot him without giving him any chance for his life. In this gruesome killing, Selman's bullet penetrated Hart's forehead and ranged upward, tearing off a great piece of the top of his skull. His brains were spattered in every direction, with bits falling into the skillet in which the steaks were cooking. They dug a hole and rolled the body into it.

Collins recovered sufficiently to regain control of the gang but Selman would not yield to him. He gathered a few of the Rustlers favorable to him and the two groups engaged in a running fight for eighteen miles.

As my brother, Will, was riding from our Rio Feliz ranch to that on the Hondo he met Tom Collins. The latter had two mares that were obviously ridden down as a result of the fight with the Selman division. Collins forced Will to give up his good horse in exchange for the two exhausted mares, then escaped on Will's horse. Will understood Collins' situation too well to protest, though Gray was his favorite mount.

The mares were too nearly spent to be ridden so Will walked and brought them home with him. He changed his saddle from one to the other two or three times because of the condition of the animals.

When he told Mother what had happened he was so chagrined that he cried. She told him that no horse was worth his life and that he had done the only thing possible under the circumstances.

She received a letter from Collins in which he said that he had been forced to take Will's horse in order to save his life, and that it was the best he had ever ridden. He said Gray was worth at least $500 and that he would send Will $100 in gold to pay for the mount.

But the gold never came.

21

Bob Olinger as I Knew Him

AS NO FULL AND UNPREJUDICED ACCOUNT of the Lincoln County War exists [in 1927], many of the participants have been misunderstood and even misinterpreted. To the present generation none of this seems more nearly true than in the case of Bob Olinger. Emerson Hough in his *The Story of the Outlaw,* published in 1905, gave a lengthy account of the Lincoln County troubles with which he had become familiar through hearsay during his stay at White Oaks in 1883 or 1884. For some reason which I am unable to explain, Emerson Hough chose to depict Bob Olinger in the darkest colors. Hough had every opportunity to make inquiries and to ascertain just what sort of man Bob Olinger was, but he possibly contented himself with getting his information from some envious, hostile person.

The unfair picture of Bob Olinger became greatly intensified at the hands of Walter Noble Burns in his *Saga of Billy the Kid.* Burns' tendency to write in the style of the dime novel led him to endow Bob Olinger with all the attributes of the conventional villain of melodrama. In the face of this misrepresentation I feel that the time has come to break a silence I have kept for nearly fifty years, despite many requests to break it, and to try to set a friend in truer light.

The Olingers came originally from Ohio to the West and settled for awhile in the Indian Territory. When Bob Olinger came to New Mexico about 1876, he joined his brother Wallace who had come to the Seven Rivers section of Lincoln County a few years previously and had gone into the cattle business in partnership with W. A. Johnson, son-in-law of Hugh M. Beckwith. As Wallace did well with his cattle it was logical for him to send for his younger brother, whose full name was Robert Ameridth Olinger, and their mother, Mrs. Stafford [Safford]. I give these details about the Olingers because I wish to make it clear that Bob and Wallace Olinger did not belong to the class known in those times as renegades, but in reality were decent, industrious folk who had come to New Mexico because of business opportunities.

Bob Olinger was a quiet young man who worked faithfully for a time as foreman on the Beckwith ranch. He was not drawn into any of the earlier incidents of the Lincoln County War. He was not, for instance, in the deputy sheriff's posse under Billy Matthews that went out to the Feliz ranch in February, 1878, and whose visit led to the killing of John H. Tunstall. That posse had been largely recruited from among those living on the Rio Pecos and in the vicinity of Seven Rivers; but Bob Olinger did not go along although his brother, Wallace, was summoned and did become a member of the posse. It is almost certain that Bob Olinger knew of the getting together of the crowd and, if he had really been the bloodthirsty, swashbuckling kind of young man he is said by some to have been, he would most certainly have gone.

Bob Olinger made his appearance first in the crowd of twenty or twenty-five Seven Rivers Warriors who, under the leadership of Marion Turner, started toward Lincoln in the summer of 1878 to settle this trouble or fight it out. At the Feliz ranch, Marion Turner's crowd unexpectedly came across three men belonging to the Brewer side, Frank McNab [Macnab], Frank Coe, and Al [Ab] Sanders. Despite the great difference in numbers shooting began between the groups. McNab was killed, Sanders wounded, and Frank Coe hemmed up in a cave [an arroyo]. It was Bob Olinger who vigilantly kept the arroyo under the range of his pistol. He told me afterward how Frank Coe would thrust out his pistol every few minutes and take a shot at him; then he would shoot at Coe. Although his bullets could not reach Coe they cut away a good deal of the bank which protected the man. When Coe's supply of ammunition was exhausted he called out that he was willing to surrender. Bob Olinger used to say that he was glad to end the affair in that manner, for he and Frank Coe were not in any sense personal enemies. Their shooting at each other was owing to the fact that they were on opposite sides of the feud raging in Lincoln County.

Frank Coe was taken prisoner and carried with the Seven Rivers Warriors to Lincoln where he was placed in the Murphy store and left with Bob Olinger as guard. The next morning when shooting began at the other end of the town Bob Olinger itched so to get into it that he left his prisoner to shift for himself. In doing so he showed his respect for the amenities of warfare in a nice [sic] way. Knowing that Frank Coe was unarmed and at the mercy of any of Marion Turner's men who might want to kill him, Olinger, before leaving him, handed back Coe's pistol and said, "Take this, Frank, and use it if you need to protect yourself."* I mention this incident to show what strain there was in the Olingers.

Bob Olinger was in Lincoln during the subsequent fighting which lasted three days and terminated in the burning of the McSween house and the killing of McSween. His part in the fighting docs not seem to have been especially outstanding as was that of others including Marion Turner, Joe Nash, John and Jim Jones, Bob Beckwith, Andy Boyle, and Buck Powell. Toward the end of the fight when the McSween house was being consumed by fire, Bob Olinger was in the group in front of and near the McSween place and he witnessed the driving of the men from room to room of the residence by flames until they were forced to make a break from the kitchen.

Their bursting from the door was the climax of the three days' fighting. Numerous shots were fired by each side and Bob Beckwith was killed. One account states that his gun hung fire and that he was killed accidentally by a man on his own side; another says that when he went forward to receive the surrender of some one who had called out that he wished to stop fighting, that one of the McSween men shot him. Bob Olinger and Bob Beckwith were close friends

---

*This incident as related by Frank Coe to his daughter, Mrs. Edith Coe Rigsby, was attributed not to Bob Olinger, but to his brother, Wallace. This version was corroborated by William Johnson, son of Captain William Johnson, and also by Bill and Sam Jones. Is it possible that Bob Olinger told Lily Casey that it was he who performed this generous act in order to ingratiate himself with her? Reportedly they were engaged to be married.

and it was logical that Olinger would resent the killing of his friend. I do not believe that the death of Bob Beckwith should be attributed to Billy the Kid;* and, as Bob Olinger was in a position to know the facts of the affair, that his statements should be accepted. I am aware of stories to the effect that there was strong animosity on Bob Olinger's part toward the Kid because of Bob Beckwith's death but think they are creations of fictitious origin. I can certainly testify that Bob Olinger's account to me did not coincide with them. He talked much to me about the Lincoln County War, and he had a different explanation from that usually accepted as to the trouble between Billy the Kid and himself.

Shortly after the burning of the McSween house Bob Olinger accepted an appointment as United States deputy marshal. The circumstances of his being selected for this office are creditable both as to his courage and his desire to be of service in checking lawlessness. A notorious band of outlaws was making its rendezvous along the Pecos and in the nearby mountains, especially in the Guadalupes and the Davis range. They frequently descended upon stages on the line running from Fort Concho, Texas, to San Antonio, Texas; and upon one occasion staged a holdup at Pegleg, Texas. The Texas Rangers were doing their best to cope with these bandits, but were too few in numbers to accomplish much. Company "D" was stationed in that area under command of Captain D. W. Roberts, and it was expected to patrol the vast stretch of country in the western part of the state, known as the Llano Estacado (Staked Plain) and also the Pecos Valley. This troop was responsible also for Fort Stockton and Ft. Davis, near the Rio Grande. Uncertainty as to the location of the state line between New Mexico and Texas increased the problem of the Rangers, who were obligated to remain within the confines of their own jurisdiction.

The emergency created by the Pegleg robbery provoked the participation of the federal government which, of course, was not subject to state lines. The Post Office Department procured the appointment of several United States deputy marshals for the purpose of capturing stage robbers, counterfeiters, and moonshiners. West Texas and southeast New Mexico were infested with criminals

---

*Bill (William) Johnson, grandson of Hugh Beckwith said that the family always believed that Robert Beckwith was killed by Billy Bonney.

playing hide-and-seek with the Rangers. Bob Olinger was appointed as one of the deputy marshals and received his commission at Fort Stockton, Texas.

From the first he was active in carrying out the dangerous duties of his office. When a warrant was placed in his hands he did not hesitate to attempt an arrest, regardless of how desperate the man might be. In some cases he had to "capture the man by killing him," as the quaint but grim phrase of the time was. I think the first occasion of this sort was Bob Olinger's undertaking to arrest Tom Hill, alias Peter Grain [Crain?]. Hill resisted arrest and Olinger shot him. In telling me about this case Bob said Hill was the first man he ever killed and that he regretted doing it, but that under the circumstances he could do nothing else.

Olinger's detractors have made much of his killing John Jones. They cite this as his liking to kill regardless of lack of provocation. The facts are not so damaging as represented. Bob told me of this occurrence and I think I know whereof I speak. Bad feelings had been created between the two by meddlers who carried stories to each, primarily regarding the killing of John Beckwith, the younger son of Hugh Beckwith, by John Jones at Seven Rivers in 1879. Realizing that a quarrel was imminent Bob Olinger refused to go to John Jones' cow camp to discuss their grievances, but sent word that he would meet Jones at the cow camp of Pearce [Milo Pierce] and Paxton — neutral ground. John Jones, a large and fearless man, arrived, armed to the teeth and seeking trouble. When he dismounted he cocked his rifle and throwing it across his arm, walked toward Bob Olinger, who had come out of the house and was standing at the door.

When John Jones said, belligerently, "I came to settle with you about those lies I've heard you told about my killing John Beckwith," Bob Olinger stepped quickly toward Jones and asked, "What sort of settlement do you want, John?" Jones fired, but the bullet missed Olinger because he was very close to John. Olinger fired in self-defense.

The killing of John Jones was very unfortunate, but it was not premeditated nor done in a cowardly manner. When two hot-blooded, armed men quarreled, the likelihood was great at that time that the matter would terminate in death. The previous friendship of these men and their families made this shooting doubly unfortunate. I know well that this tragic death was a source of much regret to Bob Olinger, for he told not only me but many others how he felt about this killing.

I wish to present a positive denial to the charge that Bob Olinger treacherously killed a Mexican, Pas Chávez, when the man offered his hand to Olinger in friendly greeting. Bob Olinger was not present when Pas Chávez was killed at Dan Dow's stage stand. Buck Guyse and Dave Peverhouse, deputy sheriffs sent out to arrest Chávez, said that he resisted arrest and that they had to shoot him.

As a law-enforcing officer Bob Olinger was considerate and generous. In 1880 I received a letter from him saying that if Dave Peverhouse was at our place, or if we knew of his whereabouts, he should be informed that his family was at Pope's Crossing and needed his assistance. Peverhouse was "on the dodge" because of trouble in Texas and was at our home on the Hondo in preparation for leaving for Arizona. When told of Bob's letter he was excited and worried, fearing it was a trap, but was finally convinced of its truth.

Mother had planned leaving for Van Wyck's at Seven Rivers to deliver a wagon load of flour, and she offered to take Peverhouse. He had been expecting his family for some time but his wife had been delayed en route by detours to evade pursuers in search of them.

I met Bob Olinger in December, 1877, shortly before the Lincoln County War. I was helping my brothers take our cattle into Texas and we stopped a few days at Seven Rivers. When I first saw him he was looking through a pair of field glasses* at a man who was cutting off the water at the springs. When he was introduced I noticed spots on his face caused by an attack of smallpox from which he was recuperating. I, too, had suffered from that disease not long before, so each of us felt a bond of sympathy and interest for the other.

Because I was in Texas I did not see Bob Olinger again for a long time, but after my return we met in Roswell a time or two. It should be remembered that during the Lincoln County War Mother was in Texas trying to recover her cattle that were held by the Rustlers. When she went to Seven Rivers on this mission she stopped at the home of Mrs. Safford, mother of the Olinger boys.

---

*After Olinger's death Lily Casey was given his six-shooter, field glasses, and gauntlets.

Bob was so helpful to Mother that she thought very highly of him, and after our return to the Hondo he frequently came to the ranch.

Bob Olinger was at our home the Sunday before he was killed by Billy the Kid. He spoke of the Kid but not in an unfriendly way. I recall a Mexican girl's having come to the house to see Bob whom she heard was visiting us. She asked him whether or not she should marry the Kid when he was freed. She explained that a law in Old Mexico required that this procedure would save a life and asked if that were true in the Territory. Through an interpreter Bob explained that such was not the law in New Mexico and that she could not save Billy by that means.

The news of Bob Olinger's death at the hands of Billy the Kid was a great shock to our family. We learned of it from Captain and Mrs. J. C. Lea who stopped at the Fritz ranch on their way from Roswell to Lincoln in a hack. They also told that the Kid had escaped from jail and that he had killed both guards. Mrs. Lea was afraid to go on to Lincoln and begged her husband to turn back. He decided to go to Picacho, get Old Man Cline [Kline], Old Man Kimbrell, and some others to go to Lincoln with him.

We, too, were excited and eager to go to Lincoln and learn exactly what had occurred. Mother was unwilling to leave home though she was greatly concerned about Bob's death. She permitted us older children to drive up to Lincoln in a hack. We reached the town late in the day, and found that the reports we had heard were only too true. Bob Olinger and J. W. Bell had been killed by the Kid in a very brutal and revengeful manner. We never saw this friend of ours again. The commanding officer at Fort Stanton had sent down and had the bodies of Olinger and Bell, the other guard killed by the Kid, taken to Fort Stanton. The next day Bob Olinger, being a U.S. deputy marshal, was buried in the cemetery there, but Bell's body was sent over to White Oaks where his family lived.

Much has been said and written about the hatred existing between Billy the Kid and Bob Olinger, and various explanations of it have been given. As I have already indicated, a favorite theory dates the ill feeling between these two back to the killing of Bob Beckwith. But such was not the case, and I shall give the real cause as I learned it from Bob Olinger himself.

After Olinger killed John Jones at Pearce and Paxton's cow camp under the circumstances already related, Billy the Kid, seeking probably to curry favor with the Joneses, told Old Man Jones that the first time he got a chance he would kill Bob Olinger. Just why the Kid should have wanted to espouse the cause of John Jones and become the avenger of his death I have never been able to fathom, for Marion Turner, John, and Jim Jones were supposed by a good many people to have been among those most directly responsible for the death of McSween.

But Bob Olinger was not vindictive about the matter and he did not seek to retaliate upon Billy the Kid. When Pat Garrett became sheriff and started his pursuit of the Kid, Olinger was never a member of the posse that Garrett kept in the field. Neither was he present when the Kid surrendered to Garrett at Stinking Springs. But Garrett had become acquainted with Bob Olinger and had formed such a high opinion of his qualities that when he wanted a trustworthy guard for the Kid, he picked Olinger as one of the two men most likely to see that the Kid did not escape.

Several stories exist about Olinger's rough treatment of the Kid while the latter was in his custody. I think, however, that these must be greatly exaggerated. Guards and prisoners will talk, and naturally their remarks sometimes grew acrid without their being much reality of feeling back of it all. It would be easy for an outsider, especially if he were partisan, to ascribe to such remarks more of an animus than there really is. I do not profess to know what Bob Olinger said to his prisoners, but I do know that it would not be in keeping with his general character to deliberately taunt and torment a prisoner about his approaching execution, as the accounts say he did the Kid.

In all likelihood Olinger was a careful guard and disposed to be strict with his prisoner. He noted with disapproval that the other guard, Bell, was inclined to be easy going with the Kid, and he felt duty bound to drop a word of warning on this score to Garrett. After the Kid made his escape, utilizing to his advantage the probable carelessness of Bell, Garrett was ready to admit over the dead bodies of the two guards that the terrible outcome might have been avoided had he heeded the advice Olinger had given him.

One thing I do know, however, and that is that Bob Olinger went to his death bravely and courageously as became a worthy peace officer. He was across the street from the old Murphy store in which the Kid was kept a prisoner, when he heard the shot that killed Bell. His first thought was probably that some of the Kid's friends were attempting a rescue, for he had told me on his last visit to our place that he feared such an attempt might be made. When the hotel keeper shouted, "They're fighting at the courthouse," Bob Olinger dashed across the street to his death, foolhardy brave to the last.

22

School–teaching on the Peñasco

MY INCLINATION FOR TEACHING showed itself when I was a small girl. There was nothing I liked better than to say to my playmates, "Let's play school," and if they agreed, I always assumed the role of teacher. I felt that this was mine by right, for I was farther advanced than the rest of the children of our family; and those of the Mexican renters who played with us had hardly put their feet onto the road of learning. I will admit that I got a good deal of enjoyment from the punishment my position allowed me to inflict on the others, but at the same time I greatly enjoyed feeling that I was trying to instill some knowledge into the minds of others.

The first chance I had of being a teacher in a real sense came in 1882, when I happened to go away from home for a visit to a family named [Jack] Wilson that lived on the Upper Peñasco, near what is now Mayhill,* New Mexico. At that time I was nearly grown and rather large for my age. On this portion of the Peñasco, there was quite a settlement of American families, some from Missouri, like the Coes and Mahills,* and the others mostly from Texas, like the Jameses, the Bateses, and the Orial Means family. In all these there were quite a number of children and up to that time there were no school opportunities. The public school system was in its infancy

---

*The family's name is Mahill. The village, Mayhill, is named for them but was misspelled.

in the Territory, and of course was very laxly managed in an extensive county like that of Lincoln. Of what service were the three commissioners in a county as large as that? A Mr. Bryan, commissioner for that part of the county, lived some distance away on the lower Peñasco, and paid little attention to the upper Peñasco.

While I was at the home of the Wilsons, the families in that section got together and agreed to start a school of their own. They built a schoolhouse and raised enough by subscription to pay a teacher $50 a month for six months. How they selected me as teacher I do not know, but they came to me with the offer and I agreed to teach for them. Mrs. Mahill agreed to board me for $10 a month with the understanding that I was to be like one of the family and help with the work morning and evening. This seemed to be the best arrangement I could make for boarding, although the two-mile walk from the Mahills to the school promised to be formidable when the heavy winter snows came.

The log schoolhouse was built by the men of the community quickly enough and equipped with some roughly made tables and benches. My table was a little more substantial than the others, and somebody furnished a chair for my use. About twenty pupils were assembled, and then the school was ready for work.

Of course some of the older boys determined to try me out. They talked a lot about how they would run away from school if I tried to punish them, and then boasted that I could never catch them, for they could outrun me. I confess that my heart sometimes sank into my shoes as I thought of what these boys might do. About five or six of the oldest ones always brought their six-shooters and Winchesters. Though still in their teens they had attained that much of manhood on the frontier. There was reason for them coming armed; they had to ride in from different ranches a long distance away, and there still lurked the fear of Indians. Of course on arrival at school they laid aside their arms and did not put them on until they were ready to start homewards. But it was not reassuring to a greenhorn teacher as I was to think that these boys might make trouble if they became so inclined.

I resolved firmly that I would nip in the bud the first attempt at rebellion, and I succeeded in doing so in a manner that established me in authority. About a week after school commenced, little Frank Mahill got contrary, and refused to make the figure 6 according to directions. He seemed determined to follow his way which was to start at the bottom with the "o" then move upward with the stroke* instead of the reverse method which Uncle Ash Upson had taught me and which I was passing on to my students. As he was the youngest and rather spoiled child of Mrs. Mahill with whom I stayed, I talked more nicely and coaxingly to him than I might have done had it been anyone else, but with no results. Frank resolutely stuck to his method of making a 6 and I realized that I would have to take issue with him over the matter.

All the other pupils were interested in my tussle with Frank, and it flashed into my mind that I had better give first attention to the door, and with my legs none too steady, I walked over and closed it, locking it as I did so and putting the key into my pocket. I knew somehow that by that action I had conquered the school completely. Without saying a word, I walked back to the desk where Frank stood with his slate, and taking it in my hands, I remarked, "Now, Frank, let's learn how to make those 6's in the right way."

Frank's attitude had been changed, too, and soon he was making his 6's as well as could be expected, starting at the top and rounding out the bottom last. Never later on did I have the least difficulty in exercising proper authority in the school room. The large boys never gave me any of the trouble they had so much boasted of; of course, I had to get after some of the smaller children for minor offenses and sometimes I had to punish them. But on the whole my pupils and I got on very well together, all due, I think, to my having had the courage to lock the door and put the key in my pocket.

The equipment was meager as it could be. I used a cow bell as the school bell, and my register was an old store "blotter." I was inclined to insist upon all the ceremonies connected with going to school. Every morning I carefully called the roll, requiring each one to answer by one formula or the other: "Present and not tardy," or "Present and tardy." I also made them form a line of two's and march in and out of the building. The subjects I taught were the elementary ones of reading, writing, spelling, geography, and arithmetic. I did say something to some of the parents about teaching grammar, but they disapproved, saying that it was just foolishness.

---

*A method still used in parts of Germany.

It was arithmetic I took greatest delight in teaching. Elmer Mahill was pretty good at arithmetic and the most advanced pupil I had. I made it a practice to go over the next day's lesson with him every night, and in that way killed two birds with one stone. I got the good will of Mrs. Mahill for my helpfulness to Elmer and I made sure that I had all of the more advanced sums worked out before I went to school the next day.

Naturally I had some material in the school that it was impossible to do anything with. I remember one large boy of nineteen who had such an impediment of speech he could hardly talk at all. He was an exceptionally good boy and tried hard to learn, but with that handicap it was difficult for him to make progress. I used to feel so sympathetic that I would almost cry at his efforts to talk. His name was, I think, John Sheets. There was another pathetic case of a little nine-year-old girl so tongue-tied that I could not understand what she was trying to say. And, to make things worse, others from the same family had picked up the habit of talking like her. I was almost distracted at times by the effort to understand this group of children.

This family was as ignorant a set as I have ever encountered. It would not be far wrong to say that they were degenerates. The father was very mean, really cruel, to his children, and frequently used a large club to knock one of the boys down for some slight offense. As the old fellow had been married four times, there were four sets of children in his household. Each of the first three wives had borne him a son, and the fourth had presented him with three younger children. All were subnormal and one or two of them certainly were feeble minded. I have never encountered a more wretched conglomeration than this family.

To illustrate the old man's ignorance that made him a laughingstock in the neighborhood, here are two amusing quotes. Most of the settlers on the Upper Peñasco used to say, when asked what direction the stream flowed, "It runs nearly parallel east and west." But when this man was asked, his reply invariably was, "Hit runs nearly paralyzed with the sun, east and west." Another time when he got in a tight place for money, he decided to sell his mule team. In telling it to a friend he said, "I got to have some money, so I'm going to prepose of one team of my mules."

On the whole my experience at school teaching was pleasant.

I had something more of a taste of social life than I had had on the ranch. During that winter what were called "storm dances" were very popular among the people on the upper Peñasco. During Christmas week especially they went from house to house in a series of these. They not only expected the different householders to let them come in, but they also expected a liberal layout of things to eat. The only thing to do was to make the best of it and comply with both demands; otherwise there was a good chance for trouble.

One night the crowd of dancers went to the house of Mr. Wilson. His wife was from the East — Illinois, I believe — but Mr. Wilson himself, while originally from Alabama, had been in the West long enough to know its ways and customs. When his wife began to show she was displeased at the crowd's coming to her house, he simply told her she would have to make the best of it, and went ahead to give the party as cordial a reception as was possible. He took everything out of the spare room, it being the largest one in the house, and let them dance. All went well until about eleven o'clock, when the dancers became hungry. Not seeing any preparations for giving them anything to eat, some of them went to Mr. Wilson and told him what they expected. He replied, "Well, I don't know whether my wife will cook anything or not." Several in the party replied to this, "We're going to have something to eat for our women and children, anyway; or somebody will go into the ditch. If you don't want to cook for us, just show us the chuck and we'll do the rest, for we're pretty good cooks, and our women can make bread."

Mr. Wilson saw the significance of these remarks, and looking at his wife, who was still disgruntled over the whole business, he told her that she had better get in an amiable frame of mind. He added that if she was not willing to do the cooking, he would turn the kitchen over to those people and let them do it themselves. But Mrs. Wilson remained in a bad humor, so I thought it was time to step in and do what I could to avert trouble. Mr. Wilson and the boys were good meat cooks and there was a newly killed beef hanging on the porch. With the help of some of the women I knew in the party of dancers I managed to get some biscuits made. Then we made an enormous quantity of coffee, not only enough for all the coffee pots we could find but for the teakettle as well. Thus the dancers were fed, but realizing that their request had been complied with unwillingly so far as Mrs. Wilson was concerned, they decided to end the dance as soon as they had eaten their fill. It was not a pleasant situation, but I think both parties were to blame. I am convinced that my cooperation had something to do with averting trouble for the Wilsons.

Although my school was very successful, toward the end I encountered some opposition from Old Man White and his son-in-law [?] Curtis, both great rascals and troublemakers. White was in reality a German, and no one seemed to know whether he had become a naturalized citizen. He claimed possession of a large tract of land, and was always trying to sell some of it to greenhorns from the East or elsewhere. He had somehow gotten in his toils an English family by the name of Windsor, and had them come up from El Paso where he had discovered them, and buy some of his land. As these English people knew nothing about our land lines and measurements, it was easy enough for Old Man White to trick them into buying what turned out to be rough, undesirable land among the hills. Among other inducements he held out was that one of the ladies in the family could have a school to teach. While I was teaching, he tried his utmost to get the people to let me out and put this English woman in, arguing that I was too young and inexperienced. But my friends among the people of the Peñasco remained true to me, and I kept the school until the end of the term. Such treatment, however, did not make me inclined to try it for another term.

I remember those Windsors distinctly. They were directly from England, and it was reported that they belonged to the nobility and were very wealthy. I used to see them when they came down to Al Coe's for the mail. I liked to help Mrs. Coe with the mail and to talk Spanish with old Peso,* an Indian who brought the mail over into our section once a week from the post office on the reservation (South Fork). When some of the Windsors came down for their mail, I used to enjoy their peculiarities of speech and dress. When Old Man White was trying to get the English woman substituted for me as teacher, one of the arguments my friends made for retaining me was that they did not want their children taught by a lady who spoke English in the way she did; United States English, they said to

---

*Peso was the last Mescalero chief.

Old Man White, was good enough for them and they did not want their children to learn to talk differently from them.

White and Curtis were almost a curse to the community. They always took a side opposite that of the majority of people, and so were consistently fomenting discord and trouble.

23

The Sutton–Nixon Killing

WHEN I WENT TO MAHILLS, Will took me over in a buckboard. In the back of the vehicle he carried a very large, domed trunk covered and lined with heavy canvas in which were my clothing and other necessities. In this trunk I kept also a revolver and field glasses that had belonged to Bob Olinger, and which were brought to me after his death by his brother, Wallace.

It was during this term of school that young Tim Valentine was killed by Sutton and Nixon. They appeared on the Peñasco from God knows where, and stopped at Old Man James' place. Nobody asked a man's name, from whence he came, nor why. James needed hands for the harvest that was ready to begin so he employed them. Shortly after that he decided to go back to his old home in Texas to visit his aged father. Since he was taking Mrs. James it was necessary to find someone to stay at the home with the children. He induced Mr. and Mrs. Mahill to go to his home for a month, and as I lived with them, I, too, went.

Sutton and Nixon were still there and consequently I met them. I was not favorably impressed. Both were heavy but in other respects they were unlike. Nixon was dark, with straight, coarse black hair and black eyes; Sutton was what I would call a sandy blond. He had what one of the boys described as sorrel hair, and his eyes were blue. While Sutton was "hatchet faced," Nixon's face was round, and his nose was "pug." I learned that the people along the Peñasco shared my distrust of the two.

Because Mrs. Mahill prepared meals for all I had no choice but to see them often. They were accustomed to staying in the house until bedtime so there was no avoiding conversation with them. Sutton was satisfied to remain on terms of distant courtesy, but Nixon persisted in trying to effect a closer acquaintance. If we played games he insisted upon being my partner. If the others read, he did not permit me to do so but forced his silly, uninteresting ideas on me. His insistence upon calling me "The Schoolmarm" was offensive. I evaded him as much as I could for in addition to my dislike of him I was also afraid of him.

The Mahills sensed my attitude and tried to help me but wanted to avoid the ill-will of the two even more than I did. I think they were as relieved as I when the return of Mr. and Mrs. James enabled us to leave.

Again the Jack Wilsons invited me to spend a weekend with them some sixteen miles away in the mountains. I did not expect to encounter Nixon and Sutton, but I did rather dread having to be near Mr. Wilson's employee, Bob Buford, whom I'd met at dances, and whose attentions I did not enjoy. When Mr. Wilson suggested that I go with him and Buford to get wood I objected. Mr. Wilson understood my reason for not going and said that he'd drive the wagon and that Buford might ride his horse. Under those conditions I was glad to go. Later we realized that the arrangement was a very fortunate one for Mr. Wilson.

On our way we stopped at a store belonging to Henry and Johnson. When we entered there were several rough looking men seated about the stove, and among them were Sutton and Nixon. All were heavily armed but I thought nothing of that because it was customary for men to carry weapons. The men bought liquor and talked loud. I felt out of place and feared that Nixon might attempt to start a conversation with me, so I left the store, and seated myself outside. Mr. Henry, one of the owners of the store, surmised my reason for leaving and followed to reassure me and ask me to return. With tears in my eyes I told him I did not know what to do, and that I was afraid of the drinking and what it might mean.

Mr. Henry said, "Let me give you some advice: whenever circumstances, as they have today, throw you in a place of this kind, first you should make your presence known, for any real man will protect you from annoyance. Even the worst men will seldom do or say anything offensive with a lady present. Now come back out of the cold. There's a chair in the drygoods section and I promise that you will not be annoyed."

As I walked in with him he directed me to the chair and said, "Boys, let's not forget that there is a lady present." The men glanced my way and lowered their voices, and I heard no objectionable language.

In a short time Nixon and Sutton left the building, mounted, and rode up the trail we were intending to take. Buford rode ahead, and Mr. Wilson and I did not overtake him till evening. When we got up among the deep arroyos and canyons of the Sacramento Mountains, Nixon and Sutton appeared leading two pack horses and looking back as though afraid of being followed. Buford had no reason for being suspicious of them and rode close. They asked where Jack Wilson was and Buford told them he would be there in a short time. They inquired if he were alone and he told them that I was with Jack. They rode up the road a short distance and then turned off in the direction of a spring near which a cattle company had built a cabin.

When we caught up with Buford he told us of meeting them, and we went on to the Wilson home. There we learned that these two men were trying to jump a claim belonging to the cattle company for which Jack worked. He decided to investigate and the next morning he and Tim Valentine, a very fine boy recently come from the East, started out to follow the men. On arriving in the vicinity of the cabin they tied their horses in a hollow and walked toward the house. As they did so a man came out of it but immediately returned to it. Wilson and Tim stepped behind trees to talk over the situation and decide what to do. They debated whether to go on and order the two to leave or to ride for an officer of the law to handle them. Jack was a true Westerner and knew the necessity of exercising care, so he kept the tree between the men and himself. Tim stepped from behind his shelter and fell to the ground with a bullet hole in the middle of his forehead.

Sutton, the man whom Wilson and Tim had seen come from the house and then go back, had caught sight of one or both. Inside, he poked his gun through one of the openings in the wall and awaited a chance to shoot. As soon as he saw Tim's head protruding from behind a tree, he took aim and fired. His reputation of being a dead shot was proved.

Taking advantage of the protection of the trees, Wilson made his way back to the house with the news. I deeply regretted that I had not known where Wilson and Tim were going, for I could have warned them what to expect. Mrs. Wilson had not told me their plans until I asked about her apparent worry and restlessness. To afford her some ease I offered to start with her in the direction they had gone. We had not walked far when we saw Wilson coming, leading Tim's horse. We knew what had happened without being told.

Wilson sent Bob Buford down the creek sixteen miles to a place where he could report the murder and get help. To prepare for an attack by Sutton and Nixon, we barricaded the house as best we could and stayed inside all day. I think that was the most miserable one I ever spent, for I feared Tim might be only wounded and would be suffering from both the bullet and the intense cold.

Buford returned at midnight, bringing several of the leading citizens of the country to go to the cabin to recover Tim's body. Tim was a popular young man and the story of his killing aroused the whole community. However, the people were so scattered that time was required for the news to spread, and it was nearly morning when enough men had arrived at the Wilson's to organize a search.

When fifteen men had gathered they held a council of war. Wilson felt sure that Tim had died immediately upon being shot and thought it foolish to make the trip by night and risk more lives. We sat up waiting until daybreak when the men could leave on their tragic mission. They brought Tim's body back and made a crude coffin in which they buried him. Sutton's shot had struck Tim between the eyes.

There was much talk of lynching Sutton and Nixon, not only by those who buried Tim but all over the neighborhood. The two outlaws anticipated this and took refuge with Old Man White, a known troublemaker. Meanwhile Jack Wilson had gone to the Justice of the Peace and sworn out a warrant for the arrest of the two men. It was placed in the hands of a Mr. Warren and of Sam Collins who went to White's and found Sutton and Nixon. White said he was a lawyer and could protect the renegades in his professional capacity. He advised them to give up without trouble, and they did so.

They were given an immediate hearing, and to the surprise of everybody in the country, were cleared of the charges. No testimony was taken except that of Nixon and Sutton, against Wilson.

It was suspected that because Wilson was employed by a big cow company that many of the people were biased against him. In addition, the witnesses were two to one.

After the trial Mrs. Wilson asked me to return to the ranch with her, and I did so. That evening one of the owners came and advised Jack to go to Lincoln and report the result of the preliminary hearing to the sheriff, John W. Poe. This would keep Wilson away several days, so he had to leave things in charge of Bob Buford, a comparatively new man. He, of course, could not think of leaving Mrs. Wilson, and she made ready to go to Lincoln with him. Because it was close to the Christmas holidays I decided to go with the Wilsons and make a visit at home. Needless to say, I could not risk staying alone at the Wilson place.

Jack Wilson felt certain that his life was in danger. As a precaution we left late in the evening so we could travel through some of the dangerous places of the Indian reservation, such as Dark Canyon, in the night, thus reducing our chances of being attacked. I will never forget that night and that ride. I drove most of the way so that Jack Wilson could maintain a lookout to see if we were followed. We suffered with the cold until about two A.M. when we reached the house of Cherokee Bill, a friend of the Wilsons as well as my family. Mr. Wilson shouted until he waked the fellow, then we went in and got thoroughly warm by the big fire the Indian soon had going for us. He also set out what he had in the way of tortillas, frijoles, chili, dried meat, and coffee. We were very hungry and it tasted good.

It seemed unwise to go further that night, so we managed to distribute ourselves in the two rooms of Cherokee Bill's house and get some sleep. After breakfast, but still before daylight, we resumed our journey by way of Dowlin's Mill and on to Fort Stanton. From the Fort we went on over to Lincoln, where Mr. Wilson found the sheriff. Warrants were issued for both Sutton and Nixon and in a short time Sheriff John W. Poe and two deputies were ready to start after the two men. They arrested them and brought them to Lincoln for preliminary hearings. Without friends to protect them, they were bound over to the grand jury. As it turned out, local people saw to it that both were killed before the next grand jury met.

24

Tragedies & Shooting Scrapes

THERE ARE OTHER TRAGEDIES and shooting scrapes that show the turbulent state of affairs I spent my girlhood in. I shall not try to give them in chronological order but attempt to group them according to their causes.

When I first came into the country, Indians were the cause of many killings among both Mexicans and Americans. One outstanding Indian killing was that of Oliver Loving in 1867. I had the good fortune to hear fully the circumstances from Abneth McCabe who was at Fort Sumner when Old Man Loving was brought there badly wounded by Indians.

In the spring of 1867, Loving and his partner, [Colonel] Charles Goodnight, were driving a herd of cattle up through New Mexico into Colorado. When the herd was about a hundred miles north of Horsehead Crossing, it was decided that Loving should go on ahead in order to reach Colorado in time to bid on some Government contracts likely to be let before the herd could come up. Only one man could go along with Loving, and Bill Wilson, who was with the outfit, was chosen to be escort and bodyguard. Knowing a large party of Indians was in the country, the two men traveled only by night. But one fine morning they changed tactics and began to travel by day.

About two o'clock that afternoon a large band of Indians — the number was estimated at about 500 — came upon them. The two men at once left the trail and made for the Pecos River about four miles away, the nearest shelter from behind which to try to stand off the Indians. The steep banks of the river, which in that vicinity were sometimes a hundred feet high, would materially help them to escape their pursuers. The two men reached the bluff some distance ahead of the Indians and dashed down to the bottom. There they tied their horses and crossed to the other side of the river where they hid themselves among the sand dunes and *carrizo* (Spanish cane).

The Indians, close behind them, captured the two horses. Then some of them crossed the river, and tried to slip up on the hiding place of Loving and Wilson. The two men divided between themselves the work of watching the Indians, Wilson looking up the river and Loving looking down. Loving, however, was fired upon by Indians concealed in a brake of carrizo and sustained a severe wound in the arm and side. The two men retreated to the shelter of the river bank and continued the attempt to hold the Indians at bay. All the rest of the afternoon and through the first part of the night they managed to hold their own until the moon had gone down behind a mountain, when the Indians abandoned their efforts.

Sick from his wounds and weak from loss of blood, Loving was certain he was going to die. He begged Wilson to leave him and make his escape if possible. Uppermost in Loving's mind was the desire to have Wilson get away and report to his partner Goodnight what had happened and to let his family back at Weatherford, Texas, know his fate. Loving insisted Wilson take his rifle because, as it used metallic cartridges, it would not be made useless when Wilson had to swim the river. Although Wilson was a one-armed man he was able to swim and carry the rifle. He soon had to abandon the gun, but took care to stick it in the quicksand and mud in the water under the bank where the Indians could not find it.

When Wilson had swum about a hundred yards he saw an Indian sitting on his horse out in the river, with the water almost over the horse's back. Apparently the Indian was not on the lookout for Wilson or anyone else; he seemed to be amusing himself playing in the water with his lance. But Wilson dared not let himself be seen, so he got himself under the fallen cane along the bank of the river, diving under the water. As he reached the Indian he simply drifted past him without being discovered. When Wilson was finally out of all danger, he made a wearisome three days' journey on foot to where Goodnight was with the cattle. In the swim down the river he had discarded his shoes and most of his clothing, so the journey over that rough country without shoes must have been indeed a trial.

When Wilson had told his story, Goodnight immediately started with a party of men to find Loving. Wilson had given explicit directions as to the spot where they had fought the Indians, even telling Goodnight just where to find the rifle hidden under the bank. Goodnight and his party managed to reach the spot in the very short time of twenty-four hours, but they found no trace of Loving. Naturally supposing the Indians had killed him and thrown his body into the river, they turned back to where their cattle had been left.

About two weeks later, as they were coming up on the Pecos with their herd of cattle, to their great surprise they learned that Loving was at the Fort. It seems that the night after Wilson left, Loving had managed to drift by the Indians using the same sort of ruse Wilson did. The next day he lay hidden in the reeds on the bank of the river, afraid to venture out; but when night came, he made his way back to the road five miles away, hoping to find somebody traveling along it who might give him aid. He remained by the side of the road for five days without anybody's passing along; finally some Mexicans came by and he hired them to take him to Fort Sumner. It is a wonder that the old man survived, for not only was he badly wounded, but he was absolutely without food all the while.

The doctor at the Fort did what he could for the old man but he was afraid to try to amputate the arm. Eventually gangrene set in, and when the arm was finally taken off, it was too late.

Goodnight reached the Fort a few days before Loving's death, and did all he could to save his partner's life. He even sent to Santa Fe for a surgeon, but before one could reach Fort Sumner, Loving had died.

Though Loving's was the most widely known instance of a killing at the hands of the Indians, there are several others. Newt Huggins, one of the Chisum line riders, was killed in an arroyo which has since then been known as Huggins' Arroyo. Whenever the Indians were giving trouble, a line rider had a very hazardous job. He went, generally alone, from cow camp to cow camp, his business being to see that everything was all right in the various camps. Such work required courage and Newt Huggins was one of the best Uncle John Chisum had in his employ. Nothing was ever learned regarding the circumstances of the fight that Huggins must have had with the Indians. When after a full allowance of time he did not return to Bosque Grande with his report some of the Chisum cowboys went out to search for him. They found his body in the arroyo with unmistakable evidence that it was Indians who killed him

Mexicans frequently became the victims of the Indians' blood-thirstiness. One of the most atrocious of such attacks occurred in the vicinity of the Capitán Mountains. Two Mexicans with their wives were staying with a bunch of cattle Steve Stanley and Ham Mills had out at Agua Azul. On a day when one man and his wife had gone away, the Indians swooped down on the camp and killed the man who was there. They then forced his wife to go with them. Although this poor woman was soon to become a mother they made her walk all the way. It was said that the route of the Indians was plainly indicated by bits of the woman's clothing hanging from the bushes which had caught and torn it off. Some were stained with blood, which seemed to show that the poor woman was wounded. Finally she gave out, and the Indians killed her.

The body of the woman, mutilated in a fiendish and depraved manner, was found by a party of soldiers Steve Stanley and Ham Mills had procured from Fort Stanton and sent after the Indians as soon as they learned what had happened at Agua Azul. The soldiers overtook the Indians and there was a sharp battle between them which terminated in a sort of draw. A Mexican named José Duran was killed by a shot almost directly in the center of the forehead, so there must have been a good shot among the Indians. In this fight Steve Stanley, who had gone along with the soldiers, was so wounded in the knee that he was a cripple the rest of his life.

Another case in which the Mexicans suffered at the hands of the Indians happened not far from our place — in the vicinity of the Brady Hill, to be exact.

Sometimes the killings were accidents. Everybody carried guns and pistols constantly and as there was always more or less handling of them, often in a very careless way, it was natural that these should be frequently discharged accidentally. One death of this sort, I recall, was that of a young deputy sheriff by the name of Grey. He unintentionally dropped his pistol on the floor, and the fall made the weapon go off, striking him in a vital spot. Another accidental killing was that of Mike G. Haskins in the fall of 1876. One day he and Dee Scurlock were examining a revolver in L. G. Murphy's carpenter shop at Lincoln. The revolver was accidentally discharged, the ball striking Haskins under the left nipple and killing him instantly. Scurlock was examined before Squire Green Wilson and discharged, as there was no evidence to show it was anything else than an accident. Nothing was done with Scurlock.

Another accidental death was that of a young cowboy named O'Keefe who had stopped at our place on his way up from Seven Rivers, in the lower part of the Pecos country, to Fort Stanton for medicine for a fellow cowboy who had been shot by Indians. I remember how eager he was to continue on his errand of mercy. A few days later news came of his death under peculiar circumstances. Something frightened his horse which began pitching, somehow entangling O'Keefe's rope. O'Keefe was thrown to the ground, his leg broken, and the broken bone cut an artery, causing him to bleed to death. The man for whom he ventured the trip to Fort Stanton got well.

Cowboys were always having accidents to their horses and to themselves. Often a horse would step into a prairie-dog hole, stumble, fall, and throw the rider headlong, breaking some bone. But fatalities in such accidents were rare. Usually the injured man only sustained a broken collarbone or a sprained ankle and was patched up by his companions. If his injuries were more serious an effort was made to take him to a doctor, although that could mean a journey of as much as two hundred miles. The doctors at the Fort were the only ones in the country but the Government did not allow them to leave their posts, so it was necessary to take the injured person to them. When that was not possible, then someone went on an errand of mercy, as did O'Keefe, to bring back medicine and advice as to what steps to take to help the injured man.

A great many killings were the results of quarrels — sometimes over such trival matters as to deserve rather to be called fusses. A case of this sort was when Old Man Kline, an old German ex-soldier, killed a man whose name I have forgotten at Spring ranch. Both men had been drinking heavily, and when they began to sober up, the man who was killed began to demean himself for the way he had behaved. In condemnation of himself he expressed a wish that someone would kill him for a worthless scalawag, and added that he deserved killing for all he had done. That remark imprinted itself upon the drink-befuddled mind of Old Man Kline, and he took it upon himself to fulfill the man's wish by shooting him dead. In extenuation of this killing Kline always claimed that he did not think the gun was loaded.

Another instance of a killing growing out of a quarrel was that of Yopp by Buck Powell at Robert K. Wiley's camp below Seven Rivers. Yopp was trying to pen up a bunch of wild cattle when Buck Powell emerged from the *chosa* (dugout). This frightened the cattle and made them run away. Yopp promptly began to vent his anger on Powell and abused him dreadfully for scaring the cattle and making a lot of extra trouble for him. When his anger had reached white heat, he started to draw his pistol. Buck Powell beat him to it, however, and fired first, killing Yopp. As Yopp was seemingly the aggressor, it was an easy matter for Buck Powell to come clear.

Still another killing that came from a fuss was when Bennett Howell killed Dwight Adams. Howell was one of the Chisum range foremen, and Dwight Adams a carpenter at the Chisum place who had such a hankering for being a cowboy that he quit carpentering and had gone out on the range. One day he and Howell, who had usually been on good terms, got into a quarrel while they were around the campfire. It was said at the time that Howell was sick, else he might not have been so "tetchy" over whatever was the subject of the fuss. However that may be, the two men did have a quarrel and Adams in his anger picked up a camp shovel and knocked Bennett Howell to his knees. Howell then jerked out his six-shooter and killed his assailant. Everyone seemed to sanction Howell's action; he was a small man, while Dwight Adams was a big six-footer, generally known to be pretty rough in his ways. Public opinion seemed to hold that Howell did what was right and proper in order to protect himself from bodily harm.

The gambling which was so common in those times had a great tendency to generate quarrels, with usually an attendant killing. The killing of Cal Dotson in 1872 at Lincoln might be put under this head. While a group was playing monte in the back of Pete Bishop's saloon, Old Man Clene and S. W. VanSickle got into a dispute over the game. Cal Dotson went to the aid of his friend VanSickle, and the two of them beat up Clene in what was really a very brutal manner. Pete Bishop came to his rescue and got the old man into another room and tried to dress his wounds. This good Samaritan act was too much for VanSickle and Dotson to stand, now that they were athirst for blood. They armed themselves with rocks and attacked the room where Pete Bishop was attending Old Man Clene. Pete Bishop tried to persuade them to stop, but they paid no attention, for they were both so drunk they did not really know what they were doing. Finally Bishop drew his revolver and fired first at one and then the other of his assailants, inflicting severe wounds on both. Cal Dotson lived but a short time, but VanSickle recovered. Several years afterward, he came to his death in a violent manner at the hands of a Mexican who cut him to pieces and hid his body in a haystack.

I might group with the killings growing out of a quarrel that of young Price Stone. Judge Stone had settled a little north of Roswell about 1877 or 1878. He became a large sheep owner, and had his sheep somewhere in the Seven Rivers country, in charge of an old Dutchman whose name I do not recall. Price Stone and Sterling Ashby, both mere boys, were also along as helpers. On this particular night the two boys got to teasing the old man about something; finally they got rougher than the old man could stand, and he snatched up his old six-shooter. As soon as they realized what he might do, the two boys ran for their lives. Sterling Ashby had the good luck to fall down behind some bushes, into which he crawled and hid. But Price Stone fell a victim to the old man's shot. The old man tried his best to find Ashby but did not succeed in doing so.

When the old man had quit hunting around for him, Ashby crawled away and made his escape. He headed for Seven Rivers and got the constable there to issue a warrant for the Dutchman's arrest. Pat Garrett was deputy sheriff at the time, and he came down to Seven Rivers and took the old man to Lincoln and put him into jail there. A short time afterwards, the old man was killed by the jailer. No one ever knew just why; the jailer's defense was the usual one that the Dutchman had made a break for liberty, but in this case there was a curious discrepancy in the jailer's story. As he told it, the Dutchman had in trying to get away grabbed the jailer's pistol with *both* hands. This made many smile knowingly, for the old Dutchman had but one arm; the other had been amputated up close to the shoulder. As there was no evidence in regard to the killing except what the jailer told, he was never even indicted for the affair. This old fellow was what was called in those days "addled" in his head, and it was generally supposed that the teasing of the two boys had made him completely crazy for the time being.

A few years later there was a deplorable tragedy up toward the head of Bonito River — clearly the work of a man gone temporarily insane. The man was a stranger who was boarding at the Mayberry's. He had fallen in love, it seems, with Mrs. Mayberry, and when she did not respond to his wooing he ran amuck and wiped out the entire Mayberry family, with the exception of a daughter who escaped. As the murderer was fleeing he encountered one of the neighbors rushing over to see what caused the shooting at the Mayberry place, and without delay he added this man to his total.

Some of the neighbors got together, hunted down the murderer, and "captured him by killing him."

Many killings were prompted by a desire for money. Usually these were done in a stealthy way, the favorite methods being to lie in ambush or to shoot the unsuspecting victim through a window at night.

One of the earliest killings of this variety was that of Bijido Salcido who was waylaid and killed just above old Missouri Bottom on the Hondo. He had sold a yoke of oxen to Uncle John Chisum for $50 cash, and on that day had delivered them to South Spring River ranch. As Uncle John was absent, Salcido was returning with empty pockets. On his way down he had spent the night at La Boquia [Boquilla] where two Mexicans, Videl Majeres and an unidentified companion learned the purpose of his trip and plotted to waylay and rob him on his way back.

They concealed themselves near the road at two points where it came close to the Hondo, and when they saw Salcido coming, one came out and rode along with him, talking in a friendly manner. The other man waited until they had passed a short distance, then came out and shot Salcido from behind, the bullet going into the back of his head. They turned all his pockets inside out but of course found nothing. They kept his horse and skipped out of the country, next being heard of at Fort Concho, Texas. A passer-by found Salcido's body lying near the road and reported the killing to the people at El Redepente. Some men from that settlement went out and got the body and buried it.

Another killing, virtually from ambush, that created a great deal of excitement was that of a Mexican woman in the vicinity of Arroya Secca [Arroyo Seco] at the foot of Capitán Mountain. This woman had hired herself to a rich sheepman named Mes as his housekeeper and, of course, his common-law wife. The understanding was that at the end of five years she was to receive a certain number of sheep. Just before the five years was up she was killed by a shot coming through the window. It was never proved who did the shooting, although the circumstances indicated the motive was to avoid paying over the property.

Another killing that seems to have been prompted by desire for money was that of Francisco Romero y Valencia. He was what was called a "civilized Indian" who had saved up a good deal of money. This he kept in his house, about two miles from Lincoln, and it was undoubtedly the cause of his death. When friends noticed he had not been seen for several days they investigated and found his body in his house. Evidently he had been shot a day or two previously by an assassin who had fired through the window and then ransacked the house looking for the money supposedly kept there. He must have carried it off for none was found by the investigators nor was any evidence found that would convict anyone for the killing.

Another murder that might be placed with those known as waylayings was that of the Nesbit [Nesmith] family. George Nesmith was working at Pat Coghlin's ranch near Tularosa when a prominent cowman was arrested through the activities of the Cattleman's Association. He was accused of buying cattle from Billy the Kid's gang which they had stolen from the Canadian country. Nesmith had been summoned as a witness and took his wife and child with him to Socorro where the trial was to be held. When the case was continued, the Nesmiths started back home accompanied by a man whose name I do not recall. When they did not arrive on time a search was made, and several days later their bodies were found some distance off the road out among the White Sands. Just how they were killed could not be determined because the bodies were in a bad state of decomposition.

Some Mexicans who had been riding about in that vicinity about that time with blind bridles and no saddles were arrested and tried for those killings. Their statement was that they had been hired to do this by some Americans, but they could not identify anyone. This cowman [Coghlin] was naturally the suspect, since Nesmith's testimony was likely to result in his being convicted for buying stolen cattle, but the Mexicans were unable to identify him as the one who had hired them to do the killing. They claimed that the man who came to them wore a beard, and it was generally supposed that whoever it was wore false whiskers when talking to the Mexicans.

Another motiveless killing took place at Lincoln. A Mexican named Domingo killed Dan Fisher, who had worked on our place in the blacksmith shop for about a year Fisher was just sitting in a house at Lincoln — he had been drinking some but had done nothing unseemly. This Mexican who had also been drinking some just walked in the door, took aim with his pistol, and shot Fisher in the back, killing him instantly. Of killings of this class — those that come when men lose control of themselves under the influence of whiskey — I could name dozens, I am sure, but must pass on to other types.

I do not recall many cases of suicide in those days. I can only cite the case of Lucas Gallegos who killed himself out near the Capitán Mountains in the fall of 1877. Gallegos was under arrest for killing a man at Lincoln, when Jesse Evans and his three companions were arrested for stealing horses belonging to Dick Brewer, Tunstall, and McSween. The friends of this crowd engineered a jail delivery, and Lucas Gallegos profited by it. The Pecos men, who were largely responsible for the release of these prisoners, took him with them to Seven Rivers, and from there he made his way across the line into Texas. He remained in that state on the dodge for two years then came back and stood trial. Gallegos was acquitted and remained pathetically grateful to his lawyer, Col. A. J. Fountain. When Col. Fountain disappeared, the wife of Lucas Gallegos took to her bed and died of grief. Some years afterwards Gallegos killed himself, and it was thought he did so because he was old and despondent.

There were some instances of killings *pro bono publico,* as it were. Lincoln County never had a vigilante organization as did some other places in New Mexico to take a firm hand in the extinguishing of lawlessness, although there were times when such an organization might have done yeoman's service. Occasionally public opinion would crystalize and instigate a lynching.

I must not omit telling about two hangings that took place in the early days when Bosque Grande was the headquarters of Uncle John Chisum. The first was a cowboy who killed a range boss of the remuda under some circumstances that made everybody condemn the killing. Some of the other cowboys caught the one responsible for the killing and then appealed to Uncle John Chisum for advice as to what course to take to have him punished. In fact, they wanted Uncle John to take the responsibility of meting out justice in this instance, but Uncle John was too long-headed for that. He explained the law governing the different degrees of murder, and then said, "Now, we are away out here on the frontier where we have no regular court. But we can proceed by law and organize a court of our own. We can probably make it just as fair as any regular court; we can hear evidence and be governed by our consciences. The law says a man shall be judged by his peers, and that means that you cowboys, who are the peers of the one that did the killing, are the ones to try him."

So the cowboys named a judge, a sheriff, a prosecuting attorney, and twelve jurymen. They told the accused to select someone to defend him, and then the court went into session. Evidence was presented both for and against the accused, and the case turned over to the jury. The verdict was guilty, but the boy appealed to Uncle John, saying, "Can't you say something to save me?" "No," answered Uncle John, "I have already said all I can and done all I can for you. These men would have hung you at once if I hadn't interfered and got them to give you a fair trial. I did so because I hoped something would come out in the trial to save you, but nothing of the kind has developed. These cowboys are your peers; they've been your companions and associates; they've given you a fair hearing; and this is their verdict. I don't see that I can do anything more for you. You won't be missed half as much as the man you killed will be by his widow and three children." So the sentence of the court was carried out. A long wagon tongue was propped upright and one end of the noose fastened to the iron ring on the end. Then the condemned man was placed on a horse, and when everything was ready the horse was given a smart lick.

I have heard Uncle John say that he acted in this affair as he did under the belief that it was the best course to follow. The location of county lines was so uncertain it was impossible to tell readily which county had jurisdiction. Then, too, the counties were so large it was a time-consuming matter to go to court. The counties were very poor, and as this was a cold-blooded murder, it was just as well to deal out justice and at the same time save the taxpayers money. All these were reasons that led Uncle John to advise the organization of a court.

There was another of these "kangaroo courts" which was brought into action a short time afterwards. Two of the cowboys had a quarrel over something of no importance. One was a sort of would-be bad man, and he promptly jerked out his pistol, exclaiming, "I'll just kill you for that!" And he did. The cowboys formed a court and tried the man who did the killing — Curly was his name. He was found guilty of murder in the first degree and sentenced to be hanged then and there to a cottonwood tree. This fellow died game! I often heard Uncle Mac describe how he went to his death: seeing that the cowboys were bungling the job of getting ready, he said to them, "Now boys, if you're going to hang me, I'll tell you how to do a decent job. As I am mainly concerned in this thing, I don't want you to make a botch of it. Now, bring a horse up so I can get on 'im; then lead 'im under that big limb. Put the loop end of the rope around my neck; then throw the other end over the limb and tie it. Then hit the horse smartly so that he'll jump from under me." Uncle Mac used to say that when Curly saw them bring a horse that the man who had been killed used to ride, he exclaimed, "Why, that's Brownie. You're an unlucky horse, but I guess you'll do as well as any," and with that he sprang upon the horse's back. In a few minutes it was all over.

25

The Sinewy & Powerful Arm of The Law

THIS ACCOUNT has of necessity presented many glimpses of the lawlessness that was prevalent in southeastern New Mexico in the early days. My purpose has been to refrain from exaggeration or of giving sensational descriptions of these numerous killings. Nearly all can be attributed to the condition existing at that time when the six-shooter was the law of the land and everybody went armed.

The country was so newly settled and so sparsely populated that machinery in the form of courts and officers of the law had not begun to function as they did in the older and more established parts of the country. In Lincoln County it was necessary for every man to protect himself and assert his rights. The cheap whiskey that was commonly drunk contributed to the confusion. Men who drank it became quarrelsome, and were for settling their difficulties with some sort of fight, using fists, knives, or shooting irons. Today, people probably fight as much as in former times but in a different way — they take their quarrels to court.

The advance of law and order gradually became perceptible. Courts became certain and sure in the administration of justice, although they still had to contend with obstacles and hindrances, because of the great extent of territory, the difficulty of getting witnesses, and the unreliability of juries. The greatest restraint on lawlessness, however, came from improvement in the type of peace officer. A better class of men was elected, especially the sheriffs;

and they chose honest deputies and constables unafraid to perform the obligations of their positions without fear or favor. In the discharge of their duties these men sometimes had to resort to extreme measures. At times the peace officer became the victim of a shot from a criminal, thereby sacrificing his life on the altar of law and order.

Unquestionably the most noted killing in southeastern New Mexico was that of Billy the Kid. Captured at Stinking Springs, tried and convicted at Mesilla, and jailed at Lincoln, the Kid made his escape in the spring of 1881, killing his guards, Bell and Olinger. He hid among his friends at Fort Sumner, many of whom were sheepherders. Pat Garrett, who was serving as sheriff, seemed rather half-hearted in his efforts to find the Kid and capture him. But John W. Poe had been sent to Lincoln County by the Panhandle Cattlemen's Association to help rid the country of Billy the Kid and his gang, notorious for stealing cattle in the Panhandle and disposing of them to Pat Coghlin of Tularosa. When Poe heard that the Kid was in the vicinity of Fort Sumner, Garrett, though skeptical as to the truth of the report, investigated it. He was accompanied by Poe and Tip McKinney. For some time it looked as though the Kid would not walk into the trap prepared for him, but he did just this on the night of the 14th of July. The Kid's many friends were quick to condemn Garrett and to charge him with doing it in a cowardly and unfair manner. I have never been able to follow the reasoning of those who take this attitude. Those who recall the circumstances will realize that Garrett followed the law of self-preservation. Feeling that he was about to be balked in his effort to find the Kid at Fort Sumner, Garrett decided to go to the room of Pete Maxwell and inquire if he knew anything as to the Kid's whereabouts. Leaving Poe and Tip McKinney on guard, Garrett entered and wakened Maxwell who recognized him and also the Kid as he was outlined in the moonlight. Accounts differ as to why Billy was coming to the Maxwell house, but when he spotted the two strangers on the porch he stepped into Maxwell's room asking excitedly, "Quién es? Quién es?" (Who is it? Who is it?) Garrett recognized his voice. Knowing that the Kid would shoot him on sight, there was only one thing for Garrett to do — he fired as quickly as he could in the direction of the voice. The bullet went through the Kid's heart.

I have heard many people express the idea that what Pat

Garrett should have done on that occasion was to call on the Kid to surrender. But I feel absolutely sure that had Garrett taken that course, a bullet from the Kid's six-shooter would have pierced his body before he could have yelled, "Put 'em up, Kid!" Garrett knew it was a case of kill or be killed, and took the natural and instinctive course. What had blinded the minds of many persons as to the killing of the Kid is the fact that Garrett and the Kid had formerly been friends. Such was the case, but when Garrett accepted the duties and responsibilities of sheriff and took an oath accordingly, he put friendship behind him. He knew that he had been placed in that office for the express purpose of seeing that the arm of the law got the Kid and his gang into its clutches, and he carried out the program he had assumed.

John W. Poe followed Pat Garrett as sheriff of Lincoln County and was a notable crusader in behalf of law and order. Everyone knew that Poe meant business, and he most certainly did, even though it had to be accomplished at the risk of his life. As sheriff, Poe's most famous achievement was the capture of the Mexican desperado, Aragón, after a stiff fight in which two of the sheriff's posse — Jasper Corn and Johnny Hurley — had met their deaths at the hands of this desperado. I remember well the excitement produced by this affair in Lincoln County, although it happened in Miguel [County]. In order to have my account accurate, I interviewed Judge Smith Lea of Roswell, who was living at Lincoln at the time and was a close friend of John W. Poe. Judge Lea was kind enough to write out for me an account of this fight, as it was related to him by John W. Poe:

Being sheriff at that time was a real man's job. During that period, one Nicholas Aragon and an *amigo* of his came down from San Miguel County, stole a bunch of horses on the Rio Hondo in Lincoln County, and carried them to a canyon near Anton Chico in San Miguel county. Part of the horses belonged to residents of Lincoln county, who heard who had stolen the horses and where they were being kept. So they swore out a warrant for both Aragon and his associate, which was given to Deputy Sheriff Jim Brent. Brent with his posse was successful in arresting both men, getting back the horses. The two men he landed in jail at Lincoln, and the horses he returned to the owners.

Later Aragon escaped from jail. When Sheriff Poe heard that he was near Anton Chico, he sent one of his deputies, Jasper Corn of Roswell, who was as brave as the bravest, up into that section with instructions to take such help along as he needed and, if he succeeded in locating Aragon, to arrest him. Corn took his brother-in-law, Bill Holloman, and went into the neighborhood where Aragon was supposed to be. He heard that Aragon was frequenting a certain woman's home near there, and he went to the place expecting to find him. As Corn approached the house he saw Aragon run out of the back door, and with the aid of the protection afforded by a rock fence, make for his horse which was hitched, all saddled and bridled, some distance from the house. Seeing that Aragon would reach his horse before he could head him off, Corn opened fire with his pistol from horseback, his horse running at full speed. Aragon returned the fire with a Winchester rifle, taking rest off the rock fence. His first shot struck Corn's horse on top of the neck, and the animal fell as though it was killed. In this fall Corn's leg got caught under the horse and was badly broken. But with one leg pinned under the horse, Corn fought until his pistol was empty. Aragon's second shot struck Corn in the stomach, making an ugly wound from which he died thirty-six hours later without receiving a particle of medical aid.

Aragon then hid out for some time, but later Sheriff Poe heard of his being again in that neighborhood. Taking with him Jim Brent, Johnny Hurley, Barney Mason, Billy Bufer, and Jim Abercrombie, Poe went up into that section. They arrived at the house where Aragon was supposed to be about midnight on a bitter cold night. Poe knocked on the door, and received no answer although he heard someone stirring around inside the room and whispering to another person. Poe then called out that he was the sheriff and was there with a warrant for the arrest of Aragon.

A woman replied saying that only she and another woman were there and that Aragon was not there. She said that she and the other woman were willing to come out. Poe told them to open the door at once and come out, and they did so.

Poe then told Johnny Hurley, who spoke Spanish fluently, to take the women into a part of the house that angled off from the rest of the building and was used as a kitchen, and make them a fire and see if he could get any information from them. The rest of the sheriff's party continued to guard the main part of the house carefully. After much persuading, the two women finally told Hurley that Aragon was in there and that he was well armed and ready for a fight.

In his excitement to carry the news to Sheriff Poe, Hurley forgot his accustomed prudence and came around the kitchen in full view of the open door of the room where Aragon was, saying, "We've got him! He's in there!" Seeing the danger Poe spoke sharply to him saying, "Johnny, get out from in front of that door or he'll kill you." Just then Aragon fired, the ball striking Hurley in the stomach, inflicting a wound from which he died thirty-six hours later just as Corn did. Poe said, "Are you hit, Johnny?" and Hurley answered, "Yes — gut shot," a wound of that sort being dreaded worse than any other shot in those days. Then Hurley stepped around the corner and went back to the kitchen and lay down by the fire. He was made as comfortable as possible and had all done for him that could be done while he lived.

Meanwhile a general shooting had developed between Aragon on the inside of the house and the sheriff's men on the outside. If any of them exposed themselves in the slightest degree, they were promptly shot at by Aragon. Poe tried by peeping over an adobe wall to locate Aragon through a back window, but a shot that struck the top of the adobe wall knocking his hat off and filling his eyes with dirt, apprised him that Aragon was on the alert.

Had Poe's head been an inch more above the wall, the shot would have hit him squarely between the eyes. Bret also had a narrow escape; the brim of his hat was powder-burned. Poe and his men poured shot after shot into the door and into every window, shooting from every possible angle, hoping that they might hit Aragon somewhere or somehow. But their efforts were [so] unsuccessful in fact that they [were forced to keep up the] fusillade for sixty hours.

The second night, Jim Brent was suffering so from neuralgia that Poe sent him to Las Vegas, thirty-six miles away, for medical attention, instructing him to notify the sheriff of San Miguel while at Las Vegas and to ask him to send out some assistance. On the trip Jim Brent came to a creek which was frozen over. The horse would not step on the ice; so Jim Brent dismounted and broke the ice with his boots. Then he led the horse across. The result of using such heroic measures to get the horse over the creek was that when Jim Brent reached Las Vegas he had both feet badly frozen.

The next day, however, Jim Brent returned accompanied by the San Miguel County sheriff, who was a native, and a posse. After the San Miguel sheriff had held a parley with Aragon and assured him that he would be protected, Aragon agreed to surrender, and did so, coming out with his hands up. It was then revealed that in the course of the shooting he had been wounded three times. One shot had cut a furrow through his heavy hair and just grazed the scalp squarely over the forehead, plowing a furrow three or four inches long and then glancing off his skull. Aragon told it that this wound had knocked him down, but in a second or two he was up again and back in the fighting. A third shot had torn a big hole through the middle of the calf of one of his legs, and it was this one from which he was suffering most at the time of the surrender. Among the sheriff's posse there were no other casualties than the death of Hurley, but the bitter cold had been very trying on all of them.

Aragón was carried to Las Vegas and placed in jail there. He was afterwards tried for killing Jasper Corn but was acquitted, the ground being that he did not know who Corn was and that Corn had opened fire first. Later he was tried for killing Johnny Hurley and sentenced to the pen for life. After ten years he was pardoned, and returned to his old neighborhood, where he died a natural death some years later.

The high sheriff and his posse were not the only ones called upon to put their lives in jeopardy in behalf of law and order. The town marshal in the older days was engaged in what might properly be called a hazardous occupation. Upon him fell the perilous task of restraining drunken cowboys who either singly or en masse were bent on shooting up the town. In this connection I remember Charlie Perry who for several years was town marshal for Roswell. His most famous feat in the cause of law and order was the double killing of George Griffin and his cousin, B. Champion. This affair came directly under my observation because I was in Roswell at the time, nursing Captain J. C. Lea, who was thought at the time to be taking black smallpox, although it turned out to be simply a bilious attack. George Griffin, a cowboy from Texas who was generally known as a bad fellow when under the influence of liquor, threw the town into consternation by going on a drunken rampage. He charged up and down the only street that Roswell had in those times, and everybody had promptly housed up at the beginning of the big frolic; there was no one to say him nay until Charlie Perry appeared on the scene. What occurred after the town marshal entered the game I shall give in the words of Judge Smith Lea, who has furnished me with a vivid account of the affair.

Charlie Perry was a quick and accurate shot with either a gun or a pistol. He had killed a man or two previously in the discharge of duty and had built up quite a reputation as a brave man and efficient officer who was neither ashamed nor afraid to go after the worst of them. At the time he killed George Griffin and Champion he was deputy sheriff and city marshal of Roswell. Later he was elected sheriff, and made a splendid record in that dangerous office.

A big round-up was coming up the Pecos and hundreds of cowboys were with it. Among them was one George Griffin, a bad acting *hombre*. On account of a big rain the round-up was compelled to stop at South Spring River. The ground was made so boggy by the rain that the wagons could not move for a few days. The cowboys who were not on guard took the opportunity of coming to Roswell for a frolic. Among them on this day was George Griffin who had been making the brag all up the Pecos that when he got to Roswell, he was going to kill Charlie Perry, the city marshal. News of this threat had reached Perry before Griffin arrived on the scene, but he did not let it disturb the even tenor of his way.

The rain having subsided, Griffin and a bunch of the cowboys showed up at a sporting-house just after dark and proceeded to tank up. Griffin kept saying he had come to town to kill Charlie Perry, and as he got deeper and deeper in his cups, he began to speculate if Charlie Perry really was the brave man he was said to be, and why he did not come and try to arrest him. In his zeal for an encounter with Perry, Griffin came very near to killing two or three men, mistaking them for the city marshal he so much wanted to see. One of the girls sent word to Perry what was going on down there, and Perry promptly went down in person. He knocked on the back door, and when it was opened, stood there with the light from inside shining on him, while the girl who had sent the message told him in more detail what Griffin had been doing and saying.

Some of the cooler heads among the cowboys, knowing there would be trouble if they didn't get out of town, had finally persuaded Griffin to get on his horse and go back to camp. They were just riding round the corner of the house, when one of them, seeing Perry standing in the light from the doorway, called out, "There's Charlie Perry now." Griffin, who had his gun in his hand, shouted, "Well, I will kill him right now," and immediately attempted to carry out his threat. But one of the cowboys grabbed his gun, and before Griffin could get it loose, Perry had stepped to one side out of the light, and dropped prone on the ground to await developments. As Griffin and his companions could not see him and as they knew it would be risky business to be hunting for a man of Charlie Perry's quickness with a pistol in the dark, they quickly rode out of town.

Perry went back up town and summoned two men to go with him down to the camp to arrest Griffin. Each of them took his gun and pistol and plenty of cartridges. Just before they were to start, two of Griffin's friends, who had been in town ostensibly to get two bottles of whiskey and two boxes of cartridges, started to mount their horses for the return to the camp. Perry stepped up to them and told them to consider themselves under arrest. They insisted that they had not done anything to justify arrest [and would not submit to] such treatment and would go back to camp, Perry, to the contrary notwithstanding. Then Perry told them he was sure they had come to get information as to his movements and were going back to carry it to Griffin. He assured them he was going to arrest them and keep them in town until he had returned from his contemplated visit to the camp.

The two men continued to protest against their arrest and to insist that they were not going to be stopped from going back to camp. When they tried to mount their horses Perry quietly told them to stop, adding that he did not want to kill them, but he was prepared to do so if they attempted to mount their horses. The two men by this time had concluded that the city marshal meant what he said, and allowed themselves to be disarmed and put under guard. They were certainly two mighty mad fellows, but they had sense enough to know that the best thing was to obey orders, especially when Charlie Perry was giving the orders.

It was full moon, but the sky was so filled with floating clouds that it was alternately dark or light for a short spell. Perry and his two men started for the cowboys' camp at South Spring River. Just before they reached the bridge south of town over the Rio Hondo, Perry remarked, "Here is where we are liable to be fired on." So the three slowed down and got ready to cross the bridge single file. The event showed Perry a good prophet. Griffin and a cousin of his, B. Champion, fired on them from below the bridge, but missed them entirely. Perry returned the fire, shooting at the flash of the guns, as they were unable to see the men for the darkness. Perry's shot tore off three of the fingers of the hand with which Griffin was holding the barrel of his gun.

Perry spurred his horse on across the bridge and then fell off, lying flat on the ground to await further developments. The shooting had scared the horses of the other two men so badly that they whirled around and ran back towards town. They were so sure that Perry was killed that they did not attempt to go back but came on up to town and gave out the report that Perry had been shot.

In the meantime Griffin and Champion had dodged under the bridge and waiting until the melee had subsided, they came out hurriedly and attempted to mount their horses. Griffin succeeded in getting into the saddle, but his horse started off bucking. Perry at once sky-lighted him and fired, the ball striking square in the back of his head. As Perry's gun was one of large bore, the bullet made a big hole in Griffin's forehead. Champion's horse also bucked and finally jerked loose and ran off, leaving Champion afoot. Meanwhile Perry was going after him. They exchanged two shots at each other in the dark, but neither hit the other. As Perry was crowding him, Champion ran down under the river bank, where he could sky-light Perry.

But at this point Perry quit trying after Champion, and went up the Rio Hondo a little way in search of his horse. Finding him, he mounted and rode out half way across the big flat between the Rio Hondo and South Spring. There he dismounted, tied his horse to a little bush, and lay down on the ground to await Champion's coming along. It was not long until he saw a man coming on foot. He was sure it was Champion, because there was no one else who would be splashing along in the mud on foot at that time of the night. The clouds were clearing up by this time, and it was possible to see quite well by moonlight. Champion saw Perry's horse with a saddle on, and made for it. When he got within a hundred twenty-six steps of the animal, Perry took deliberate aim and fired, the ball striking Champion in the corner of the forehead, tearing the skull open and exposing the brain for about four inches. This terrible wound caused Champion's death the next day.

Perry then got on his horse and rode back towards town. When he reached the Rio Hondo bridge, he met a large posse who were looking for him and expecting to find his dead body somewhere in the vicinity. He got there in time to hear one of his companions say, "Right here is where he fell," but he had the pleasure of telling them that he believed he had killed both Griffin and Champion, but was not altogether sure on that point. He showed them about where Griffin had fallen, and there was his body shot through the head as described above. He said he was certain he had hit Champion, for he had distinctly heard the ball strike him. So they went out to where that shooting had occurred, and found Champion lying there unconscious and wounded, as described above. Thus ended the wild and reckless career of George Griffin.

As time passed, incidents such as this became less and less common. The country began to be settled by a more law-abiding class, and the rougher element drifted elsewhere.

Evil men still roamed the country, robbing and torturing innocent people. One victim was Uncle Jim Chisum who least deserved such abuse.

I always felt a large debt of gratitude toward Uncle Jim since he acted as guardian for the Casey children after our father's murder. His kindness and gentleness guided us through those very bad years and he continued as a source of strength and counsel after his service in that capacity was no longer needed.

James Chisum came out from Bolivar, Denton County, Texas, with his three children, Sallie L., Walter, and Willie, and joined his brother John at the South Spring River ranch about the middle of the 1880s. Uncle Jim became his brother's range boss, a position that required him to be with the cattle for nine or ten months of the year, living in the camps. During the months that he was able to be at the ranch, Uncle Jim made it his special interest to set out trees

— cottonwoods along the irrigation ditches, fruit trees for the orchard Uncle John was developing.

When the ranch was broken up and sold to M. J. Farris, Uncle Jim disposed of his cattle interests, and in partnership with his son, Walter, went into the sheep business. For several years they did very well, but eventually grew tired of the business and sold out at a time when sheep were high. Then Uncle Jim invested in a flock of fine goats which he took down to Seven Rivers, then through the Sacramento Mountains and over into the Capitáns. It was there that he had an adventure with robbers in which he cleverly outwitted them.

He was at camp all day by himself, the herder having gone to town. Three masked men appeared and threw their guns down on him. They thought Uncle Jim had on his person or among his belongings the larger part of the money he had received from the recent sale of his sheep, but as a matter of fact this money had been deposited in a bank. The robbers demanded money, but Uncle Jim truthfully told that he had none. Then, to make sure of no interference from him while they were going through what he had on the wagon, they tied Uncle Jim's hands down to his feet, then tied his legs together, and when he was trussed up in that way they tied him to the wagon tongue. All they could find was a bundle of Confederate money, which they took to be of some value and carried off with them, leaving Uncle Jim tied to the wagon tongue. It was bad enough to try to rob him, but it was sheer brutality to mistreat in such a way an old man of more than 80 years.

It was no easy matter to get loose from the wagon tongue. Realizing he would probably die of exposure if he did not, he tried to work his hands loose and finally in desperation to gnaw at the knots. Though his teeth were not those of a young man, he was able to gnaw and pull until the rope became loosened so that he freed first one hand and then the other. He soon untied his legs and the rest of his body. It was a severe experience, for the robbers had drawn the rope pretty tight around his body. Not feeling safe in the camp alone, Uncle Jim made his way back to a ranch in the vicinity and remained there until the next day.

For three years, so Uncle Jim told me himself, he had stayed with his herd of goats. He was in camp with them all that time and did not sleep a single night in a house — a remarkable record of endurance on the part of a man whose years were already past the four-score mark.

After his experience with the robbers in the Capitáns, Uncle Jim took his herd down into the Guadalupe Mountains where there was considerable free range. The ensuing winter was exceptionally severe, and during a blizzard which brought sleet along with it, Uncle Jim could not find his way back to his camp. To keep from freezing to death, the old man tramped back and forth among the goats. When he grew tired and sat down, he would almost immediately feel the devastating sleepiness creeping over him, and would resume walking. The next morning his herders found him still tramping around among his goats. It is a miracle that he survived a night so severe that twenty-five hundred of the goats died from exposure.

But this experience impressed him with the dangers he was confronting in his advanced age, and perhaps led him to decide to give up the goat herd. He would never admit that he was dismayed by the hardships and the loss, but merely vouchsafed as reason for his retirement that he was "tired of the business." His son Walter went down to where he (James Chisum) made his home with his daughter, Mrs. Sallie L. Robert, until his death a few years later, March 17, 1908.

When his daughter wrote me, "Pa is sick and wants to see you," I went at once, for Uncle Jim had always been like a second father to me. I found him very feeble, but he still had that indomitable spirit that refused to admit physical infirmity. He was just tired, he put it, and would soon be rested up. He told me that he had never killed a man in his life, although it had been spent on the frontier. He believed that his record was clear in this respect. Although he had fought Indians several times, he said he had never killed one that he knew of. He also averred that he had never robbed, stolen, or cheated anyone out of a dollar in his life, and I am convinced that this statement was true. He was a man who embodied in his life the finest qualities of the pioneer.

PART III

John Simpson Chisum

26

The Texas Period

John Chisum was one of the men whom the Southwest should delight to honor. At present there exists no account of him that will bring his personality and achievements properly before later generations. Yet as the compiler of *History of New Mexico, Its Resources and People* puts it, "The story of John Chisum's life has never been half told, and if written in detail would present a clear, correct, and forceful picture of pioneer times with all the various characteristics of frontier life — its dangers, its privations, hardships, its terrors, its pleasures, its prosperity."

I hope I can in a half dozen or so chapters develop a sketch of his career that will hereafter make it impossible to voice such a reproach. It is surprising the ingratitude later generations are sometimes guilty of toward those who in pioneer days laid the foundation of subsequent development. Such a pioneer was Uncle John, as I always called him, and he deserves high place as one of those most active in the development of the Southwest, especially New Mexico.

Without intending to be boastful, I feel I can rightfully say I have special qualifications for what I am attempting. For a long stretch of years, Uncle John was a close friend of my family. My father and Uncle John were warm friends, even before we came into New Mexico. After Father was killed, Uncle John was very helpful to my Mother in the perplexities she fell heir to by trying to keep together for us children what Father had accumulated. As a child,

I had many indications that Uncle John took an especial interest in me, and when I became a young woman, I was made to realize that his interest had continued. By his kindness and generosity Uncle John gave my sister and me a quit claim deed to a piece of land he owned adjoining our place. He would have certainly been my guardian, had it not been that he was absent from home. So his brother, James Chisum, became my guardian, and this fact served to keep up the connection between the Chisums and the Caseys.

I had also the good fortune to spend several months at the South Spring River ranch several times when it was in the height of its prosperity. During this time I often rode with Uncle John when he was making trips to look after his interests. He always liked to talk, and on such occasions he spoke freely on all sorts of matters about himself and his business. It was through these conversations that I, though but a girl in her teens, came to know more fully about his life and character than many an older person. Even now I do not exactly understand why he was inclined to talk to one so much younger in years in the free and full way he did, but he always said, "You are long-headed and have hoss (horse) sense (common sense)." Sometimes I have thought that in those last years of his life, with so many perplexing things on his mind that he had to open up to someone, and I, being the one at hand, became the party of the second part in these conversations. Then, of course, I did not bother myself with the why's and wherefore's of the situation but felt myself honored, and I cherished in my heart all his words I could. I wish now I had at the time kept a diary or notebook and made a full record, but fortunately my memory is still active and vigorous and returns me many of the things we talked about.

Also, fortunately, I am able to reinforce and supplement my memory with certain written material. Entertaining the idea of some day attempting an account of him, I have treasured some of his letters that I think are helpful in showing the type of man he was. Nothing shows a person as well as his letters, and this general rule will apply to Uncle John. I wish his letters were more abundant, so that this biographical sketch might be even more largely autobiographical through them, but I shall have to be content with my own meager assortment, for I have not been able to locate others.

I have had, however, one piece of rare good fortune in my efforts to gather documentary material about Uncle John. I was able

John Chisum, the New Mexico Cattle King, was a close friend of the Casey family, interested especially in Lily Klasner to whom he confided much about himself and his business although she was many years his junior.

Courtesy of Ola C. Jones

to unearth an extended account written by Uncle John himself of what might be called the climax of the difficulties and persecutions he underwent in New Mexico at the hands of those who were jealous or envious of his prosperity and who used their power and influence to drag this cattle king of the Pecos valley from his throne. For a number of years Uncle John had kept a diary, but I was always given the impression by those speaking of it that he had either destroyed it himself or that someone into whose hands it had come had destroyed it.

Search on my part bore fruit, for I found the manuscript to be still in existence. While it is all too brief and is concerned simply with one period in his long and adventurous life, it reveals in a high degree Uncle John's personality and is well worth reading. This is not the place to elaborate on this manuscript or its value. I have simply been led into referring to it in order to show that I have done my best to find and consult available documents, in addition to using what facts I can bring forth from the storehouse of my memory.

John Simpson Chisum, to use his full name, was born in Hardeman, Madison County, Tennessee, on August 15th, 1824. His parents were Claiborne and Lucinda Chisum. His mother died, and his father married again shortly. I do not recall the name of the stepmother, but I recall that Aunt Cintha, as they were taught to call her, was living at the time I knew Uncle John and that he always held her in the greatest affection even though he was far away from her. Uncle John's father was a farmer in Tennessee, and as a small boy Uncle John helped with the various tasks that a boy his age could perform.

In 1837, when John was thirteen, the Chisums moved from Tennessee to Texas, and located on Mud Creek near what after-wards became the town of Paris, Texas.* Uncle John always said the Chisums were of the pioneering and forward-moving type of which there were many among the Tennesseeans. They were not the sort to remain in their locality when fresh lands were beckoning to them from the Southwest, especially Texas. I remember that once in his later years, Uncle John went back to Tennessee and returned full of contemptuous disgust for the sort of people he found there. He remarked that the country had a world of acorns, the finest mash in the world, but the people did not even have hogs to eat them. This seemed to him the acme of shiftlessness. He also commented on how much of a decline that country was in. He mentioned as the probable cause the fact that the people had married and intermarried until the stock had degenerated. These criticisms indicate the type of man Uncle John himself was — quite the opposite of the stay-at-home, get-along-as-best-can.

To Claiborne Chisum and his two wives were born several sons and daughters. Besides Uncle John, the first wife bore his brothers, James, Pitzer M., Jefferson, and a sister, Nancy E. The second wife had two boys, W. C. (Tony) and R. C. (Bob) and two girls who died while quite small. When Claiborne Chisum died in Paris, Texas, Uncle John became the head of the first family in a very literal sense. In fact, until his death, the family group was a sort of patriarchy, with Uncle John as the undisputed head of what might be called the Chisum brotherhood. He was the bellwether of the flock, and what-ever he proposed the others did. He was not only better endowed with business ability than the other brothers, but he was also more well-balanced and freer from certain shortcomings and failings com-

*About 75 miles west of the Arkansas-Texas border.

mon to men in those days. He always felt a responsibility for the rest of the brothers, and his first thoughts were for their welfare. His devotion to his brother Jeff, who was afflicted with epilepsy, was particularly affectionate. Everywhere he went, he managed it so that Jeff should be well cared for when not under his watchful eye. If Uncle John needed helpers in his business affairs, it was always to his brothers that he turned.

I remember Uncle John telling about the first business venture he ever undertook. When he was a boy at Paris, the town had to get its supply of water from Mud Creek. Uncle John undertook to haul water from the stream to the town, and thereby earned a very tidy sum for a boy. It was characteristic of him that he had an eye for the main chance, as the expression is, and possessed a high degree of business shrewdness. He had the knack of taking advantage of any opportunity coming his way.

It has been said by some who were inclined to belittle him, that he was only a cattleman, the implication being that he was not competent to be anything else. Such was not the case, as the variety of things he engaged in before embarking into the cattle business on a large scale will indicate. While he lived at Paris he was generally known as a contractor, said to have been the first one in the place, and the first courthouse of Lamar County was a monument to his skill and integrity in this occupation.

By 1851 Uncle John, now 27 years old, was a candidate for the office of county clerk against John R. Craddock, who had been the incumbent for several years. Mr. Craddock was very popular, having given good service twelve years, so defeated Uncle John by a small majority. But Uncle John even then showed that spirit of determination and perseverance which brought him ultimate success; he bided his time until the next election and again became a candidate for the office. This time, although his competitor was the same Mr. Craddock, Uncle John won the election. He gave such satisfaction in the duties of the office that he was re-elected.

But finding that his health was beginning to suffer from the confining work, he decided to retire from the office. It was about this time that he felt the lure of the cattle business, which, with shrewdness and foresight, he now believed would become the leading industry of Texas. He had been dealing in cattle in a small way previously, getting together one or two herds of moderate size and sending them towards Shreveport, which was then a distributing point for Texas cattle. But in 1857 an opportunity presented itself for forming a partnership with Oliver Keep of New York City, who had come to Paris, looking for someone to handle the investment he intended to make in Texas cattle. Uncle John agreed to buy cattle with Oliver Keep's $6,000, the understanding being that Uncle John was to manage the cattle and have a share of the profits.

Uncle John went to what was then called the Colorado country in southern Texas, and bought cattle for almost a song — $6 a head, with calves thrown in! These he drove into Denton County and established a ranch there near the town of Bolivar. He used to say that the present site of the city of Fort Worth was a part of what he then claimed as his range. Oliver Keep furnished him more money, and Uncle John bought wisely and thriftily. I have heard him say that at one time he bought 1,000 head of cattle at $2 a head, delivered. He remained in Denton County until 1862, attending the cattle operation.

But when that part of Texas began to fill up and desirable range was no longer obtainable, Uncle John moved farther westward. He realized that success in the cattle business as then conducted was impossible without a free and unlimited range, and this he sought to find in the Concho country, near where Fort Concho* was later established. Uncle John was again on the vanguard of the frontier, for his was the first ranch of any importance established in that section.

During the Civil War Uncle John was one of the those designated cattlemen expected to supply the Confederate Army with all the beef possible, the stipulated price being $40 a head in Confederate money. Uncle John wisely used the money he derived from this source while it had some value, and purchased lands and horses.

When the Civil War ended, Uncle John felt confident that he no longer needed a partner. So when the agreement between him and Mr. Keep came to an end, Uncle John declined to renew it, making Mr. Keep an offer to buy out his interest or to sell to him, saying that he had made up his mind that in the future he would either run only Chisum cattle or go out of the stock business altogether. Mr. Keep accepted the offer, and in this way Uncle John became well established in the cattle business.

---

*Near present San Angelo, Texas.

In addition to his cattle business, Uncle John had gained an interest in Cheatham's store at Trickman, in Coleman County, not far from Concho County. At first he was a clerk for Cheatham and served so faithfully for six to eight years that he eventually was made a partner, the firm becoming Cheatham & Chisum. This store-keeping experience gave Uncle John much that was interesting to talk about in later days.

While in Concho County Uncle John first became interested in the opportunities that New Mexico afforded for cattle raising, not so much for better range as better markets. How this fact was first brought to Uncle John's attention is an interesting story. It seems that he had a cousin by the name of Tol Chisum who got into trouble in Texas; that is, he killed a man. Tol Chisum had tried during the Civil War to evade conscription, but someone had told on him, and he had been forced to go into the Army. When the war ended, he came back to Texas and hunted down the informer and killed him. To escape any consequences Tol Chisum fled to New Mexico, but finally came back to Texas and stood trial. The outcome was that he came clear.

While Tol Chisum was in New Mexico he wrote Uncle John about the chance to secure the contract for furnishing beef to the Government at Fort Sumner. At that time there were between eight and ten thousand Indians under charge of the Government at the Bosque Redondo, and some 1,500 to 2,000 soldiers at Fort Sumner to look after them. So there existed an opportunity for someone to get a large and profitable contract. Uncle John was quick to see this was a chance to dispose of the cattle which had been accumulating in Texas.

But before deciding to drive some of his cattle over, he sent his brother Pitzer with James Patterson into New Mexico to investigate the situation thoroughly. Uncle Pitzer came back and said he liked the country and the prospect of a market for cattle. Uncle John used to say that this information was somewhat expensive, for he had provided Uncle Pitzer with $2,500 for the expenses of the trip, and what Uncle Pitzer did with it was lose it. He said he got robbed and I guess he did. Uncle John Chisum then came into the country himself. Since he was seriously thinking of driving a herd through, he needed to acquaint himself thoroughly with the country. Especially would he have to learn the location of the watering places and the chances for grazing.

I have heard Uncle John speak often of things connected with this, his first trip into New Mexico. He came with a party of eight or ten men, among who were Old Man Hubbard and Hunnicut Allen. They were all, like Uncle John, interested in blazing a trail up the Pecos in order to see what possibilities southeastern New Mexico offered for the raising of cattle. Texas at that time was overcrowded with cattle, because during the Civil War there had been no outlet to any market and the herds had multiplied rapidly. So the cattlemen of Texas were eagerly seeking markets in every possible direction. Those in the western part of the state, like those in Uncle John's party, were hopeful of finding a way to send their cattle westward into Arizona or northwards into Colorado, if there were no markets nearer at hand.

Uncle John and Old Man Hubbard were full of practical jokes, and Uncle John always enjoyed telling about one in particular that took place on this trip. The whole party was made to enter into a solemn written compact that each one would during the trip kill some kind of game and then bring it to camp and dress and cook it. Then when it was served, everyone was bound to eat some of it. This agreement gave great impetus to hunting, and the variety of birds and animals brought under the designation of "game" was astonishing.

Uncle John's experience with food rapidly became enlarged; chicken hawk, he found, was fine and tasted much like chicken; rattlesnake was not bad and tasted much like eel; skunk was palatable and tasted something like rabbit; jack rabbit was edible though rather tough, except for the hind legs; prairie dog was chewable though it tasted of weeds; and so on with deer, antelope, buffalo, catfish, suckers, prairie chicken, and several other sorts of fowls of the air, animals of the land, or fish of the sea.

The *ne plus ultra* of this huntsman's dietary came when someone in the party shot a buzzard and brought it to camp as his contribution. Of course all the rest of the crowd were game and tried to live up to the compact, but Uncle John admitted that he, along with the rest, had to give up before buzzard meat. He took a portion of the meat, but found it the toughest, most leather-like meat he ever put in his mouth. It was possible, he said, to get it chewed somewhat, but as to swallowing it, that was impossible. So all gave up, and the bill of fare was light for supper that day.

As the party went up the valley of the Pecos River, Uncle John readily sensed what a wonderful opportunity that country offered for cattle raising, and he quietly made up his mind that he would become lord of that vast domain of 300 or more miles by and down the river.

In most accounts of John Chisum, mention is made of the fact that he never married. The reason usually given is a love affair in his early life in Texas, one that ended unfortunately but no account I have seen tells the circumstances. I shall give the story as Uncle John himself once told it to me. I remember the occasion very well. I was at the time (1882) at Mrs. Milo Pearce's on the Hondo a few miles below Roswell, helping look after the sick in the household, when on a Sunday Uncle John came in his buggy. He called to me to ask if I did not want to go with him on a trip he had to make to the Berrendo, a few miles from Roswell. He urged me to go, saying, "I'm pretty blue today — something unusual for me — and I want company — someone I can talk to. I thought that as you have been shut up with the sick you might like to get out. So come along and go with me." Of course, I was delighted to do so, and was soon seated in the buggy by his side.

When we had gone a short distance, Uncle John said to me, "Lily, I'm full up today," and turning my head toward him at these words, I saw that this old man of nearly sixty who had all his life faced dangers and hardships without faltering, was about to break down. The tears were in his eyes as he continued. "I've just received last night the saddest news I ever had in my life. It is the hardest thing, I believe, that I ever had to bear. I can hardly stand it. The woman I once hoped to marry and the only one I ever loved is living in California in dire poverty. If I only had that scrub of a man she married out on this prairie for a few minutes, what I would do to him would be a-plenty! Any man who will take a woman and bring her into worse conditions than she was when she married him, is a low-down cur, not even worthy of the name of a man."

I was all interest and sympathy immediately and said, "Tell me all about it, Uncle John, won't you?" This he proceeded to do at considerable length, and I shall try to give the story as it came from his lips:

"When I was young and in the prime of life, I was a great ladies' man. At that time I was in Denton County working for Mr. Cheatham as clerk in his store. The girl who most caught my fancy was a fine looker — a better class country girl, full of health and vigor and life. She was what I call a harum-scarum type — not rough but full of mischief and ready for a joke at any and all times. To tell the truth, she was very much like you in that respect, Lily, and maybe that is why I have always liked you especially well. She was a girl I could not make mad, and neither could I get ahead of her. Her name was Sue Holman, and I always called her Sue.

"I went with other girls, but they were only friends. Sue was the one particular one with me and I certainly thought a lot of her. But I was then working for wages in the store, and a clerk's wages were not very large. I didn't feel I was in a position to marry and have a home of the sort I wanted to give my wife. So for several years we remained just sweethearts; I shouldn't say that we were actually engaged, though all our talk and plans were centered around the understanding that as soon as I had accumulated enough to have a home and take care of a wife, we would pledge our troth and shortly afterwards be married.

"On the basis of such an implied understanding, we got along finely, enjoying each other's company and having a good time. But there happened to appear on the scene a strange young man from a city somewhere — a sort of dude he was, and well dressed — who took a great fancy to Sue. My partner, Mr. Cheatham, noticed his attentions to her and one day he took me to time about it, saying, 'John, look here. Why don't you marry that girl? You may never get a better one, and if you don't, look out or that city fellow will get her.' 'No,' I replied, 'I don't feel that I'm earning enough to give her as good a home as she has now, and I'm too much of a man to ask her to marry me under those conditions.'

"Mr. Cheatham then said, 'Well, now, look here. You've been working for me about eight years and I've never had anyone to give better satisfaction or to take more interest in my store and business. My wife says the same, and we both think the world and all of Sue. We've been talking this matter over, and we realize that since we're getting old, we need new blood to take care of us and this business. Now here is what we have decided to do: I want to take you in as full partner and let you pay out for your share from your part of the income of the store. I'm sure you can easily do this in a short time. Now I want you to accept my offer, and then I want you and Sue to go and get married at once.'

"I was almost taken off my feet by the good fortune that came my way in this offer and I at once said, 'All right, Mr. Cheatham, I'll agree to both your stipulations.' Mr. Cheatham was much pleased and said, 'All right, John, we'll inventory the goods right away and charge half to you. I'll give you plenty of time to pay for your share. You can count on having for your own use at least half your share of the income of the store.'

"Thinking that all would now be plain sailing as regards Sue and me, I wrote at once and told her of my good fortune, giving her full particulars about the agreement Mr. Cheatham and I had made. I never for a moment doubted she would be willing to marry me without further delay, but some women, you know, are very long-headed, even in regard to marrying. Somehow Sue did not feel like making the venture with me just then. She replied that she was entirely willing to become engaged to me, but that she would rather wait a year and see how the arrangements with Cheatham turned out. I never did believe in long engagements, and for that reason had never in the past proposed to any girl. I'll admit I had never before thought enough of any to want to ask her, but at the same time I had not felt myself in a position to marry in a reasonably short time if accepted.

"Just as soon as I could get away I went over to see Sue, and we talked the matter over from all sides. She would acquiesce in my views on every matter except on that one point of an immediate marriage. So after I had exhausted all of my persuasive powers on her I said, 'Well, Sue, if you won't agree to become Mrs. Chisum soon — that is, within a reasonable time, say enough to make a wedding dress and notify the neighbors — then the only thing is for us to break up. I don't believe in long engagements, and I want you either to become mine entirely in a short time or I want us both to be in a position under which we feel entirely free to go with whom we please.'

"Sue agreed to this, although I think she was taken aback at my firm attitude. I think one reason she didn't want to marry at once was that she was having too good a time. She was the belle of the section and going to all the social affairs, especially with this city dude that was hanging around her. I admit I was a little sore at her and I made my position more of an ultimatum than she antici-pated, but she would not alter her attitude. I think she expected it wouldn't be long before I came around and tried to make up. But I was too proud to do anything of the sort. I plunged into the business with all my might and main. I took on the cattle business besides that of the store and consequently I had to be away a good deal. So I did not see Sue for a long time and the next thing I knew she had married that city dude and moved away to where he came from. So I plunged deeper and deeper into work and tried to forget her.

"A year or so after she married I happened to meet her somewhat accidentally. There was a good deal of sickness in Trickham, and she and I happened to meet one night at a neighbor's where we had both gone to sit up with someone who was sick. The patient was sleeping most of the time, and we had plenty of time to talk. Our conversation was about first one thing and another, until finally she said to me in the kindest and friendliest way, 'John, why don't you get married?' I was surprised at the question coming from her, because I supposed she understood fully what was the reason, but not wishing to cause her any regret, I tried to turn the matter aside by replying, 'Why, Sue, I can't; nobody will have me.' 'Oh, yes, someone will,' she answered, 'there are plenty of good girls. You ought to get married; you'll be happier. I'm sure there are plenty will say yes!' Then she said, 'I'll help you.'

"Up to that time our conversation and actions had been just what might have passed between old friends, but when I had to answer her offer to help me find someone, I couldn't resist saying, 'How could you help me to get married when you wouldn't have me yourself? How could you advise any other girl to do what you wouldn't?' As soon as I said it, I realized I had cut her to the quick. She broke down and began to cry. I made some excuse to go into the patient's room, and didn't come back. I had gotten new light on the situation between us. Up to that time I had taken my medicine like a man, as I thought, and had accepted my defeat under the impression that Sue preferred the other man to me. Now I realized that she had married him not out of love but rather to spite me.

"Shortly thereafter I left Denton County and went into Coleman County and finally on to Concho County. I lost all track of Sue until last night there came to my ranch an old man who knew her out in California where she and her husband had gone. From him I learned that her life out there had been one long series of hardships. Her husband turned out to be a poor provider, and what is more he wasn't even kind to her. Sue had opened up her heart to this old man, who was a friend of long standing to her and her people, and she had told him it was the regret of her life that she had not taken me. She blamed herself for being so hard-headed when I came to ask her to marry me, and said she had repented a thousand times the decision that made us break up."

At this point Uncle John paused and then said, thoughtfully, "I guess Sue is not the only one to assume some of the blame. If I had been patient, I think maybe everything would have come out different, for I know now that Sue really loved me. But I was young then, and that was the first time I had actually courted a woman in earnest. I didn't understand their skittishness, as I might call it, as well as I do now. Under the circumstances I didn't feel I could stay in her vicinity; to do so would only add fuel to my disappointment. So I took myself off to the frontier and put civilization and women largely behind me. Here I am, rich, and called the cattle king of the Pecos Valley. And there is poor Sue, in California, having a hard time. It almost kills me to think of it."

27

Trouble With Indians

JOHN CHISUM'S VISIT to inspect the land in New Mexico convinced him that it might become the Promised Land for him, and he determined to take advantage of the opportunities the undeveloped Pecos Valley revealed. Returning to Texas, he gathered a herd of about 900 beef cattle and started back to New Mexico with them for an experimental venture.

The first drive was made safely despite the fact that it lay through country infested with Indians. The herd was driven to the Bosque Grande* in August of 1867, and Uncle John wintered there. The next spring Uncle John sold his herd to the Government contractors. At that time the contract for Fort Sumner was in the hands of Stadtahr & Co. of New York, and their subcontractor was Jim Patterson who had established a ranch at Bosque Grande. Uncle John sold to Patterson and took in payment drafts for $28,000 on the New York firm of Stadtahr & Co. But before the drafts were presented this firm failed, and the drafts were, of course, worthless. The loss was a heavy one for Uncle John but he knew how to take misfortune philosophically.

As I look over his career, he seems always to have been undergoing losses. He made a great deal of money, but he also lost

---

*Spanish for Big Woods, a grove so unusual that it was named. This one was about 35 miles north of Roswell.

a great deal. Sometimes, as in this instance, it was simply one of the accidents of business; at other times it was from depredations of Indians or American outlaws, hazards of business arising out of the peculiar situation in the country at that time. Again it was occasionally from displaced trust in a friend or business associates, for he was the kind of man who has abiding faith in the integrity of those whom he selected as friends.

Not daunted by his financial loss and knowing that there were plenty of cattle obtainable in Texas, Uncle John made an agreement with Mr. Patterson who, after the failure of Stadtahr & Co., secured for himself the Government contract to furnish the large quantity of 7,000 head of cattle. Everything that could be converted into meat was to be accepted under this contract and the prices were as follows: for cow and calf, $16; for two-year-olds, $9; for three-year-olds and dry cows, $18; and for four-year-olds and up, $25.

Under this contract Uncle John bought up several herds. In the course of the next year or so, E. B. Peters went in with Patterson. The firm was called Peters and Patterson, with E. B. Peters trail boss. Patterson had the contract for beef at Fort Sumner alone, but, because they were partners in the cattle, Uncle John formed a sort of partnership with them, the terms of agreement being similar to those made with Patterson. Charles Goodnight wanted a large number of cattle for his extensive operation in Colorado and Wyoming. According to Goodnight's statement the understanding was that he was to allow Uncle John $1 profit over Texas prices for the time, effort, and risk involved in getting the cattle to Bosque Grande, where they were to be turned over to Goodnight, and that in addition, after the cattle had been sold, the partners were to divide the profits equally.

It was in connection with the first herd that Uncle John drove up from Texas to deliver to Goodnight that there occurred what was possibly the greatest loss he ever sustained at one time from the Indians. In this herd were some 1100 or more steers that had cost $18 or $20 apiece in Texas, and would bring perhaps $36 at Fort Sumner. Uncle John himself drove the herd as far as Horsehead Crossing on the Pecos, and there turned it over to his brother, Pitzer (or P. M. as he generally called him), to drive the rest of the way to Bosque Grande. Uncle Pitzer knew that the Indians had broken away from the reservation and were stealing and killing everything in the way of meat they came across. He asked the officer in command of a detachment of soldiers stationed at Horsehead Crossing for an escort, but the request was refused. All Uncle Pitzer could do then was to go ahead, depending upon the men who were with the herd to protect it from the Indians.

He continued without being molested until he reached Black River at the mouth of Dark Canyon, at the point of the Guadalupe Mountains. It was at this locality, it will be remembered, that the Indians three years before "took" my father's cattle when he was coming to New Mexico. On the night of the 12th of June a large band of Indians appeared and stampeded the Chisum herd. Uncle Pitzer and the cowboys made as vigorous a resistance as they could, but were powerless before the large number of Indians, who drove off practically all of the herd. In the fight several Indians were killed, and one of the cowboys wounded.

The news of this disaster reached Uncle John after he had gone to Texas for more cattle. As usual he accepted the loss and went on with his preparations for picking up another herd for delivery. In the course of time it was put together and taken by Uncle John to Horsehead Crossing. When he met Pitzer he simply turned the herd over to him, without making reference to the loss of the former one, and said with a smile, "Well, P.M., here's another herd. Try her again." This time the cattle got through without mishap and were delivered to Charles Goodnight.

It was from these hastily collected herds that the oft-repeated stories regarding the great variety of brands in the Chisum herds got started. Knowing that Goodnight would be in close quarters if he did not receive the cattle which he counted upon Uncle John for delivery, this new herd had to be put up as quickly as possible. To one who knew how herds were put up, it was easy to understand the great variety of brands in a given herd. A man operating a store as Uncle John did at Trickham would take in payment of accounts a good many cattle which would bear the brands of the original owners. He might also purchase some from his neighbors, which likewise would bear the brands of the original owners. In those days in Texas anyone driving a herd through could pick up all stray cattle belonging to his friends. The country was full of them, and the rules in Texas made this a common custom: the man driving them paid the owner for them when they were sold. While he might not go to another man's range and take one of his mavericks, if the same maverick attached itself to his herd as it went through, the owner of the herd had a right to put his brand on it, sell it, and pay the owner of the range for the maverick. This was the custom of the country.

Another custom contributing to a variety of brands was that owners of small herds would send their cattle with a much larger herd, thus being relieved of the problems of delivery. John Chisum was considered to be honest, and many of his friends were glad to let him take their cattle with his, confident that they would receive full returns of the sale in course of time, which might be many months, or even a year, ahead.

These simple and natural customs explain the mixture of brands in the Chisum herds. To imply these mixtures were evidence of crookedness on the part of Uncle John is to do an injustice to a man whose uprightness in business transactions was well understood by all who came in contact with him.

Uncle John was careful to protect himself in his transactions, and whenever it was necessary for him to prove the fallacy of aspersion such as those of which I write, he could always produce bills of sale or power of attorney to show that the cattle in question were rightfully in his herds if on his range.

Uncle John's partnership with Charles Goodnight continued for two or three years, and proved so profitable that at the end of that period Uncle John felt it was to his best interest to conduct the business on a larger scale. According to Goodnight's estimate, in the three years their agreement was in effect, Uncle John bought in Texas and delivered to him some 15,000 or 16,000 head of cattle. As one of the customary steps toward the enlargement of his business Uncle John bought from Jim Patterson the buildings and store the latter owned at Bosque Grande, and proceeded to make that his headquarters. By this time he had decided upon leaving Texas and was busy bringing all the cattle he could to New Mexico. This required a good deal of time and it was not until 1872 that the job was completed.

One of the deciding factors in Uncle John's establishing himself in New Mexico was the danger from Indians. Of course there was also the desire to take advantage of the vast range up and down the Pecos for a hundred miles or more which was covered with the finest kind of gramma grass, thick and heavy, and "belly deep to a horse." But it was evident that the great drawback was the danger of Indian raids. These were, of course, just as likely to occur in Texas, but a point in favor of the location at Bosque Grande was that he was under the shadow of Fort Sumner and the proximity of the soldiers was a check upon the Indians.

There was still another phase that must have appealed to his sagacity. A herd at Bosque Grande would obviate the long drive from the Concho to New Mexico. The great problem was good water; and that term implied running or living water. From the head of the Concho River the next good water to be had was at Horsehead Crossing on the Pecos. In the stretch of 96 miles between these two sources there were only two watering places, Mustang Ponds and Chino Ponds, and sometimes Rock Tank in Castle Gap. And the water in those, if found, was not good; it was stagnant. It did quench thirst but was not wholesome. Unless the snows had been heavy, even these two places could not be depended upon as a source of water, and sometimes cattle had to walk 96 miles without a drop. As a result of this condition, the herds were made up of only the stronger cattle, beef steers above three, four, and five years old being preferred. Dry cows, too, were sometimes taken. Clearly it would have been a great gain to have a thriving herd on the Pecos Valley range and be relieved from making this long and hazardous trip.

When Uncle John made Bosque Grande his center of activities in New Mexico, he had the only ranch on the upper Pecos. But about this time Robert K. Wiley established a camp at Eighteen Mile Bend on the Pecos, some 200 miles south of Bosque Grande. Even though Uncle John and Wiley were on friendly terms, Chisum felt that he must have plenty of elbow room, and he bought Wiley out, and thereby became sole overlord of the vast range of the entire lower valley.

There is a good story that goes along with this buying out of Wiley, which deserves retelling. I shall give it as recorded by James Cox in, *The Cattle Industry of Texas and Adjacent Territory.**

Several years after Chisum had located his ranch on the Pecos River, Mr. R. K. Wiley was the next to locate a herd of 9,000 cattle just below Chisum,

---

*Also quoted by J. Frank Dobie in *A Vaquero of the Brush Country.*

when, Lo! and behold! a blinding snow storm and blizzard, that was terrific, struck the Wiley herd at night, and when Bob Wiley emerged from his dugout the next morning, with his best and longest range field-glasses, not a hoof was to be seen. He was all broke up; his cattle, not yet accustomed to that high altitude, had taken to their heels and drifted into Chisum's range, and with a look of abject despair, told his tale of woe.

To John Chisum who always enjoyed a good joke that did not lacerate, this look on Bob Wiley's face and his recital were side-splitting and amusing. He fell down on the snow, rolled and laughed until he made himself almost sick. Riley could not see where the fun came in, but bore up in the trying ordeal as best he could until John Chisum asked him what he valued his cattle at, and when he replied, $65,000, a sale was at once closed, and Wiley returned to the settlements across the Staked Plains a wiser and happier man through the kindness of his lifelong friend, honest John Chisum.

After establishing himself at Bosque Grande, Uncle John continued to suffer from Indian raids. It is impossible at this time to gather up the details of these raids, or even to catalogue all of them. The best I can do is to mention a few of the most notable ones. In June, 1872, Uncle John was driving through the country a bunch of mules and horses, which the Indians stole. There were about 120 horses, valued at perhaps $100 each, and 30 large draft mules, valued at $150 each. The estimated loss from this attack might, therefore, be placed at $16,500. In April, 1873, the Indians again got away with 70 horses and 35 mules, the total loss being approximately $13,500. About three months later, he lost in the same way about 75 horses and 25 mules, their value being about $9,510. These were stolen by the Indians in the vicinity of Adobe Walls on the Canadian.

In August 1873, the Indians descended upon the Bosque Grande, and rode right up to the corral in front of the store. Their intention was to drive off the 125 valuable saddle horses that were in the corral. The few men at the corral made a vigorous fight against the Indians, shooting at them from the protection of the store. After a rather long fight, the Indians succeeded in stampeding the horses, and got away with the whole bunch, and drove them toward the Indian Territory. In this fight, some of the Chisum men were killed, but several of the Indians passed into the category of "good Indians." The loss in money from this raid might be said to have been $33,550. In that same month, the Indians again went through that section, and coming across a roundup party under charge of Uncle Pitzer Chisum near the Twelve Mile Bend of the Pecos, they made an attack and got away with about 40 head of cattle. The same day they encountered another Chisum roundup party under charge of

Felix McKittrick whose men put up a vigorous fight, the Indian loss of which was never known. One of the Chisum cowboys was killed.

In the fall of 1873 the Indians again went on a rampage. They stole about 60 head of horses from a branding outfit of Uncle John's that was in camp at Eighteen Mile Bend on the Pecos, and they also killed about this time a line rider, Jack Holt. For about a year, there was a letup in Indian depredations, but in the fall of 1874, trouble arose again from this source. This time the Indians raided a Chisum camp in the vicinity of Comanche Spring (Ft. Stockton, Texas), but they got only seven head of cattle and two good saddle horses, together with some saddles, blankets, pistols, and the like. About two weeks later — on the 18th of November — the Indians again raided the camp at Comanche Spring, and took 58 horses, 36 mules, and two head of beef cattle. This loss of horses was a serious matter, for at that time they were high priced, and hard to get. To replace his losses Uncle John succeeded in getting together about 60 or 70 more but these were in turn scooped up by the Apaches. The result was that for some time Uncle John was seriously handicapped in his work by lack of mounts. So in that year very little branding was done, the number of calves tallied falling much below that of the preceding year, having dropped from 8,228 to 5,000.

The Indians were primarily after horses, yet they ran off and killed many thousands of cattle. Uncle John made claims to the Government for Indian losses to the amount of $143,995; but I do not believe that even this big sum represented all the losses he sustained. It would have been a hard matter to keep track of all the attacks by Indians and the losses from each. In some cases it would have been useless to make claims for damages; the Government did not pay claims for losses when the Indians were hostile; it paid only for losses such as came within the scope of the governmental policy in this matter, and let the other be charged to profit and loss.

There must have been many stories of hairbreadth escape and deadly encounters in these fights with the Indians, which unfortunately are lost to us. The Chisum cowboys were to a man sturdy fighters, well acquainted with the habits and ways of the Indians, and they must have taken a heavy toll of Indian lives. It is remarkable that in all these many fights so few cowboys were either killed or wounded.

The Chisum men and others among the settlers in that section gave the Indians an impressive lesson that showed them they should not continue their raids. In 1874 the Indians had done much stealing in the Seven Rivers country. The men of that part of the country got together and decided to give the Indians a lesson not easily forgotten. Uncle John Chisum was not in the party but his employees were. I remember hearing my father and Uncle John talk of the proposed move against the Indians. Father urged him to use his influence to prevent it, but I do not think Uncle John did so. A large party was assembled and started for the reservation. They came past our place, and it was upon this occasion that I first saw Jesse Evans and Jimmie McDaniels.

I do not know the details of the encounter between these men and the Indians. The report was that a good many Indians were killed, but I cannot say how many. At any rate the lesson, though severe, was wholesome for the Indians. From that time they gave less and less trouble. Particularly did they evince a great respect for the Chisum employees. Because Uncle John was the biggest cowman in the section, the Indians thought the whole crowd was composed of his cowboys.

28

Trouble With Cattle Rustlers

THE GOVERNMENT'S ATTEMPTS to keep the Indians in check became more and more successful, and danger from this source decreased. But a new and even more troublesome source developed from cattle rustling. That was the time when rustling was the order of the day. In fact it had become a sort of profession and had developed a science of its own. Although laws were becoming stricter in regard to mavericking and brand burning, the Southwest had not come to the point where it was willing to call a spade a spade and bestow the ugly word, "stealing" upon the operations of the rustlers. The professional rustler who stole a bunch of cattle was said to "have got off with them" and it was usual to hear it said about men that "they made a good haul," as though they had been successful in a legitimate business. Perhaps no other industry ever suffered such a drawback as did the cattle business from rustling.

The existence of so much easily appropriated property in the large herds of Uncle John Chisum could not fail to be inviting to men seeking wealth through ill-gotten gains. Apparently not only the weak and lawless but even the strong and unscrupulous set out to reap in their respective fashions where they had not sown, and Chisum herds became their harvest fields. At first the smaller fellows came to use the Chisum herds as their sources of supply; but I doubt that Uncle John paid much attention to this sort of stealing. It was easy for a man of his generous nature to take a lenient attitude toward such nibbling at his property. He used to say that it was better to lose some cattle than to fight over them. Later he became the target for the thievery encouraged by strong and unscrupulous persons as were in the Murphy and Dolan crowd. The ones who did the stealing were still the little fellows, but they were encouraged and supported by the big ones. When this came about Uncle John felt called upon to assert his rights and to use means to protect himself. I shall try to give some idea of the situation and how he attempted to meet it.

It was about this time that Uncle John Chisum decided it would be advantageous to have his headquarters more nearly in the center of the extended stretch of country he claimed as his range.

In February 1875, he started to move down from the Bosque Grande and establish himself at South Spring River, about six miles south of the present town of Roswell. I remember it was in February of that year also that I first saw this place. Mother had sent Will and me down with a load of flour that had been ground at our mill for the Chisum ranch. We left home early one morning, and, taking the river road, reached the ranch in the night after driving all day. We put up with a family by the name of Beaver Smith, who were in the employ of Uncle John, and early next morning, having delivered the flour and loaded the wagon with things Mother wanted from the store at the ranch, we started on the return trip.

We had hardly seen anything of the ranch, for with the curious sense of values children have, we were consumed with a desire to return by the longest way. It led through the little settlement of Roswell. My brother and I wanted to see something of which we had heard — shingle roofs on the two houses Van Smith and Aaron Wilburn [Wellburn] had built at Roswell. At that time these were the only buildings in the country with roofs of that sort, and they were a source of wonderment. We also would be able to see our teacher, Uncle Ash Upson, who was at that time associated with F. G. Christie in taking care of the store and post office at Roswell. As I recall it, we stayed but a few hours in Roswell and took dinner with Uncle Ash. Then we drove up to Dan Dow's stage stand on the road back home, arriving there late at night and putting up there for a little sleep. The next day we resumed our journey, and arrived at home about noon.

From our brief stop at the South Spring River ranch, and with my interest centered on it, I did not bring away many details regarding the ranch but I distinctly recall the old house. I designate it as the old house because it was the one standing on the place when Uncle John bought it in 1874 from Jim Patterson for $2,500 to be paid in cattle, and because this house is to be carefully distinguished from the long house built later — about 1882 or 1884. In nearly all accounts of the Chisum place and in nearly all the photographs purporting to be of it, it is the second house that appears. But it was the first house that figured largely in the exciting events of the times, especially those of the Billy the Kid encounters during the Lincoln County War.

The old house was built of adobe and was larger than such houses usually are. It was practically square with four rooms on each side, and enclosed in the middle was a yard or patio.

The original owner had evidently wished to build a house that would afford protection against Indian raids, for it had certain features significant of the time. In the walls, for example, long planks had been laid as a means of preventing Indians or thieves from cutting a gap in the wall by sawing with a rawhide or horsehair rope as they did to break into corrals.

The roof was flat and made of dirt. The clay used had been brought from twelve miles north of Roswell, because the soil in the immediate vicinity of South Spring River contained so much alkali that it was little protection against rain. On the roof was a two- or three-foot wall or parapet, which the Mexicans called a *pretil* in which were portholes. A few men concealed behind such a wall and equipped with good arms and an abundance of ammunition could have stood off a whole company of soldiers, to say nothing of a band of Indians.

The story about the building of this house was that it was done by Old Man Pedro Sánchez, a rich Mexican who became notable in that area because he had a double son-in-law. An American named Hutchinson had married Pedro's daughter Onsanna. When she and her twin babies died they were buried in one of the rooms of the house. With little delay the widower married her younger sister, Juanita Sánchez. I remember well Pedro Sánchez and Mr. and Mrs. Hutchison, for they always stopped at our place on their way to Lincoln before they moved. I last saw him at the stage stand at Centralia Station, which he kept on the plains, the Llano Estacado.

Just before leaving Bosque Grande and moving to South Spring River, Uncle John made arrangements to sell nearly all of his cattle to the large livestock organization of Hunter and Evans, of St. Louis. For nearly thirty years Uncle John had been in the cattle business contending with all sorts of drawbacks and hardships, and it was no wonder, as he said, that he was tired of it and wanted to quit.

Conditions in New Mexico were getting worse and worse and he saw the difficulties he would have in protecting his herds as the small cowmen came into his range. He might laugh about old Charlie Woolsey, for example, who had gone up on the Peñasco with one yoke of steers and had branded seventy-five calves the first year, but he knew that this was simply an indication of the mavericking that was destined to go on at an increasing rate. Business judgment made him realize that the only way to protect himself as well as those to whom he owed money for cattle he had taken charge of to dispose of along with his own, was to sell out to parties who could handle the cattle under better conditions than were probable in New Mexico.

At that time Hunter & Evans, while primarily commission merchants, were also engaged in cattle raising. They held large beef contracts for the Indians, and to provide the needed cattle to turn in on these, they kept their large range in western Kansas stocked with a great many cattle. They were very glad to increase their number of cattle by buying what Uncle John had.

I do not know how large this herd was nor the terms of the sale, but the statement current at the time was that Uncle John received about $50,000. One stipulation was that cattle to the value of $27,000 were to be turned over to Uncle Pitzer Chisum as payment for being Uncle John's range boss for nine years. There were supposed to be about 60,000 head of cattle on the range controlled by Uncle John, and naturally the work of gathering and turning over this immense number required several months. In addition to sending the bulk of the cattle northward in different droves from time to time, Uncle John undertook to see that 12,000 head were delivered at the San Carlos Agency in Arizona, where Hunter & Evans had one of their beef contracts.

While this was transpiring Uncle John remained as actively engaged in the cattle business as ever. During the years 1875-1877 he was superintending the transfer of his cattle to Hunter & Evans assisted by his brothers and their force of men. It was not possible for him to realize the rest and enjoyment of life he had looked forward to when he located himself at South Spring River.

He still had to face the old difficulties and dangers. When all the cattle turned over to Hunter & Evans were checked there were 50,000. Uncle John Chisum's greatest trouble with the cattle rustlers was from people living in the vicinity of Rocky Arroyo and the Seven Rivers country. This scope of land was just about in the middle of the Chisum range, and was the hanging-out place for a very rough and lawless element. Old settlers of the place like the Beckwiths and Reeds were inclined to be law abiding, but they could not keep some very rascally fellows from coming into the community and connecting themselves with local people. Uncle John's range boss had more than one row with parties in that section of the country. One of these I shall record.

Just a little time before the Lincoln County War he heard through his friend Bob Gilbert, who had a farm on the Peñasco and was a sort of spy for Uncle John, that there was suspicious activity in progress in the corrals at Beckwith's place in the vicinity of Seven Rivers. Uncle John could not go down at once to investigate, as he had to make a trip to Arizona, I believe. He sent Pitzer, Jim Highsaw, and a few of his cowboys to Seven Rivers. They discovered a thousand jingle-bobbed ears of cattle buried in a certain corral. The conclusion was inescapable: some 500 head of Chisum cattle had been treated to brand changing and driven off somewhere — probably to Mexico. An equally large number of cattle freshly branded with the arrow ←—≪ turned up at the Murphy-Dolan camp in that vicinity. Obviously the feathers and tip had been added to the long rail of the Chisum brand.

About a year later the situation became so acute that Uncle John had to make another raid down in that area. This time he went with blood in his eye, and took along a number of his cowboys, well armed.

On still another occasion Uncle John learned through one of his detective agents at El Paso that some cattle stolen from his range had been sold at that place. So, taking his range boss, Jim Highsaw, with him, he started on the trail of these stolen cattle. The trail was a little old, but they were able to follow it to El Paso, and to get a description of the cattle and also of the men and the

horses they rode. When Uncle John and Jim Highsaw reached El
Paso they found some of the cattle still in the possession of men
who had bought them from the thieves, and they replevined them.

When the two returned they met Dick Smith, a small cowman
on the lower Pecos, in the vicinity of the Chisum camp. Highsaw
told him of the trip and charged Smith with stealing the cattle. The
latter resented the accusation and promptly reached for his six-
shooter. Highsaw was the quicker; he shot and killed Dick Smith.
The outcome might have been expected, for Highsaw was quick as
lightning on the draw. He was also cool under any circumstances
and took no chances. Those who knew him considered him to be a
brave but dangerous man. He was not quarrelsome, but if accosted,
shot to kill. He practiced continually with his pistol and could
twirl it over his finger, cocking it meanwhile, and as it came over,
aiming and preparing for a second shot.

The killing of Dick Smith caused Uncle John some criticism,
but had this been his only problem it might not have been serious.
When Murphy and Dolan came into the contest, the situation
became acute. It was impossible to class this firm with the small
cowmen. They were certainly among the big ones, for they held
government contracts which required the furnishing of a large
number of cattle to the Mescalero Apaches on the reservation and
to the soldiers at Fort Stanton. For awhile they maintained their
Fair View ranch at Carrizo Springs, more than fifty miles west of
Lincoln, but in 1878 they moved their cow camp to the Murphy-
Blake Spring in the vicinity of Seven Rivers.

To fulfill their contracts in the easiest and cheapest way, they
had made a practice of hiring some of the worst characters in the
country to conduct systematic stealing from the Chisum range.
Their cow camps at and near Seven Rivers were evidently intended
as a more convenient base for their operations. Uncle John could
easily perceive the sinister design back of this, and if the controversy
between him and these invaders had not been forced by circumstances into a different channel, he might have had to use more
violent measures for the protection of his property.

The killing of the young Englishman, John H. Tunstall, in
February, 1878 produced an alignment of most of the citizens of
the county either with the Murphy-Dolan crowd or with the
McSween element and led up to the Lincoln County War. Uncle

John was not a participant in the struggle. On December 22, 1877, he started to St. Louis on a business trip, and had got as far as Las Vegas when he was arrested at the instigation of powerful citizens of the Territory. Rather than submit to demands which he considered illegal, he endured voluntary imprisonment lasting until about the middle of March. Hence he was not in the country during the earliest stages of the Lincoln County War. After his return to South Spring River, McSween took refuge in the vicinity for a short time. The McSweens did try, without success, to gain the active support of Uncle John.

It is true that in the later part of the War the McSween fighting men took refuge at the South Spring River ranch when they were hotly pursued by a party of Seven Rivers men under Marion Turner, a deputy sheriff. When this occurred the Chisum brothers were away from the ranch — Uncle John in the East and the others down on the range. Mrs. Sallie Robert, Uncle Jim's daughter, sent news of the impending fight to her father and he hurried back to the ranch with his outfit, and informed both parties that they could not fight there, because of his children's being in the house. Marion Turner took his forces to Roswell for the time being; the McSween crowd left for Lincoln, and Turner's crowd followed them. At Lincoln the two parties fought it out in the famous Three Day Battle.

These facts tend to prove that Uncle John was not active in the Lincoln County War. The statements frequently made to the effect that the war was the outcome of trouble between the big cowmen like John S. Chisum and the smaller ones seems to me to be beside the mark. If that had been the single cause of the trouble, I feel sure there would have been no Lincoln County War. Uncle John was even then moving his cattle out of the country and it is not likely that he would have resorted to bloodshed over rustling when he was deliberately seeking to escape it by removing his herds.

To conclude the troubles and annoyances Uncle John suffered in New Mexico from thieves and robbers, I shall give an account of the time when, in a very literal way, he was the victim of stage robbers while he was traveling from Santa Fe to Las Vegas. He stopped overnight at our house on his way back, and I heard him tell about this experience shortly after it occurred.

He had been sleeping on the stage when about 2 A.M. he

realized that the stage had come to a stop. One of three robbers held his gun on the driver, another on the passengers — Uncle John, a preacher, and a little lawyer. Neither of the other two would have had the grit to pull a setting hen from her nest. To Uncle John's dismay it looked as though there would be no resistance. This was disturbing for he was carrying a big sum of money.

While trying to think of a ruse, Uncle John pretended to be asleep; this caused the other passengers to step out first and submit to a search at the hands of the robber. The only weapon Uncle John carried was a No. 1 range marking pocketknife, sharp. A plan formulated: when the robber searched him he would stab him in the heart, leap on the second robber who was holding the gun on the passengers before he could fire. But this plan did not include the third bandit who was holding his gun on the stage driver. Because Uncle John could not count on any help from the other passengers, he did not consider his plan feasible.

When ordered to get out of the stage he managed to drop, unobserved, a roll of money amounting to about $2,000 on the ground. To hold the attention of the two robbers, one of whom was searching him, he started a conversation with them. He called them "boys," and "my boy" and this seemed to disturb them for they suspected that he had identified them. They got a bottle of whiskey off Uncle John and invited themselves to have a drink with him. However, they required him to drink first.

They evidently knew who he was and expected a big haul, but their search resulted in a few dollars in small change. They were about to take it when Uncle John said, "Now, boys, you've taken my last cent. Can't you leave me enough for breakfast? I'm a stranger in a strange land and may have to go hungry. You wouldn't have me go hungry, would you?" The robber who had searched him was ready to hand back seventy-five cents but the other protested. Uncle John continued, "It's rough to refuse a man barely enough for a night's lodging." The other robber ran his hand in his pocket, brought up a dollar and a half, handed it to Uncle John, saying, "Well, I never refused a man a night's lodging in my life."

They took the fine watch Uncle John was wearing. It was not only expensive but a gift from his good friend and former partner, Charles Goodnight. When asked why he did not save the watch as he did the money Uncle John said that he feared the robbers had noticed the chain while he was in Santa Fe, and that he did not think it wise to seem completely destitute of both money and jewelry.

About 1876 or 1877, John Slaughter, a big cowman from Texas, killed a man named Gallegher near the Chisum place at the head of South Spring River. Slaughter charged Gallegher and his partner, Boyd, with stealing a large number of cattle from him in Texas. These men had driven off a number of the Slaughter cattle but had made use of a fraudulent bill of sale to protect themselves. This bill of sale appeared to have been legally certified by the county clerk, for it bore his name and seal, but the supposition was that they had got the fellow drunk and made him put his seal on the paper, or possibly had stolen his seal and forged his name. They had prepared a document that enabled them to satisfy the inspectors and different agents along the route from Texas into New Mexico. Slaughter and Uncle John were on good terms and cooperated with each other. Uncle John held papers from Slaughter that empowered Chisum to cut out of any passing herd and hold under his brand any Slaughter cattle that might be found, unless covered by a valid bill of sale.

On his way back to Texas John Slaughter made camp at the Chisum headquarters. While there he was informed that Gallegher and Boyd were in the vicinity with some cattle having his brand and apparently covered by a bill of sale. Slaughter got angry for he knew the bill of sale to be bogus, but he did nothing about it at the time.

A day or so later, Gallegher and Boyd came up to the Chisum store, and hearing about Slaughter, tanked up on whiskey and started for John's camp. Slaughter recognized them as they approached and got ready to receive them. Taking up his Winchester he walked around to the back of his wagon and laid the gun on the box which provided a dead rest. He called to the two men approaching, "Hold up! Don't come any closer or I'll kill you." The two paid no attention to the warning but continued to advance at a fast lope. Slaughter fired, the bullet striking Gallegher in the thigh, and causing him to fall from his horse. His partner, Boyd, ran.

Slaughter promptly sent one of his men to the store to get someone to come and examine Gallegher and find how badly he was hurt and to carry him to the store for treatment. Since Gallegher had received a mortal wound there was not time for a doctor to make the trip from Fort Stanton. McCabe and others about the store did the best they could to make the wounded man comfortable and to staunch the flow of blood but their efforts were unavailing. About midnight Gallegher died of loss of blood.

Slaughter came to the dying man and declared himself very sorry that he had hit him and asserted that he had tried to shoot the horse. He added, "You know me, and you know I'd never let you ride up on me armed after you had robbed me of cattle." To this Gallegher replied, "I was drunk and didn't think. I was just coming to talk things over."

"Well," said Slaughter, "you ought to have sent someone to tell me you wanted to talk. I didn't know; and you can bet I'm not going to let any man who has wronged me ride up to me armed and get the drop on me."

After Slaughter left, Gallegher admitted to McCabe that he had made the mistake of his life by being led into this trouble, the blame for which he laid upon his partner. He asked McCabe to remove a ring from his finger and take his watch from his pocket so that they might be sent to his wife in Texas. He spoke tenderly of his wife and two little girls, and said that his only dread of death was because he must leave them. He was buried at the old Chisum place, near the ditch.

Slaughter was never apprehended for this killing. The circumstances gave support to his statement that he felt certain that the two men were coming to kill him and that he had, therefore, felt called upon to shoot in defense of his life. His regret over the outcome of the shooting was also accepted as genuine.

29

Antagonism From the Ring

In addition to his annoyance and losses from Indians and cattle rustlers, Uncle John suffered at the hands of the powerful Santa Fe ring of those days. This ring, a group of politicians and businessmen, sought to control the courts and everything else in the state and to get their hands on as much of the resources of the state as possible to exploit in their own interests. In other words, they were greedy for personal gain and sought to obtain it by fair means or foul, most frequently the latter. Some members viewed with jealousy the success of Uncle John's cattle running venture, and sought to cause him all the trouble they could. I suppose, too, that growth of his business, conducted in a legitimate way, formed an irritating and annoying rebuke of their crooked methods.

Hostility reached its climax the later part of 1877 and the early part of 1878. Thomas B. Catron — then United States District Attorney and commonly regarded as one of the most influential members of the Santa Fe ring, if not really its guiding spirit — instigated trouble for Uncle John in connection with some notes which had fallen into the hands of certain tools of the ring. Rather than submit to what he considered high-handed injustice, Uncle John spent several weeks of January and February 1878 in jail at Las Vegas. To while away the tedium of this imprisonment he began the writing of a defense of himself, which he evidently intended some day to have published as an explanation and a vindication. Feeling that this episode deserves to be given as far as possible in his own words, I'll quote from this interesting piece of autobiographical writing.

* * *

Las Vegas January 16th 1878

I WAS IMPRISONED AND FOR WHAT

Feeling it an imperative duty I owe to myself and my friends to make as full and correct statement of the whole transactions as I possibly can, giv- my readers all the facts and circumstances just as they occurd.

My object in doing this is not to heap reproach upon the characters of our appointed officials whose sworn duty it is to deal justly with evry citizen of the Territory but it is to place myself properly before the business world and in order to do this, I must give as near as possible all the facts connected, together with all the circumstances connected ther to.

In order to do this you will have to be patient and let me fully explain and when I have done this then judge me as you would be judged.

Now in order to make this matter plain to my readers I will have to go back to the Spring of 1867. At that time I was living in Danton [Denton] County Texas. A Mr. Wilber came to my house in March 1867 and stated to me that he and a man by the name of Clark was going into the Beef Packing Business at Fort Smith Arkansas and he wished me to go in with them as an equal partner in the Business as I was a stock man. To this I did not accept he, Wilber, insisted. I still refused telling him that was out of my line of Business, he still insisted saying we could pack from 10,000 to 15,000 Beeves in the season and that the profit would be immense & etc.

I finally asked him how much money him and Clark could command. He said both together could raise $25,000. That amount I informed him would not buy the salt & Bbl. and that if he went into that business with that small amount of money his firm would proove a curse rather than a blessing both to them & the stock men.

I finally agreed if he and Clark would raise $66,666 2/3 and would invest it in a Packing house, salt and Bbls and other fixtures necessary for the packing of Beef and when I saw that was done I then would furnish $33,333 1/3 in Beef at cash price provided they

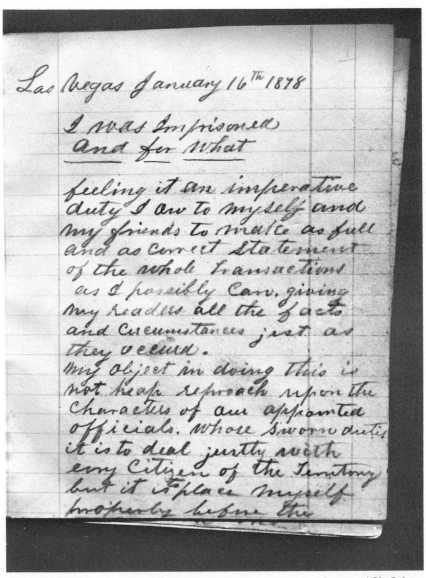

Las Vegas January 16ᵀʰ 1878

I was imprisoned
And for what

feeling it an imperative
duty I ow to myself and
my friends to make as full
and as correct statement
of the whole transactions
as I possibly Can, giving
my readers all the facts
and Circumstances just as
they occurd.
My object in doing this is
not heap reproach upon the
Characters of our appointed
officials. Whose Sworn dutis
it is to deal justly with
every Citizen of the Teritory
but it is place myself
properly before the

John Chisum's personal diary, started while he was in jail in 1878,
set forth his views of the manipulations of the Santa Fe Ring.

would agree not to attempt to pack over 5,000 Beeves the first season.

To these propositions and restrictions he protested against saying he and Clark could not raise the amount of money. I then advised him to imbark in some other Business that would not require so much capitol.

he finally concluded that he would go and see Clark & if they could raise the amount I required them to raise they would write me at once and in three weeks we would meet at some point and draw the writings. he requested me before leaving to write down what I would do and what I required of them so he Clark could see for himself just what I proposed to do and what I proposed for them to do.

This I did and signed. I kept a copy of same. I also stated to Wilbern [Wilber] at the same time that I had never saw Clark and did not know what kind of a man he was and that I claimed the priviledge of finding out something about him as a man and that it was more than likely that when I got his standing as a business man and a gentleman that I would not wish to associate myself in business with, no difference how much he might be able to controll. This was also agreed to, and Wilbern left. That day I wrote to a friend of mine in Arkansas making inquiries of this man Clark. The answer was Clark has got nothing and let him alone.

This then settled the matter with me and if Wilber had written to me as he agreed to it would have made no difference to me I should refused to have any thing to have done with them. from that day to this I have never seen Wilbern and I never did see Mr. Clark in life.

I was at home in Denton County for three months after Wilbern left but having not received a line from him nor Clark I of course came to the conclusion all idea of the packing business was all abandoned under my proposition to them.

In June following I left Denton County and went to Concho County some 200 miles west and in July I started to New Mexico with a herd of Beef and got to N M in August 1867. Their I remained until 5th of April 1868 and started for Texas. I arrived in Coleman County Texas 8th of May 1868 — and then and not until then I learnt that Wilbern and Clark had been packing Beef at Fort Smith under the name of Wilbern Chisum & Clark.

My brother hearing that such a firm was packing Beef at Fort Smith then a distance of 300 miles he knowing where I was and fearing something was wrong. So he went and found it was so. They were in the Mercantile business also a large Sign over their Store door & also over their Packing house and even on their Bottle of Cocktails was labled Wilbern Chisum and Clark (these lables they had maid in N.Y.) As soon as Wilbern found out that my brother was their he went to him and said Myself and Clark have taken the liberty to use your Brother Johns naim but dont say any thing about it we will make a big thing & not hirt him but if you speak of it it will ruin us. But my brother exposed the whole thing that evening and the next day they were closed up and the swindle exposed.

On the 10th of May 1868 I started to Austin Texas taking with me the copy of the proposition I had maid them in the Spring 1867. I showed it to Goven Peas [Pease] and asked him if that made me a partner of those men. he said no and asked me the circumstances. I stated them. He said if I had been in the Country and was knowing that these men were using your name & by so doing was getting peoples property & that I did not let it be known that I was no partner that the law would make me responsible but that if I had been out of the state and did not know this the law would not make me responsible.

But he says you yet have a duty to perform & that was to publish them and let it be known that you was not a partner and would not be responsible for contracts that they had maid nor for those they might make hereafter. This I did in 3 news papers, one in Arkansas & 2 in Texas. At the time this pretended firm of W. C. & C. was closed up they had put out notes to the amount of 80 or 90 thousand dollars with the signature of W. C. & C. A large amount of these notes were given to stock men of Texas who had started herds of cattle late in the fall with the expectation of driving into Ilinoys. And by the time they reached Fort Smith it was then getting late and their cattle was dying with poverty and the country for 300 miles north of Fort Smith was all burnt off and no feed at all and to make it across was impossible to go back to Texas they could not and to go up or down the river they could not. In fact their stock was so weak an poor they could not go either way.

Well in such cases something must be done or we perish. What could be done, only one thing left and that was to sell to the pretended firm of W.C.&.C. These stock men knew I was in N.M. & knew I did not have any interest in the concern but they was compelled to do something as their cattle was dying evry day & evry night. So a traid was maid between the firm & the cattle men in this way. The firm agreed to take the cattle at certain figures per head kill & pack the cattle & ship them in the stock mens names each stock man got all that the Beef and hides his herd maid & each man went with his Beef hides & he shipped in his own name & when in market all was sold freight paid and the Beef net from $1 30 to 3.00 per Bbl hides bringing the most. Now those stock men got all of the proceeds of their Herds and the labor salt & Bbls furnished free by the so pretended firm. These stock men came back with the full proceeds of their Herds but not satisfied with that they sues on the notes and got judgment against Willburn & Clark lieving Chisum out in the cold.

Now I think you can see just how the stock men went in & just how they came out. Now right hear let me ask you do you think I would go into a business of that magnitude with men who I did not know and come into N.Mexico and stay all fall & winter with one little Herd of cattle & lieve that Business in the hands of men that knew nothing of cattle. I say does it look reasonable I lieve you to judge and in looking it over apply common sense.

As I before stated I was sude upon some of these notes before I left Texas. The Courts decided that I was no partner of the said pretended firm and was not responcible for contracts mad by them. I remained in Texas over 4 years after the maturity of these notes and by the Texas laws these notes were bared by the Statute of limitation. And after these old forged notes had been laying around for 8 years William Rosenthall of Santa Fe notoriety went to New York & other places and gathered up this commershal paper as he calls it and gets the owners to transfer them to him. So he became the owner of the notes & the plaintif in this case.

If I was to undertake to explain all of the undue advantages that has been taken in this matter it might reflect upon some of the big ones so we will just let that pass as it is too bad to tell. So we will just say William Rosenthrall complaned & because he did so I was put in jail.

Now you are told evry day that I am in debt & will not pay and I am owing Rosenthrall a large amount and have Smuggled my property in order to defraud him and that I am a bad man and aught to be kept in jail. Well as to that I will lieve for you to say. I have explained to you when & under what circumstances the notes manunfacted [sic] and how Rosenthrall came in possession of them. You now have the whole facts before you as near as I can tell them and you are left to draw your own conclusion now.

> *(Editor's note. There is no explanation why Chisum chose to continue his narrative in the form of a conversation between an imaginary interviewer whom he designated as "Reporter" and the second imaginary person whom he called "Mr. Pecos" who acted as Chisum's vindicator.)*

Reporter to Mr. Pecos. *Do you know this man John S. Chisum who did own cattle on the Pecos River*

Pecos. Yes I know him very well

How long have you known him

Some twenty five years have been very intimately acquainted with his business affairs. In fact I have been his bookeeper for ten years & am perfectly intimate with all of his business

Chisum did have a large stock of cattle at one time did he not

Yest he had a fine lot of cattle some two or the years ago

Was it his cattle that R. D. Hunter bought in 1875

Yes he sold to Hunter in 1875

Why did he sell his cattle

He was tiard of the business

How long has he been in the cattle business

Some thirty years or more

Chisum has had considerable trouble has he not since he has been in New Mexico

No Chisum is a man they cant give trouble

I hird they had him in jail last winter

Oh yes they had him in jail sometime but that did not trouble him

What did they put him in jail for

Well they had some Excicution against him that was not just & Chisum would not agree to pay them and they could not find property to levy upon so they put him in jail

You say you have been Chisum's Book keeper for ten years you aught to know whether the excicution was just or not

Yes I know all about the whole transaction and can state that the claims are not just

Who are the Plaintiff

The plaintif in one case is Van C Smith
Who is this man V C Smith
He is a son of Old Mrs. Smith and supposed to be a son of Roswell Smith he has a brother Geo Smith and is of the same Smith family you have hird of I believe they are cosins to the Jones family at any rate they are very nice men and men of Business both doing Business in Santa Fe now
What business is V C Smith ingaged in in Santa Fe
Well at this time & for a little over one year he has been ingaged in the income business
What is that you people in this western country uses frases I am not familiar with and you must allow me to ask for explinations
Well what we call income business hear is living with a good looking Mexican woman who lives in town and has a room and a clean Bed & has an income from her costimers and she divides her income with her lover This business is rather uncertain no one can make any certain calculation as to what he will get each week as it depends upon what comes in. Say some weeks $1.00 & some weeks $3 just owing to the income of the week
What business is George Smith in there?
Shortly after I got acquainted with him he got to be Post Master at a little place down on the Pecos by the name of Roswell I believe it was named in honor of Roswell Smith the same man that is suposed to be his fater. As I said he was Post Master and also in the Clearing business he discharged the duties both of Post Master & Clearing Master with such ease eligance & energy that he was mooved up higher and put in some good office in Santa Fe but I am not certain if it is in the Receivers office I saw him not long since but I did not ask him but I think it is the Receivers office
I will have to get you to explain again What do you mean by the Clearing business or Clearing Master?
The Clearing business is this Post Master to clear his Post Office of what stamps and Stampted Envelopes there is in it and buy himself a fine 60 dollar Saddle and ride it off to Santa Fe and lieving no stamps in his office is what we Western People call the Clearing business
You say you are certain Smiths claim against Chisum is not just and yet their is judgment against Chisum you say. I cant understand that can you explain

As I stated to you I was Chisums book keeper and I know his books shows V.C. Smith to be in debt to Chisum $599.00 besides a note V. C. Smith gave Chisum in some cattle trade for near $700.00. Neither the note nor the account have been paid to my certain knowledge and I have hird Chis say often that them papers alluding to Smiths notes & account was dead head property that he never did expect to get a cent of Smith as he Smith had gone through with evry thing he had

If that be a correct statement of facts how do you think Smith came to sue Chisum?

I can only give you my honest opinion about the whole affair and that is this Smith in the first place is in debt a great deal about Santa Fe and his creditors were satisfied they never would get any thing out of Smith So I think they put him up to sue Chisum at Santa Fe a distance of 300 miles from Chisums Ranch & knowing Chisum was from home more than one half of his time & that it would be very uncertain as to whether Chisum Could attend Court or not & as they had nothing to loose so they was on the safe side

Where was Chisum at the time judgment was rendered against him at Santa Fe

Chisum at that time was at or near Elpasso in Old Mexico after a Herd of cattle that had been stolen from the Pecos River

Tell me if there is such a thing as a Santa Fe ring and if so who composes it.

I know it is said by many of the citizens that there is a Ring at Santa Fe but as the Govenor said in his last message there was no ring and I am of his opinion. If there was a ring there would some show for the people as a Ring is not solid and there would be some show to get through it, or to get on the outside or inside of it but the thing they have got there is perfectly solid it cannot be penetrated from neither side or end and it is perfectly hard & solid and when this solid substance strikes a citizen it goes right through him and lieves him in such a condition that he never recovers from it. It is so powerful that it dont only ruin citizens but sometimes it strikes whole counties. This substance whatever it is struck and killed a good Methodist preacher up in my old county of Colfax. Some of the citizens of that county made some remark about it & this same something then struck the whole county of Colfax & set it clear over the mountain into Mora County. And it took the whole of our Legislature two years to get it back into its old place and I would not be surprised if ever they hit it again they knock it clear into Colorado. So you can see that is worse than any Ring. No Ring could do that you know and the Govenor lives right their in Santa Fe and he knowes there is no Ring there.

You then give it as your opinion that there is no such thing as a Ring in Santa Fe

Yes I am confident there is no Ring there

What would you call that solid substance you spoke of as being so dangerous?

It is what we call a Substance of light. Santa Fe is The City of Light and that is what furnishes light for the whole city and for our legislators. And for all of our County officers all over the Territory and at times it reflects its light upon certain objects. It at one time reflected its light upon Grant County and the light was so dazzleing to the Eyes of the citizens that they prayed to be spaired from this great light and be attached to Arizona

Did Grant County attach herself to Arizona

No this great light said unto Grant County Though shalt not go away. Though Shalt Stay and be reflected upon as we reflect upon others

Is Smith the only plaintiff against Chisum in these troubles

Oh no there are 6 or 8 plaintiffs in all I believe

I would be glad you would go on and give me all the names of the plaintifs and as full statements as you can about the whole matter to tell you the truth I am a reporter for a large Publishing Company and ever since I got into the Terrytory I have heard Chisum spoken of in various ways and I would be glad to get all the information I can and as correct as possible. It appears from all I can find out this hole affair is somewhat Romantic and you appear to be better posted in this matter than evry other Person I have met

I suppose I know more about these matters than any other Person as I said before I have known Chisum for a long time & have been his book keeper for several years & owing to that fact Chisum makes me acquainted with all of his business transactions and in speaking of who are the plaintifs against Chisum — I would state that R H Tompkins of Santa Fe is one

Is he a plaintif for a large amount

No not over fifteen hundred dollars I dont think

Can you explain upon what grounds he Tompkins is plaintif
Yes I have hird Chisum explain. It is in this way. It appears that
Rosenthrall sued Chisum on some forged notes that were 8 years
old and had sude him in Santa Fe some 300 miles from where
Chisum lived and Rosenthrolls aim was to get judgment by defalt
and had instructed the Sheriff of the county in which Chisum lived
not to serve the notice on Chisum until just five days before Court
in Santa Fe that being the law. Five days notis was good & the
Sheriff of the county having been paid extry to follow these instructions did get servis on Chisum just as instructed and Chisum knowing
he could not possibly get their in time for the Court he gave a man
fifty dollars to carry a telegram 165 miles to the nearest office and
the dispatch was to this man Tompkins to have the case continued
if possible. In a few hours after this dispatch left Chisum found out
that the man Rosenthrall had sent to receive the papers from our
Sheriff would be detained by heavy rains & would fail beyond a
doubt to get the Sheriffs return to Santa Fe in time for Court & knowing no other evidence except the Sheriffs return with his signature
thereon was evidence in Court of Servis. So in an hour or so after
the first dispatch left Chisum started the second one in which he said
to Thompkins dont let the case be tride they have no service according to law. If they contend they have force them to show it — both
dispatches reached Tompkins in due time
This man Thompkins is a lawyer then is he
Well he has licesens to appear before the Courts but is what we call
a reflector
*You must explain again I cant understand what you mean by a
Reflector*
Give me time and I will You see the Court at Santa Fe met and . . .
[illegible] no legal servis on Chisum, and the oposite Atty of which
they were 4 or 5 contendid for a trial. Thompkins rose and said
I ask for a continuance in that case as you have no servis on the
defendant. Oposite council contendid they did. Thompkins called
on them to show it, They tride & russeled among their paper but
failed could show none & had none & Thompkins knew it. But
instead of letting the case put its self off he Reflected and made a
compromise with the other Attys on the opposite side and in that
compromise he compromised two months of Chisums rights away
in the compromise he agreed that Chisum should file his answer

two months before the next Court when the law its self gave Chisum until the first day of the Court to file his answer. So you see he Reflected and forced Chisum to show his hand two months before the law compelled him. So by his Reflecting he forced Chisum to show them his hand two months before the law compelled him to. So you see he was reflecting for the other side as all reflectors do in this Territory. Now you know what we call Reflectors in this country *Is it for his servises at that time that he is now Plaintif against Chisum* No after Court at Santa Fe was over he Thompkins wrote to Chisum that after a long hard fight he got the case continued. Chisum then wrote to Thompkins to know of him what he owed him for his servises. Thompkins then wrote to Chisum that he considered himself imployed in the case and that he would give the case his attention for $2,800.00 Chisum wrote to Thompkins & said I am not able to imploy you. I will have to get a cheaper lawyer. Thompkins writes back No I am not going to be discharged at this stage of the case saying his fee was not too much & also saying to Chisum You are sude for $28,000. Chisum writes back and sayes if you will examine the papers you will find I am sude for $18,000 on forged notes 8 years old. Thompkins writes back that I have examined the papers and find I am correct it is $28,000, and in my compromise with the opposite attys I agreed that you should file your answer by the first of December. And Court was to set in Feby following. By this time Chisum became disgusted and said to me that a man that could not figure up the amount another man sude for and would compromise two months of his rights away certainly could not be much of a lawyer and that he did not intend to imploy him or have any thing more to do with him. So things passed on until in November Chisum went to the City of Light or Santa Fe and there he saw Mr. Thomp. After the usual compliments was passed Thompkins said to Chisum you were right about the amount you are sude for. I have just been and examined the papers again and find you were right and now I will put the fee say at $2,000. Chisum sayes Now Thompkins you must excuse me I cant imploy you in this case and I would be glad if you would tell me what I owe you.

Thompkins sayes No I am in the case now and cant be got shut of in that way. Chisum then sayes Mr Thompkins it is unpleasant for me to tell you while I regard you as a nice man still you must allow me to tell you that I dont regard you as a lawyer and I dont want you & I am not going to have you Now what I want is this. I want no trouble but don't want you as a lawyer. Now tell me what you will take to let me and my business alone. Thompkins said I will take $500. Chisum said I will not pay that amount to get shut of you. Well said Thompkins what will you give. Chisum said I will give you $100 if you will let me and my busins alone from this on. Thompkins said I will take it & Chisum paid him. So the matter ended & Chisum supposed he had got [rid] of the Reflector but not so.

Two years after that Chisum got a letter from Thompkins Stating that he Thompkins had had another long hard fight in this same case of Rosenthralls and that on part of the notes they got judgment and a portion they had failed. Now I want you to send me $1,000 — To this Chisum made no reply as he Chisum had had no Correspondence with Thompkins since he had bought his piece from Thompkins & had paid his $100

What time was this $100 paid by Chisum too Thompkins and did Chisum take Thompkins receipt for the same?

Chisum paid the $100 in November 1875 and took his Receipt for the same.

What steps has Thompkins taken to collect this last amt he claims off of Chisum

Well as near as I can tell you this was his proceedings against Chisum In December 1877 Chisum started to St Louis on some business and got to Las Vegas on the night of the 24th of December 1877 and upon arrival hear found that Mr. T. B. Catron of the City of Light and he being one of the greater Illuminable lights of the whole City had Telegraphed hear to know if Chisum & McSween had passed Las Vegas yet. This Telegram was sent to one of the Small lights of Las Vegas. The Small light reflected & said no. So all was quiet in the great City of Light. But that night Chisum & McSween arrived and the little light reflected and said they are hear. So on the night of the 25th of December the Great light reflected to the Sheriff . . . and said unto him Reflect and hold McSween until I can get a warrant against him.

The Sheriff understood his mission & reflected upon McSween & said unto him Though Shalt not leave this City for the Great light has reflected upon me and in command of that Great light I hereby command you not to leave this City If you do I will reflect. Chisum was traveling in company with McSween and his lady all going to St. Louis on business and of course in a hurry as all travailers are So McSween & his lady & Chisum waited 48 hours and no warrant came for the arrest either of Chisum or McSween and by this time all hands were getting impatient as they were anxious to pursue their journey. But still they did not want to act hastily in the matter and they saw that there was another light acting in concert with the Great light of Santa Fe. This little light . . . could Reflect but when he Reflected it was something like a lightning bug but he would strain himself & spread his wings and Reflect the best he could but still his light was very dim.

At any rate he was called in consultation and the Sheriff . . . present. The matter talked up in the presence of the Sheriff and the aforesaid little light . . . and the Sheriff . . . said to Chisum and McSween, I have helt you hear for 48 hours and now if I dont get a warrant or some papers by which I can hold you legally within 15 minutes I will release you and you can go thy way rejoicing. He the Sheriff . . . had just Reflected over the Telegraph wires to the Great light and said unto the Great light Reflect again for I cannot hold them without papers any longer. So this Great light Reflected back to the Sheriff aforesaid and also to other lights all over the City of Las Vegas and said unto them Still hold them we will send papers when we get them. Chisum & McSween said unto the Sheriff aforesaid you are wrong in trying to hold us without papers and we feel we have now waited long enough and why is it you still wish to hold us The Sheriff said using his own language that the Ring at Santa Fe Telegraphs to me to hold you and I must obey.

Chisum & McSween then called all of the legal light of Las Vegas together and they being familiar with our Situation all agreed that we had been detained long enough upon a simple Telegram and advised us to go on our journey. And the little light . . . more particularly advised them to go and pay no attention to the Sheriff and his Telegrams that for them to do otherwise was foolish. So in accordance with our feelings and advice of all the legal lights of Las Vegas they hitched up and started for St Louis.

After going some half mile they were overtaken by the Sheriff and stopped on the public highway he the Sheriff having with him

from 30 to 50 of the poor native . . . with him. Some armed with
pistols some with rocks & some with clubs all making one desperate
charge upon them and surrounded the ambulanch they were traveling in.

Chisum was jerked out head foremost & fell upon his face on
the hard road and siezed by the throat . . . he still helt his grip until
Chisum said to the Sheriff Will you please be so kind as to loosen
the grip of this . . . cur The Sheriff spoke and the cur loosed his holt
so Chisum breathed once more the fresh air of New Mexico they
brag so much of.

McSween also was jerked out of the ambulanch and drug off by
a lot of the gang & Mrs McSween left siting all alone crying in the
ambulanch without a driver or even a protector. The Sheriff and his
possey very much excited McSween was somewhat confused Chisum
laughing and cool. He looked the gang over and noticest one
. . . that had on a clean shirt & had just arrived at the scene
of excitement. Chisum asked him if he would be kind enough to drive
Mrs McSween to the Hotel which he consented and drove her there.
Chisum and McSween were then marched to the Court house
McSween put in jailors room & Chisum in the Court house and
arrested under a charge sworn out by the Sheriff of resisting the
Sheriff of San Magil [Miguel] County in the discharge of his duties
as Sheriff aforesaid. This was about 12 o'clock on the 28th of January 1878. [December, 1877?] The Sheriff then asked Chisum if he
would give Bond for his appearance at 3 o'clock that day or if not
he would go to jail. Chisum give bond and at 3 o'clock the Court
met & Chisum present.

The court was composed of a large fine looking man wraped
in a Mexican Blanket. . . . Chisum said to the Court he would be glad
to have McSween and Mrs. McSween summonds as witnesses in
behalf of the defendant. Chisum had two objects in making this
request of the Court, one was he wanted McSween as a witness but
his main object was to get McSween before the Court to defend him.
Knowing the . . . family so well that he knew if he asked the Court
to let McSween defend him he would be told by the Court that
McSween was a prisoner and could not appear as his Counsel hence
Chisum had him summonds as a witness. When McSween got through
Testifying as a witness he then handed the Court his professional
card as a lawyer authorized to practice in all of the Courts of the

Terrytory. Then the Sheriff got up and objected to McSween defending Chisum and made quite a lengthy speech saying he was a prisoner and should not be allowed to plead law before that Honorable Court. So you see Chisum was right in his conjectures, but the Court having his mind made up as to his dicision he said the Court will honor McSweens argument in this case and nodded to the Sheriff to take his seat.

McSween went on to read the law and showed when a Sheriff was in the discharge of his duties, and when he went beyond what his duties were as Sheriff, and also said a Warrant or writ with the Seal of the Court was a garante to the Sheriff to arrest the person or persons named in the writ or warrant and without such writ or warrant the Sheriff had no right to go upon the public highway and arrest a man. Nay, he had no more right than any citizen had. He admitted it was a custom and a good one to arrest and hold a person by Telegraph for a reasonable time and that 48 hours was certainly a reasonable time. McSween and Mrs. McSween both testified that they were both in the Ambulanch with Chisum and that Chisum made no resistance whatever.

During the time Mr. and Mrs McSween were Testifying before the Court and during the time McSween was addressing the Court as an Atty. the Court set in his large easy chair with his abdomen projecting in front with his head laid back over his shoulders and his eyes closed and his mouth open. When McSween took his seat Chisum pinched him and said you might as well write the bond, for the Court is bound in spite of the law to reflect.

The next Atty that appeared before the Court was for the Terrytory. A Mr. Morrison who by the by was the same little light . . . heretofore alluded to, he was the same light that was in consultation with Chisum, McSween and the Sheriff and is the same light that advised them to go and not be held longer by telegrams and they took his advice and started and soon they were overpowered by a set of ignorant and blood thirsty Mexicans.

He then appeared for the Terrytory and made 4 long speeches against them and he said in the closing of the 4th speach May it please the Court you know where I stand you know what great Responsibilities are now wresting upon my Sholders as a light giver of this Terrytory. It is uslis for me to tell you what your duty is you know it and now discharge it but a Bond must be required of Chisum.

The Court said Chisum's bond is $500. I know the Bond will not be sustained in the District Court but Situated as I am I am bound to require a Bond and then he Reflected and the Court dismissed. This was at 12 o'clock at night.

Did Chisum give Bond

Yes he gave the Bond that night so he told me

What became of McSween

That night a warrant came for his arrest

What was the charge in the warrant?

He was charged of the imbezzlement of Ten Thousand dollars in money belonging to the Fritz Estate

That is a very cerious charge Do you know whether he is guilty of the charge or not

. . . he was . . . guilty [not completely legible]

Who swor out the warrant against McSween?

A woman by the name of Mrs Showland [Scholand]

Who is she?

She is a sister of Col. Fritz and is one of the heirs of the Fritz Estate.

Upon what grounds did She swear out the warrant

Well I am not so well posted about that matter but hear is the way I understand that business from McSween. Col Fritz Estate was entitled to $10,000 Insurance polocy and it appears that the polocy money could not be collected. L G Murphy the surviving partner of Col Fritz and the Administrater and Administratrix had been trying for two years and had failed to collect it and the Administrater & Administratrix Imployed McSween & gave him a power of Atty to collect said polocy. McSween went on to New York in the winter of 1877 and last August the money was paid. Since McSween received the money he has paid over some 2/3 of the amount so collected and the balance of the money now in his hands is due to Heirs in Germany & McSween is ordered by the German Consil to hold the money for said Heirs until further orders from him and it appears that L.G. Murphy the Surviving partner of Fritz is now indebted very largely to indebt to [sic] the Fritz Estate and being very hard pressed for money to pay some of his friends at Santa Fe who by the by composes the greater portion of the great Territorial Light concluded as McSween had started with his lady to St. Louis that it would be a good time to Black Mail McSween out of the money due the Heirs in Germany.

McSween feeling it his duty to protect those he represented

suffered himself imprisoned and after he had suffered in the Cold Dungeon 4 day & nights was then let out and told if he would pay over the money he could go on to St Louis. McSween refused to Compromise saying he was guilty or not guilty. And after being kept at Las Vegas some 8 or 10 day he was carried before Judge Bristol for an Examination.

Why did not McSween give Bond and not lay in jail
The Great light at Santa Fe had Reflected upon the Sheriff and said to put him in jail and take no Bond.

What became of Chisum I have lost sight of him
Immediately after his Trial alluded to The Sheriff said to him I have an Execution against you and in favor of Grizelachowshie. Chisum said I am not prepared to pay it now. The Sheriff said you must point out property so I can levy upon it. Chisum said I have no property here to point out to you. The Sheriff said I will have to put you in jail and at the same time showed Chisum law that was passed in 1846 but Repealed shortly after its passage. The law refered to was if a person was in debt and could not pay and refused to Render a Schedule of his property they could imprison him five days. At the time of his showing Chisum this venerable law Chisum noticed a letter in his hand from one of the Legal lights of Santa Fe and in said letter was the no. of the page containing this venerable law of 1846. The Great Light was Reflecting upon the little light and show-ing him what page to turn to find the good but venerable law of 1846.

Chisum says to the Sheriff I can make out a skedule of what I have. Sheriff agreed. Chisum made Skedule. The Sheriff took the Skedule and next day he Reflected back to the Great Light at Santa Fe and when the Report of the Skedule reached the City of Light there was a great excitement and gathering of all of the great lights and Small light and . . . seeing there was no Long Horns grazing upon the Skedule Reflect back to the Sheriff and said this Skedule is not enough and put Chisum in jail and take no Bond and the Sheriff upon recieving this instruction went Strait into the Multitude then assembled at Las Vegas and took one of his deciples whose Sir name is Richard Dunn and went Strait way in the Tabernicle of Theodore Wagoner and said I am commanded by the Great Light of the City of Light to place you in prison and no Bond allowed you. Chisum arose and went Strait to the Prison and was locked up followed by the Sheriff and his deciple.

After spending two days and nights in the Dungeon Chisum

was ordered out into the Clerk's office and command by the Sheriff to Render another Skedule saying the one that had been Rendered was not large enough. Chisum said I Rendered all I had and you have had me locked up ever since and I have not accumolated anything more and I cannot Render any thing different from the one you have. So Chisum was placed back again in the Dungeon.

After Chisum had been kept in the Dungeon 4 days and nights & yet no charge of any kind whatever and no Bond allowed him he wrote to Govener Axtel and Stated the Situation he was placed in that he was helt Arbitarirly that he was not charged as having Committed any Crime whatever. And he would most Respectifully ask his Excelency to please Examine into his detention in the Las Vegas jail. To which the Govener replied and said I cannot parden you You have the Right of Haibes Corbus.

Chisum was permitted the next day to go to his hotel but a gard with him & over him and after being there a day or two in that Situation one evening the Sheriff served a Capias upon Chisum which was the first paper that had been served upon him altho he had been in jail then about 6 or 7 days. This Capias had been swoorn out by the Old Reflector R. H. Thompkins for $1,500 his servies. *Let me interupt for one moment is this the same R. H. Thompkins that Chisum gave the $100 to in order to get shut of?*
The very same Old Reflector that Chisum bought his peace from but you see he is hard up and is now anxious to Reflect upon Something and knowing that Chisum had gave him $100 he thought by Reflecting he might get another $100 and so he Reflected but as I said before this Capias was served on Chisum just at night and Chisum asked the Sheriff what was the amount of the Bond he required & the Sheriff said $3,000 but I will be in in the morning & we will fix the Bond. Next morning Chisum had the Bond wrote but the Sheriff never made his appearance but still Chisum was helt a prisoner. Things stood for two days in this shape but after that elapse of time the Sheriff Reappeared and served an injunction and a Rit of Rex wherein R. H. Thompkins, Wm Rosenthrall, V. C. Smith, Grezelchowskie, Wm Babb & J. Y. Pey & W. W. Lewis were plaintifs and a Bond required of Chisum in the sum of $25,000 or as the Judge of the first District said lock him up Chisum being unable to give Bond was locked up in Las Vegas jail.
I now understand the Thompkins case against Chisum and also

V. C. Smith's. I also have a tolerable correct idea of this man Rosen-
thrall but there is several plaintifs that you have not explained why
they are plaintiffs. Are you also familiar with their cases
Yes I am very familiar with all of his cases and can explain them
fully to your satisfaction but it will take considerable time.
Time is no object I want the full history.
I will now Explain to you why Grzeelachwskie is plaintiff but in
order to do so I will have to back to 1873. At that time there was a
cattle firm of the Stile of Reed Brothers & Co and said firm borrowed
$5,000 out of the second national Bank at Santa Fe. Chisum, Grzel-
achowskie and Peat Maxwell were indorcees on the note. Shortly
after Reed Br. & Co. gave this note to the Bank all of their cattle &
other property was attached by a worthles party by the name of
Buck & Sam Stanton & all of said firms property was seased and helt
by the Sheriff of Lincoln County and the attachment having been
swoorn out in Lincoln County and the firm and their propeity all
being and residing in Don Ana County, Chisum took the ground
that the attachment was void. Chisum proposed to Capt. Ford who
was then present & Representing Grzelachowskie that for him to
go and say to Chauske that the attachment was of no effect and
to say to Chauskie that Chisum now proposes for him and Chauskie
to make the Bond required by the Sheriff of Lincoln County for
$30,000 and by doing that they could get the property out of the
hands of the Sheriff & get it into their own hands & thereby make
themselves safe.

Reed Bro. & Co. was indebted to Chouskie 3,700 over and
above the note in Bank and also was due and owing Chisum 4,800
in addition to the amount of $5,000 he had indorced for at the Bank.

Ford makes known Chisum's proposition to Chauskie but
Chauskie said it was a large Bond & that he would not help make it
that was too large a risk. Chisum then had no one the stand by
him & knowing the attachment would not be sustained and also
knowing if the property remained in the hands of the Sheriff for any
length of time would be consumed in the way of expensis & would
be of no benefit to any of Reed Br & Co creditors in view of all
these things he himself made the Bond for the $20,000 and took
the cattle & other property out of the hands of the Sheriff and at
the same time he took from Reed Bro & Co a Bill of Sale to himself
of the property so repleved by him. This was in July 1873. Chisum

at the same time having claims enough against Reed Br & Co to cover said property but instead of his applying the property or the proceeds to his own use, not turning the cattle into his own herd and the horses into his own cavay and as he could & should have done. But instead of that Chisum kept said property in as safe place as possible entirely Seperate from his other property at the same time keeping a Suffient number of good & reliable men in charge of said property. And furnishing them provisions of evry kind and paying the men their wages all out of his own pocket. This he done from July 1873 until in January 1874 seven months in all During this time the attachment had been tride and not sustained and the property so attached was no longer subject to the order of the Court & Chisum released from the obligation of the $20,000 Bond. The property released in the possession of Chisum and he holding a Bill of Sale of the same. And also as before stated Reed Br & Co was owing him $4,800.

Now this is the portion of the narrative he says he is ashamed to tell to the public but so it is and it all truth and must be stated. Now instead of Chisums turning that property into his own herd and giving Reed Br & Co credit for the same as they were willing he should and applying it to the payment of his own debt this Chisum did not do. *Why did not Chisum do that. It certainly would have been nothing but fair and right and a duty he owed to himself. Chouskie certainly could not have expected any portion of it after refusing to help Chisum Bond the property out of the hands of the Sheriff.*
That was the advise I gave Chisum at the time. Chisum said yes as I had to Bond the property out of the hands of the Sheriff myself I would be perfectly justifiable in applying it to my own debt but that is all the property Reed Bro & Co has in this Terrytory and I think it would look a little more gentlemanly to divide it amongst their Creditors and besides this was evry thing Reed Br & Co had and Chisum thought it but right for them to have something left them to live upon as they had large families to support and not even a milch cow left them to give them milk.

So Chisum as before stated sent the Herd so attached to Reed Bro & Co up to Chouskies ranch some 140 miles from where the cattle was being helt and as they passed Chisum's ranch going to Chouskies Ranch Chisum cut out 58 head of the cattle and Branded them in his own Brand and turned them loose in his Range with his other cattle. These head about paying Chisum his expencis on the cattle since he had taken them out of the hands of the Sheriff.

Chisum then instructed the men in charge of the cattle to take the remainder of the cattle about 580 head to Chouskies Ranch and turn over to him at the then market price $3,700 worth of the cattle and to see that the cattle so turned over were Branded in Chouskies Brand and the remainder of the cattle left after paying Chouskie & not having his Brand upon them which was 216 head. And to tell Chauskie to let the remainder run there with those turned over to him until Spring & subject them to Chisum's order. All of which Chouskie agreed to and the 216 head left in Chauskie's possession in that way & with that understanding, he Chauskie having received & Branded the $3,700 worth which had paid him in full of all demands he had against Reed Br & Co and that amount of cattle so received was then & there put in Chauskie's Brand & the 216 was not to be Branded but helt until Spring and then subject to the order of Chisum.

Chauskie now was paid a debt of $3,700 that he never could have collected had it not bin for Chisum & Chisum himself was unpaid. You see the kindness & friendship Chisum showed Chouskie. The next Spring Chisum sent men & an order to Chauskie for the 216 head of cattle left as stated before, but Chauskie refused to send them.

Upon what grounds did he Chauskie refuse to send Chisum the cattle?

Chouskie refused saying some of the cattle he had Branded had been stolen by the Mexicans, some had died, and some had rambled off and upon the whole he did not think he had any more than what he had paid for and he would keep what he had and so he did and never has paid for them yet.

Is that possible. He must be a very strange man. Who is he and what is his occupation and what to you know about him?

To begin with I will say he is a Polander by birth and a Merchant by profession and by the by is a very nice genteel man, very polite and nice in his manners and is well educated. In fact he was educated for the Preast Hood.

Did he ever serve in the capacity of a Preast in this country?

Oh yes he served in that capacity here for a long while.

Is he now a Preast

No not now he was expelled from that Honorable position Several years ago.

For what was he expelled for

They tell me that he had too many young black eyed girls on his program and for his great preference for them was cast a side & he went into the Mercantile business.

Is he a married man

No he has no legitimate wife.

Has he never been married.

No I think not.

He has no children then

Yes he has several but they are Ililitigemate

How Old is Mr. Chauski now?

About 65 years I would suppose

You have not as yet explained to me how he Chauskie became plaintif against Chisum in this case. If I recollect rightly you spoke about a $5,000 note given to the 2nd National Bank at Santa Fe.

Yes a note was given by Reed Bro & Co for $5,000 and Chowskie Pete Maxwell & Chisum all indorced the note and Reed Br & Co failed to pay the note and the Indorcees confessed judgment on the note. By this time the note had been in the Bank a year or over. Chisum paid on the note $2,750 and instructed the Bank to Collect the remainder of the note off of Chauskie and so they did. Then Chauske sude Chisum for the amount he Chauskie paid & got judgment for the same and is now plaintiff for the same.

*   *   *   *   *

(Cetera desunt)

This justification that Uncle John penned while he was in jail at Las Vegas remains incomplete, possibly because of his release from custody shortly afterwards. It would be interesting to know how this came about, but I fear all information on that point is lost, just as the world will never know from Uncle John's pen the occasion why the other plaintiffs in the group of six or eight alluded to become among the gadflies the parties higher up were using to harass the cattle king of the Pecos Valley. One thing is certain, however: Uncle John fronted the situation with his usual coolness and even temper. He wrote in his defense, "Chisum is a man they cannot worry," and that was literally true. Convincing evidence of the spirit in which he took the whole affair can be seen in a few letters which he wrote during his stay in the Las Vegas jail to his friends in the infant town of Roswell, especially to Ash Upson.

These letters evidence his abiding belief in the integrity of his cause and his determination to let time render the right verdict. The sense of humor which manifests itself in this correspondence was a helpful shield with which to withstand the assaults of his enemies; his pose as a senator tending the affairs of his constituents is an especially delightful expression of his disdain for his imprisonment. Evidently Uncle Ash Upson had written Uncle John sympathetically, possibly referring to the fact that this martyrdom he was now undergoing might be a stepping stone to political office, perhaps a senatorship. This led to an ironic reply from Uncle John which is very revealing of his general mood.

Las Vegas, Jan. 21st, 1878

Friend A. M. Upson

My dear sir
As a Senator from your district I must snatch a few moments to say a few words to you one of my most dear friends. Although, Ash, you was not a supporter of mine in the last great political struggle I had in your District, and while I cannot now award any credit to you for the high and honorable position that I now occupy, still I hope my clear, clean record will be such that at the next general election I will merit and receive your hearty and welcome support. Now, Friend Ash, I hope you will see from this letter that I am not a man to bear malice. No! Far from it. It is true you fought me long and hard, but, knowing as I do, that you did it upon fair, square principles, today I can extend the right hand of friendship — just as much so as though you had extended to me all the support and influence you possessed. It is a great pride for me to look back upon my past life and see that my course has been onward and upward, and today I am as the giant oak waving its majestic head far above the shrubs and underbrush of the common forest. And today, my Friend Ash, I am permitted to enjoy blessings that are only bestowed upon the unfortunate portion of mankind.

I am boarding at the Wagoner's Hotel, but have my meals brought to my rooms, as most Senators do, you know, Friend Upson. It is unpleasant for a Senator to be ushered into the dining room of a hotel in these large cities. The tramp of the waiters, the clashing of knives, forks, spoons, and dishes is well calculated to confuse and disturb the brains of a Senator. And taking this view of the matter, I take my meals in my own private room.

I could tell you of the many responsibilities that are resting upon the shoulders of a Senator, but it is no use. You are a public man and know all these things. Just suffice it to say the Senator's brain should be kept cool and clear. This Terrytory being very large, it was thought best to establish a branch house in this place, which will explain to you why I am here. As we have no dailies here now, I cannot post you as to what is going on in Santa Fe.

The bond in the Chisum case was before the House yesterday. It passed both houses, but was vetoed by the Governor (the Sheriff); so it is now a settled fact that Chisum will hold his seat until the full term expires which is about the middle of March. So if you should want anything put through just let me know. I am here to represent you and your people.

Tell Jacob Harris to take good care of Mrs. Harris and the Harris children. Give Mr. and Mrs. [Heiskell] Jones and all the little Joneses my regards.

It is natural for us all to think at times that we are badly treated and sometimes I think I am treated a little wrong but I reckon not. The good people of this country certainly would not do wrong; so I will just conclude all is right and be happy.

Now, my Friend Ash, you see I have a long session before me, and it may be that I may never see you again and if I should not, let me say to you that I hope your course may be upward and onward as it always has been and when you are done with the turmoil of this life and have gone down into the grave, may your life here have been such that your gray hairs sink into the grave crowned with honor and success. And may the little Upsons gather around the grave and point the finger of pride and say, "This is the resting place of my one affectionate papa." Write.

J. S. Chisum

The second letter refers to a matter which may have been a contributing cause in the persecution that the Generalisimo stirred up. Marion Turner evidently had possession of some place that the Generalisimo held a mortgage upon and hoped to secure for himself, and Uncle John confessed he was responsible for Marion Turner being on the place.

Las Vegas, January 28, 1878

To M.A. Upson, Marion Turner, and J.P. Jones [James (Jim) Jones]

Dear Friends

As my writing material is scarce I will have to ask you to be content with a family letter. I wrote Friend Upson a few days ago. Today I received your three letters in one envelope, and in answer will say I am not sentimental and not afraid of my friends becoming lukewarm or going back on me, for my conscience is clear. I have committed no crime. I have done nothing to cause a friend to go back on me at a time when I am struggling for my own right and not interfering with any one person or true friends. I have nothing to claim for Chisum. I can only refer you to my past conduct. I am willing to be judged by that. We all owe duties to one another and we should not shrink from those duties because trouble comes up, for a man that will shrink from his obligations is not worthy of the name of a man. I owe certain duties and obligations to my just creditors in Texas and those obligations I have fulfilled, and for so doing I am today in prison. Let it be so; I am willing to suffer (if you should call it suffering). I would rather stay here for five years than to have wronged them. My conscience tells me I have done right; and I can, as I do daily, look them in the face and tell them to punish me if they can. I ask you no difference. It's as you say; you can do me no good. No one can now. A bond of $25,000 was required of me. I made bond for $82,000, but they still hold me by force, not by law. One man cannot ship them but I think I can worry them to death.

Now, Marion, the place you hold was mortgaged to the Generalisimo by V.C. Smith from what I can find out. Think I was instrumental in your going on the place, and I suppose he is now applying the lash to me for it. Now what I want you to do is to hold the place until Gabriel blows his horn. That is my pluck, and I hope you have some about you, and if so, hold to the ship and let them apply the lash to me. I can stand it. *Don't you flinch*. Their only hope now is to punish me until I will give them something, but they can go to hell for me. They are now trying to trap me and get me to Santa Fe for a trial, but I have trapped too many mavericks to go in the corral they have for me.

I am my own lawyer and counselor. I have a cat that is faithful. It never leaves my room and is full of fun and I have a fiddle and am well fed and don't ask them any odds. If at any time I should conclude any of you could do me any good I would not hesitate one moment in calling on you for any favor in your power, believing as I do that you are true friends.

My kindest regards to all. I am your humble servant,

Yours as ever,
John S. Chisum.

P.S.

I hope peace and harmony will prevail through the neighbors. I will be down the 1st of April as fresh as a rose and as bold as a hollyhock. So fret not about me. I am in the land of Nod, surrounded by the Jews, and the Gentiles are afraid to speak.

Yours,
J.S.C.

A.M. Upson,

Las Vegas, Jany. 28th, 1878

My Dear Friend

I write as events take place. I am still in the Senate. This has been an exciting day in the House. Chisum has another bond for $40,000 now before the House of Lords. (Sheriff and _____). This bond is in strict conformity to the law in every respect and is at this time up for consideration. This is now 8 o'clock at night. Leverson, of Colorado, who is the maker of the bond, is at this time before the House of Lords, urging the acceptance of the bond. Still later Leverson came in. Bond not accepted. So I am still elected for another term, but I let them rip — I can stand it. I am satisfied now they will not accept any bond that can be made. I will be dragged from here to Santa Fe in about two weeks, and I suppose put in prison their until after Court and then perhaps brought back here or perhaps kept their until just in time for Court here. Can't tell now and don't care, as all jails are good and no difference to me. But such a thing might be possible that they might carry this thing far enough after a while. I am looking on very coolly and am anxious to see how far they will go. My regards to all.

I am as ever,
Yours,
J.S. Chisum

Las Vegas, January 31st, 1878

Dear Ash

It was with pleasure I read your lengthy and interesting letter of Jany. 27th. Knowing, my friend, as you do my great press of business, you will understand it is impossible for me to address you at length. If I took time to do so, I would not be doing my constituents justice. And to them I owe all. I must stand by them. It is my great aim and purpose while I serve the people in this capacity to leave behind me as clear, clean record as possible, as I do not now think that I ever will serve them again in this capacity since I find the many heavy responsibilities, arduous duties that devolve upon a Senator, are now fast weighting me down. And moreover, my friend, I always did believe in rotation in office of profit or honor. And why should I at my age and station of life still cling to the busy hum and buzz of political life?

My friend, no one but a Senator knows the many troubles and trials a Senator has to contend with. The Resumption Bill, the Silver Bill, and the Green Back Cause, and a thousand other bills all coming upon and crowding the Senator's brain until his head fairly echoes with anxiety to accomplish what he thinks is to be the interest of the constituents. He is not like the farmer, the stockman, or the mechanic who occupy a middle station in life, going about through the day discharging the various duties assigned to him with ease and pleasure and at night and noon returning to his humble cottage and their to be met and greeted with the pleasant smile from his bosom friend. And Ash, that is not all. Only think of the little ones gathering around to make the happiness so great that even this Senator's pen fails to describe it. Oh! my friend Ash, listen to me and never become a Senator.

As I said, I have no anxiety in serving the second term. Why should I? Is there not a great number of young men now in the Valleys of the Pecos possessing Congress heads, who should be permitted to partake of the great honors of the world? Have I not passed through all the vicissitudes of life? Was I not in my young days tossed upon the wild frontier of Texas and from the early date 1837 until 1872, did I not struggle with the Indians, thieves, mustangs and bull mavericks and did I not come out conqueror? And in 1872, did I not come to this Terrytory, still struggling with Indians, thieves, and bull mavericks, the most dangerous animal that now runs on the plains? Still with all these troubles to contend with, did I not have an eye open to honor and fame?

Am I not standing today upon the very pinnacle of fame? And I say, my friend, Ash, is this not enough? What more should I crave? Taking this view of the matter, I hope my constituents will excuse me from serving the second term.

Some excitement in the House today. A Mr. Chosky who lives between here and the City of Light, or perhaps you know it better by the name of Santa Fe. He is a Dutchman and is an old settler of 20 years. He came and took his seat in the Lower House. He killed a Mexican. He said it was an accident and I suppose it was.

The sheriff took a fright last night came to the conclusion that a big lot of my friends were going to take me out of jail and he sent in his Inaugural Address to the Speaker of the House. He recommends that no person go in to see Chisum unless written permission from his Excellency is given and that no letters come in or go out without being read by his Excellency. He, it appears, expects to be attacked any moment and has run the quarantine. He is a full blood and can't neither read nor speak English. Well, as my time is precious, I will close. My regards to all the family, Marion included.

I am yours as ever,
J.S. Chisum.

30

A Cattle King's Business

ONE OF THE THINGS of interest to the present generation is the various activities of a man like John S. Chisum operating a large-scale cattle business in the old trail-driving days. Fortunately, an old cash book, covering the years 1875 and following, throws light on this matter. This book, in Uncle John's handwriting, is suggestive of the simplicity with which he kept a record of his business. Hardly more than a memorandum book, yet it contains his own private digest of money transactions running into the hundreds of thousands of dollars. Though he was not the sort of man to trust to his memory in financial matters, at the same time he was not one to cumber himself with elaborate records of various affairs. The entries in this book bear witness to this: they are always for lump sums and rather large amounts; there is not much attempt at keeping track of things through itemized statements.

Such an attitude was altogether in keeping with the spirit of these old cattlemen. They conducted business on what might seem to a modern businessman a very free and easy plan. Those old timers trusted their fellow cattlemen, and among them a man's word was as good as his note of hand. Banks were so rare as to be practically nonexistent, and their services were dispensed with. Most of these men kept their money on deposit with different stores, the integrity of the owner being the main protection for what frequently were large amounts. When a cattleman needed to make disbursements, he gave what were called orders against these deposits. Credit was well nigh universal, and one man frequently stood good for another's accounts.

Perhaps an illustration will make this plainer. Suppose a man like R. K. Wiley or Peter Robinson was sending a herd through the country in charge of some of his employees. In order to make it possible for them to procure what they needed in the way of supplies or expense money the boss would have orders to go to the different stores that lay along their route. When the man in charge of the herd came to a store, the fact that he was boss of the herd was authority for him to get anything he needed and have it charged to the account of the owner of the cattle. It was certain, too, that the bill would be paid when presented, and no dispute would arise about the amount. This old account book contains many entries which show that Uncle John in his own case sought the same sort of accommodations from other stores he was glad to extend at his own.

Another evidence demonstrating the confidence that these old cattlemen had in one another was the way they would leave their cattle in each other's hands. If the owner of a herd should encounter difficulties of any sort and be unable to take along all of his cattle, he would simply leave the extras on the range of some friend. Many times have I heard Uncle John say, "Well, So-and-so left some of his cattle on my range. I told him it would be all right and that when I gathered my herd together I'd get up his cattle, too, and take them on and sell them." Such a transaction would be conducted without the fuss and ceremony of drawing up a lot of legal papers. In still another way the confidence underlying business dealings in those days was shown. Uncle John frequently bought cattle from other cattlemen, but he seldom paid cash, the understanding being that payment was to be made after the cattle had been sold. This account book shows many cases of business transactions in all of these ways.

Uncle John's conception of a summary of assets and liabilities was about as simple as that of a certain old-fashioned businessman, who said to a present-day accountant presenting him with a bulky and complicated audit of the business, "Don't bother me with all that junk. Simply tell me how much money I have in the bank and how much I owe. That's enough for me." In like manner Uncle John seems to have merely wanted to know what his disbursements were and what his income was. In the case of disbursements the total runs to $253,234.06; in the case of receipts the total is [illegible].

The greatest source of income was from the delivery of cattle on Government beef contracts. In 1875 Uncle John made delivery to Hot Springs, Fort Stanton, and especially to Fort Bowie, Arizona. To this latter place he regularly sent cattle in July, August, September, October, November, December, and January. His entries in regard to these may be cited as typical:

	No. of Cattle			*Total Pounds*	*Amount*
Aug.	Voucher	Bowie	89	67,074	$ 1,676.85
Sept.	"	"	122	92,589	2,314.72
Oct.	"	"	110	82,089	2,050.22
Nov.	"	"	103	77,364	1,934.10
Dec.	"	W	—	95,430	2,383.50
Jan.	"	—	86	68,859	1,721.47

At the same time he was making deliveries with equal regularity to Camp Apache and to places designated simply as "Colorado." He was also sending cattle to the San Carlos Reservation in Arizona. The entries for these deliveries at the latter place follows:

				Total Pounds	*Amount*
July	Voucher	San Carlos		268,233	$ 6,725.82
Aug.	"	"	"	281,800	7,045.00
Sept.	"	"	"	215,450	5,386.00
Oct.	"	"	"	301,203	7,530.07
Nov.	"	"	"	258,678	6,966.85
Dec.	"	"	"	305,905	7,547.62
Jan.	"	"	"	499,410	12,485.25
Feb.	"	"	"	332,706	8,317.65
Mar.	"	"	"	368,700	9,217.50
Apr.	"	"	"	314,609	7,865.22
May	"	"	"	306,900	7,672.50

The aggregate amount in these deliveries and sale of cattle the last six months of 1875 and the first six months of 1876 seems to have produced a gross income of $221,721.95.

Also recorded is the number of herds sent by Uncle John at different times and under whose charge they were. From the dates I am inclined to think that these entries mostly belong to the spring of 1878 when he was transferring his cattle from the Pecos country to the Canadian country. Two of these entries may be quoted for the light they throw on the value of cattle in those days in comparison with present prices.

Drove by Goodman, May 26, 1878

1620	yearlings at $8	$12,960.00
706	two year olds at $12	8,472.00
117	calves at $2	234.00
1082	cows at $14	15,148.00
181	three year olds at $16	2,896.00
79	beeves at $20	1,580,00
10	good bulls at $20	200.00

Drove by R. Ford, May 27th, 1878

8	good bulls at $20	160.00
1678	yearlings at $8	13,424.00
607	two year olds at $12	7,284.00
264	calves at $2	528.00
1394	cows at $14	19,488.00
210	three year olds at $16	3,360.00
122	beeves at $20	2,440.00
		$46,684.00

Some items of the expenses incident to such a large business can be had by turning to the expenditures section of the old account book. Evidently Uncle John conducted his business on shares; that is, he handled cattle for other cattlemen and when he received payments for them, he settled with the owners of the cattle. This explains such entries as "July, 1878, W. C. Parks, $1,000; F. Chapman, $3,000; S. R. Scoggins, $18,000; R. K. Wiley, $7,000; and Sampson & Hendricks, $4,152.29.

There were also expenses connected with sending the herds. The large number of entries indicate accounts were settled with stores along the route which had been authorized to furnish various articles and necessities at different times to Chisum men.

Wages paid to employees was another large item of expense. These men were perfectly willing to let their wages accumulate, and sometimes they would go a year or so without having a settlement. When some reason arose which made them want their money, they would make a request and settlement would be made. The old account book shows many entries that are clearly for wages, such as "Thos. Ewing, $456; Richard Smith, $50; C. Brady, $88; and F. McKittrick, $200."

Although Uncle John was not a land grabber in the sense some others of that time were, he did acquire a good deal of land. At South Spring River he bought from James Patterson forty acres with the two houses that were standing there, and he added to this by purchase the homesteads of James Hudson, Pedro Sánchez, Manuela Ortiz, Manicio Sanches, and Florencia Luna — five homesteads aggregating eight hundred acres. Then in course of time the different members of the family together with various ones of the employees took up desert or timber claims, which eventually were acquired by Uncle John or were to all intents in his possession. Uncle Jim Chisum, Uncle Pitzer, Walter Chisum, Willie Chisum, William Robert, and Mrs. Sallie Robert all took up claims, as well as the employees, Old Man Adams, his son, Dwight Adams, Bennett Howell, William Hutchinson, Alex Blair, Dick Burleson, William Hunt, and even the ten or twelve Mexicans who worked more or less regularly on the place.

It is impossible to say how much land Uncle John held title to in his lifetime but I am able to give the amount owned by the Jinglebob Livestock Company that, after Uncle John's death, became the incorporated name of the extensive business that he had built up. From an old tax receipt I learn that this company owned 11,221 acres, valued at $27,724. The amount of real estate owned by this company was not much changed from what it was in Uncle John's lifetime. While the amount may appear to be large, yet it is small comparatively, when the holdings of some others is taken into consideration.

I often wondered why Uncle John did not acquire more land when it could be had so cheap. He certainly let go by wonderful opportunities to acquire some of the best water supplies of the Pecos Valley. I can give no reason except his policy was always "live and let live." So when he had enough land for his own use, he was entirely willing that others might have what they wanted of the rest.

It would be hard to make any reliable estimate of the number of cattle Uncle John owned in any particular year. In fact, I doubt very much whether he himself ever knew other than approximately. In January, 1877, he seems to have told the editor of the Santa Fe *New Mexican,* who happened to meet him as he was coming back from a trip to Arizona where he had been in search of ranges farther to the west and farther from the lawlessness that was dominating Lincoln County, that he then had some 60,000 head. This was probably an underestimate, for Uncle John was not one to tell fully the details of his business, especially to a representative of the newspaper that was the chief organ of the Santa Fe Ring that caused him so much annoyance.

One thing, however, is certain. The handling of such a large number of cattle scattered over his extensive range naturally required a large force of helpers. In this same interview with the editor of the *New Mexican,* Uncle John is represented as saying that the number of his helpers was ninety, and that he had also in proportion horses, wagons, camp equipment, and provisions. This force of helpers was scattered over the range at different camps, and they were all kept busy working the cattle. By 1876 Uncle John had largely ceased going to the camps; the direct oversight he entrusted to his brother, Pitzer Chisum. By that time he seldom went with his herds when they were sent through, and when he did go he generally used a good mountain buggy drawn by two horses, which enabled him to make the trip faster and with less wear and tear than going horseback.

When at the headquarters ranch he found himself with the proverbial thousand and one things to look after. There were business letters to write, usually a good many. In connection with the store, he had to attend to many things. Although clerks were always reliable, Uncle John expected to be kept informed regarding what had been sold and what stock needed to be replenished. The tally book must be kept up to date as the official record of the cattle business. There were endless accounts of one kind and another of the day, not to say hours, that were spent in interviews with employees and others about all sorts of matters. It was a general saying among his helpers that "the old man himself" would do for them more than anyone else, and so everyone made a point of seeing him. It was a general rule that cowboys from the various camps down along the Pecos should report every week or ten days. The line riders came in with their reports, too, showing whether everyone at the different camps was alive and well and actively at work.

When Uncle John's business was at its height, he was fulfilling contracts every month with at least one and sometimes more than one large herd. Getting a herd ready for the road entailed an amazing amount of work and responsibility, and in directing this while meeting all other demands, Uncle John must be credited with possessing an unusual degree of this ability. As I know the steps usually taken, I shall give an account of them. All of his men would go down the Pecos to the end of his range, say Horsehead Crossing, and work back up, picking up from the cattle that had come down on the river for water those suitable for the herd that was about to be put up. They would also brand the calves. The required number were then taken to a locality some three or four miles from South Spring River ranch, and held there for several days until the herd was "fitted up." That expression implied not only selection of the fifteen to eighteen men who were to go with the herd, but also equipping them properly. The herd boss had complete charge and authority. Some of those upon whom Uncle John relied for bosses were McKittrick, E. B. Peters, James Patterson, George Teague, and Jim Key. Besides the boss there were twelve or fifteen cowboys, the two horse wranglers, and the cook. All these had to be supplied with bedding, saddles, bridles, leggings, and the like. Even the red bandana handkerchief so dear to the cowboys of those days had to be provided. This particular article of attire was not for purely decorative use, as is generally implied in descriptions of the cowboy, it served a very useful purpose: the cowboy would tie it over his mouth, and so keep out the alkali dust which was so trying to the lips.

Many horses had to be gathered, for each cowboy must have his mount of from six to ten horses — two or three for night use, and four or five for day use. As no feed for the horses was taken along, they had to sustain life by grazing. Grass-fed horses cannot stand as much hard work as those fed on grain, so the cowboys had to have enough horses for each man to change often and rest the horse he had just been using. The chuck wagon had to be equipped with cooking utensils and provisioned with food enough to last at least until the outfit could reach the first store on the route. An important part of the *impedimenta* was two shoeing kits with plenty of horseshoes and nails. This was absolutely necessary to prevent horses from becoming tender footed and lame from the loss of shoes.

When everything was ready the start would be made as early in the morning as possible. For the first day the journey would generally be a short one — the pace was never more than fifteen or twenty miles a day because beef cattle, as these generally were, if driven too fast would become thin. Usually a Chisum herd going westward would reach Missouri Bottom by the night of the first day; the next day's journey would take it to the Hondo; and the third up to our ranch on the Hondo. This distance of about sixty miles was not a particularly difficult drive, because the road was right up the Hondo all the way which made it possible to get water. At our ranch a herd would stop for a day or so while the men "recruited up" on supplies, for ours was the last store they would reach until they got a good deal further westward. Leaving our place, the first night probably would be spent at the San Patricio flats, the second night in the vicinity of the Upper Ruidosos, the third night near the Indian Agency, and the fourth night would bring it to Tularosa. Then would come a long and waterless stretch around the end of the White Sands, ending at Shedd's ranch. From there the herd was driven across the Rio Grande Valley and on into Arizona, to whatever was its destination.

Uncle John frequently accompanied the herd as far as the Agency, then would return to South Spring River. He felt his personal supervision was necessary on this part of the trip for two reasons. One was the danger at Boquilla from the Mes gang attempting to stampede his cattle at night, and the other was the need for seeing that the cattle did not do damage to the crops of the farmers along the Hondo and the Ruidoso. As a further safeguard during this part of the trip Uncle John generally had extra men accompanying the herd, who would stay with it as far as the Agency.

31

Heyday of the South Spring River Ranch

UNCLE JOHN HAD REALIZED that the multiplication of attacks and opposition such as the preceding chapters have presented might eventually prove overwhelming in spite of their manifest injustice. So he had been farsighted enough to trim his sails before the approaching gale and had, as he put it in his self-defense, "covered his property" in order that it might not be snatched away by those persecuting him. From his point of view, it was a case of the end's justifying the means. He felt that his enemies were so desirous of dafrauding him by trickery and underhanded means that it was only fair to circumvent them if he could. So he kept his property out of his own name, although he continued to act as general manager of the business.

As soon as Uncle John was released from imprisonment at Las Vegas, he returned to South Spring River ranch and arranged to have what cattle he had retained after the sale to Hunter and Evans transferred to a new range farther north. He had contemplated such a move for some time, planning to place his cattle on new range up on the Canadian in the Panhandle of Texas in the vicinity of Tascosa.

For the time being, the South Spring River ranch was virtually abandoned. Uncle John went East on a long trip and left the management of the cattle in the hands of his brothers, especially Uncle Jim Chisum. The cattle did well on the Canadian, but as Lincoln County had seemingly settled into more peaceful ways, the Chisums decided to return to the South Spring River ranch.

The famous old "long rail" brand had been sold, so they started afresh with what was called the U brand. When Uncle John first came there to live he built the "old house," as it was called, but it had never been satisfactory. For one thing, it was located on low ground and was always damp and mouldy. It had been used as a store, first in charge of Hutchinson & Sánchez, and later in charge of an old man by the name of Larimore, called "Lar" for short, who had lived with the Chisum family since boyhood and who finally died and was buried with them. While the Chisums were away on the Canadian, Larimore was left in general charge of the ranch, but being really too old to look after the building well, he had allowed the water canals or spouts to leak down the walls. The house being adobe, the water cut the walls badly, and the whole east and south wings were in such bad condition when Uncle John returned that he decided to tear them down as well as some of the rooms on the north

What gave impetus to carrying out this decision was Uncle John's turning over the old house to Uncle Pitzer who had decided after his many years of being a bachelor to get married; this made some property readjustments necessary. Uncle John bought out Pitzer's interest in the South Spring River ranch, giving him about $25,000 and a portion of the ranch, which included the old house, together with a good deal of land in the vicinity and what was called the old orchard. All this made the need for a new house acute, and Uncle John at once commenced work on it.

Well-named "Long House," it was simply an adobe building of nine rooms in a row, with a center hall the same size as the rooms. The house was but one room deep, and along both the east and west fronts ran porches extending the whole length of the building, providing a comfortable amount of shade whether it was morning or afternoon. A unique feature was that under the hall in the middle of the house ran an irrigation ditch, rather deep and always full of clear running water. In almost all accounts of the house this ditch is mentioned together with the fact that Uncle John always had it full of fish, one of his delights being to sit on the east porch of this hall in an afternoon or early morning and watch the fish as they darted and whisked about. He liked to feed them cracker crumbs, and had them so gentle they would come to his hands to eat.

On both sides of the house was a profusion of shrubbery and

flowers, planted along the banks of the ditch that ran on both sides of the house and scattered all over the yard. Uncle John was a great lover of flowers and he procured a great variety of ornamental ones. Roses were his especial favorites and he had literally hundreds of rose bushes.

About twenty feet east of the kitchen of the main house was a camp house for the cowboys; and about fifty feet south of this was a large single-room building that might be used for any purpose the occasion might require. Its chief use when I knew the place was as a dance hall. These dances would be attended by old and young on the Chisum ranch, reinforced by some from the nearby settlement called Pumpkin Row. Music was supplied by fiddles and guitars played by any in the company with pretensions to musical skill, principally cowboys, but Uncle John and Uncle Pitzer were both good fiddlers.

The irrigation ditch that ran through the house continued on eastward for about two hundred yards to where Uncle John planned to have a park. He had scraped out with teams two ponds or tanks, as they were commonly called. One of these was almost a complete circle in shape, while the other and the larger one was decidedly an oval. Solid ground was left in the middle of one for an island, to which Uncle Pitzer, for some reason, gave the Biblical name of the Isle of Patmos. It was on this island that the three Chisum brothers planted three weeping willow trees so often referred to. Each tree was named for one of the brothers, and their being together was a symbol of their brotherly feeling for one another. It was a similar feeling that led them to plant elsewhere on the place the three cottonwood trees, which were so united that they finally grew together — another symbol of their unity.

The dirt taken out of the ponds was used to make three large mounds, packed hard and covered with Bermuda grass, and made very attractive with more bushes and ornamental shrubbery planted up the sides and on the top. To aid in getting to the tops of them, there were steps. These again typified the three Chisum brothers.

Between the two ponds was a long strip of solid earth, which Uncle John always said represented the "long rail" brand, which had been for so many years the Chisum brand. Irrigation ditches were made to lead into this strip diverging in such a way as to suggest the pointed head of an arrow, and to run out diverging so

The Long House on the South Spring River Ranch of
John Chisum was the center of the most complete and
well-developed ranch home in eastern New Mexico.

as to make the feathered stem of the arrow. Uncle John explained that these suggested the transformation made by his enemies, especially Murphy, Dolan & Co., in burning and disfiguring the "long rail" brand into the "arrow" brand.

The waste water from all this network of ponds and ditches ran off down to a large deep draw, or arroyo, and it was to this that the cattle came for water to drink. The tramping back and forth of the great number of cattle caused the soil to pack down until it was as hard as if covered with cement. Thus developed a very attractive lake, some two or three miles wide and four or five miles long. Just beyond this were several timber claims which had been taken up by the different Chisums — to the three brothers had been added two nephews, sons of John Chisum, named Willie and Walter. Also the Chisum cowboys took up several timber claims, which they afterwards sold to Uncle John. They had cottonwoods shipped in by the thousands to set out on these claims.

This arrangement of land and trees and water made a remarkable view from the east porch of the house as one looked in an easterly direction. Especially of a morning was it a never-to-be-forgotten experience to stand there and see several miles of water extending into the distance, above which was the sun topping the tree line and making the lake glimmer in the sunlight. No wonder Uncle John took great delight in getting any of his guests up early enough to see such a notable sight, all artificially made by his mind and hand.

All planning was done on a large scale. From other sections of the country he brought lavish quantities of fruit trees of all sorts — apples, peaches, plums, pears, cherries, and nectarines, to mention but a few. He also set out many kinds of berries — strawberries, raspberries, blackberries, chiefly. He seemed to want to have every known variety of fruit or berry that could by any possible chance be grown successfully in New Mexico. In special charge of this part of the place was Jim Scurlock, the story of whose death I will tell later.

Taken all in all, the ranch was the most complete and lavish estate in West Texas or Eastern New Mexico. It had no rival. There were some old *haciendas* in other parts of the Territory, belonging to Spanish-American families and usually dating back to the days of liberal grants from the Spanish government, but there was no comparison. The Chisum ranch, as it was generally called, was known far and wide, and people came from everywhere to look at it. Uncle John always welcomed visitors and liked to conduct them all over it, explaining everything and describing other things he proposed to have done. He did not feel that he had at all completed his program of development. Undoubtedly he hoped that, if it was not permitted him to finish it, other members of the family would carry his plans to completion. But for one reason and another this did not turn out to be the case. In the course of time, the place passed into other hands, and now hardly a trace is discernible of the ranch as it was in Uncle John's time.

As Uncle John's establishment was ever a bachelor's hall he always had a lady in charge as housekeeper. The first one was Mrs. Frances Towry, a double first cousin of Uncle John's who came out from Paris, Texas, with her husband, Tom Towry, Sr. and a son, Tom Towry, Jr. Mrs. Towry looked after the house, Mr. Towry had a small harness and saddle shop, while the boy worked on the range with the cattle. The Towrys stayed several years. By that time Uncle Pitzer had married, and Uncle John invited his wife to become the housekeeper. The next one was Mrs. Sallie Robert, Uncle Jim's daughter.

The housekeeper's duties were comparatively light, for Uncle John always kept a man cook. "Negro Dick" was with him for years and years in the capacity of chief cook. Upon the latter devolved the actual preparation of the food, the housekeeper having to look simply after the house. Uncle John's hospitality was always generous and open handed, and everybody who came to the country stopped with him either for old acquaintance' sake or for the chance to see a remarkable man and a unique place, so the house was nearly always entertaining company.

Uncle John's room was the first one north of the hall. Mrs. Towry undertook to fix it up the way she thought the room of the master of the house should be. She put a carpet on the floor and bought a set of modern furniture. She took particular pains with the bed, thinking that Uncle John was getting to the time in life when his sleeping accommodations should be of great importance to him. She got a fine wooden bedstead, equipped with a mattress and feather bed, and also provided a bolster, which was in those days as indispensable an adjunct as the pillows. The latter were more for decorative effect than for use, and that fact was exhibited to the world by means of what was called a "sham cover," a highly embroidered affair which covered the pillow by day but which was removed and folded up at night.

But Uncle John was a man of simple tastes to say nothing of fixed habits, so in vain was this elaborate modern bed, spread in the sight of this veteran of the range. What did he do when at home but have his camp bed put into his room and use it as a pallet? Of course Mrs. Towry protested, but Uncle John would say to her, "Cousin Frances, you surely don't expect me to put in the rest of the night, after I have been sitting up late, in folding up these pillow shams and getting the bed fixed to sleep in? When I get ready to go to sleep I want to go to bed." Then if Mrs. Towry would continue to protest he would say, "Well, you know I've a mighty comfortable camp bed, and I'm used to that sort of sleeping, anyhow."

The ranch was always humming with activity. Uncle John, the general overseer and boss of it all, had shifted his interests largely from cattle raising to farming. While Uncle Jim looked after the cattle remaining on the range, Uncle John contented himself with simply laying down the general lines of development.

Uncle John did not care for the Herefords that have since become so popular with the cattlemen; he thought the Red Durhams were preferable because they crossed better with the range cattle, were good rustlers, and seemed to adapt themselves better to range conditions. He saw to it that Uncle Jim increased the strain of Red Durhams in the herd.

By that time Uncle John had become interested — somewhat indirectly, it is true — in raising sheep. When the bitter feuds between sheepmen and cattlemen are recalled it seems strange that Uncle John should ever have tolerated sheep on his range, but there was a reason for his doing so. The cattle were frequently getting what was then called alkali poisoning from the grass growing on the Pecos flats. Knowing that the cattle, which would not feed on land run over by sheep, would be forced to go farther away from the river on the uplands and into the gramma grass where there was no danger of alkali troubles, Uncle John let Uncle Pitzer and his partner, Fred Roth, and others like the Miller brothers, run sheep in the vicinity of the Pecos River.

Uncle John gave special attention to the planting of trees.

Mexican helpers would dig the holes but Uncle John himself did much of the actual planting. If the tree was one that he was especially interested in — the gift of some friend or an especially unusual sort of tree, then he was certain to attend to its planting in person. Many a time did I hold the tree upright in the hole made for it while he himself shoveled the dirt and tamped it firmly about the roots. All sorts of trees were set out, for it seemed he was determined not only to have every kind known to grow in New Mexico, but to experiment with every kind that by any chance might be made to grow there.

All the people about the place had something to do. Generally there were from ten to fifteen cowboys who put in their time at the work necessary in connection with the cattle. There were also Mexican helpers, the number varying with the amount of work under way. I remember at one time there were about 30 of them, for just then a lot of work was going on; Uncle John was having alfalfa planted in what was called the big field which must have included at least five hundred acres. In addition to this he was planting cottonwoods on the timber claims and setting his new orchard. The ranch was a veritable beehive of activity.

But it was not all work and no play. The memory of the good times there still lingers with me, and I shall try to give some details. The South Spring River in those days was very wide and deep, and as clear as crystal. It was filled with all sorts of fish — catfish, sunfish, bull heads, suckers, eels, red horse, and buffalo fish were all present in large quantities. As might be expected, fishing was a great sport and everyone participated.

Dwight Simms, boss carpenter on the place, made two skiffs, one of which was always kept in the river. Many and many were the rides we girls took in this skiff with the cowboys, when they would go out to bait their tram net. On Saturdays and Sundays they used a dragnet, and then there was fun sure enough. The boys would get into their overalls and jumpers; two would row the boat, and three or four others would drag the net through the deep holes. When the net was pulled out on the bank the quantity of fish was a sight I shall never forget. I can only describe it as a ripple of wriggling specimens of the finny tribe, with generally a few turtles and water snakes mixed with the fish.

We of the younger generation often took the skiff and rowed

about in the moonlight. Almost always someone who had some
ability in singing would lead off in the old-time songs, while the
others joined in the choruses.

The second boat was smaller and intended only for pleasure.
It was kept in the oval-shaped pond, and by getting into the boat
we could row around the Isle of Patmos. I remember I was always
afraid that this boat might turn over and produce some disastrous
results, for the water must have been at least ten feet deep. Consequently, I had little inclination for boat rides in that pond. I remember one moonlight night when a number of young folks were rowing
around, I refused to get into the boat, despite not a little teasing
about being afraid. Finally Uncle Pitzer and his wife came down
to the pond and insisted on my getting into the boat, assuring me
they would see that no foolishness such as rocking the boat, went on.
I changed my mind and got aboard.

Hardly was I settled on the middle seat by the oars when some
foolish girl in the party started to rock the boat. That settled things,
for I would not stay in it. I picked up one of the oars and, sticking
the point into the bank, managed to swing the boat to the bank. Then
I jumped out and stayed on land despite all invitations to come back.
The others went on with their foolishness and skylarking, and before
long the boat had dipped so much water there was danger of capsiz-
ing. Then there was consternation; in fact, it almost became a
tragedy. Some of the girls got panicky and wanted to jump out and
swim to shore, but the cooler heads prevailed. The boat was brought
to shore, but it was half full of water and the girls' dresses were
spoiled. I could not refrain from greeting them with one of Uncle
John's pet sayings, "Those who won't heed must feel."

When Uncle John heard what had happened, he was provoked
and inclined to scold. I remember he turned to me and said, "Lily,
where were you? I'd have thought you had more common sense
than to let them do that." I replied, "I showed my common sense
by jumping out when they started. Those mossy heads would not
listen nor follow me." That did not please the others, and they told
Uncle John about my leaving them, and called me a piker for doing
so. I retorted to this, "Sure; who wouldn't quit with such crazy
fools?" Uncle John stopped our wrangling by saying that in the
future we must be more careful or there would be no more boat
riding in the skiffs.

What good times we had on the old ranch! How happy everyone was, even though the section was crude and lawless! Although those pioneer men and women may have had rough exteriors and rough ways, yet no people on earth could measure up to them in true friendship and good-heartedness. I really think the percentage of happiness among them was greater than it is in later times.

Sometimes, however, grim incidents occurred which served to show us that traces of the old days still remained in that section.

In accounts of the Chisum place I have sometimes read, "This is the spot where many a cowboy bit the dust," or words bearing a similar import. Such statements, however, are absolutely false. I always have been in a position to know, and the number of killings either on the ranch or in its immediate vicinity were very few. One or two of them I have mentioned elsewhere but I am confident the only man ever killed at the long house was J. W. Spurlock.

Spurlock had come out to New Mexico to escape the consequences of a killing back at home in Tennessee. The story as I heard it was that he had killed his brother-in-law in a misunderstanding about the price of a heifer from a fine milch cow. When the brother-in-law attempted to drive the heifer away, Spurlock said, "Don't you dare drive that cow beyond my gate. I'll kill you if you do!" But the other man, thinking that because they were brothers-in-law, Spurlock would not be as good as his word, drove the cow on. Spurlock grabbed up the shotgun and fired the loads of both barrels into his brother-in-law, killing him instantly.

Spurlock skipped out, and after spending a number of years as a fugitive from justice in South America, Old Mexico, and the United States, he had come to South Spring River and gone to work for Uncle John. As Uncle John had known him when they were boys back in Tennessee, he interested himself in efforts to have the prosecution for murder dropped. Spurlock seemed well on the road toward establishing his character and reputation; he was a faithful employee, and after he had been at the ranch some time, Uncle John advanced him to the position of foreman. Uncle John also brought it about that the old fellow heard from his family. Though the news showed that they were getting on well, his wife having been able to take care of the property and to get the children educated, yet Spurlock began to worry about them. This went on until he was nearly half-crazy and not responsible for his conduct.

One day, while he was in this state of an almost nervous collapse, he got mad on some account with Fred Roth, who happened to be visiting at the ranch. Roth was a great friend of William Robert, Uncle Jim Chisum's son-in-law, and he was staying at the ranch house. Later in the day on which the row occurred, Spurlock and Roth happened to meet at the gate going out of the barnyard. Fred Roth had in his arms the little two-year-old son of William Robert, but that did not deter Spurlock from throwing his six-shooter into Roth's face and commencing to abuse and curse him violently. All that Roth could do at the time, having the baby in his arms and not being armed, was to stand and take all that was said to him. When Spurlock blustered out something about "an eye," the child reached up his small hand to the menacing barrel of the pistol and moved it out away from Roth's face.

When Spurlock had abused him until he was tired, Roth went on into the house and put the baby down. Then arming himself with a Winchester, he went back into the yard, and seeing Spurlock still there, he shouted to him, "Come on now; say what you have to say; I'm ready for you." Then without more ado both began firing at each other. For a time they exchanged shots, Spurlock sheltering himself behind a wagon, Roth firing from behind a corner of the house. Roth did much better shooting, for two or three of his shots lodged in Spurlock's body, and several others went through the wagon bed. Finally Spurlock fell, saying, "That's enough. You've got me, Fred. Don't shoot any more." But Roth, wild with a desire to retaliate, ran up to the prostrate form of Spurlock and was preparing to shoot him again when Elias Bly, one of the bystanders who had appeared on the scene, stopped him. A few minutes later Spurlock died.

Those who witnessed this fight always spoke of it as a desperate one, both in the number of shots exchanged and the ferocity of the combatants. Both men were of the better type of Westerners, but they had reached a point where their differences had to be settled by shooting it out. Though Spurlock was undoubtedly the aggressor, it must be remembered that he was nearly crazy from grief and trouble. Roth simply did what any other man would have done under like abuse and insult. As soon as he was free of the baby he had been carrying, he proceeded to the defense of his own self-respect. He was a gentleman and not in the least a truculent man. He remained in the section for several years afterward, making Roswell his home, and doing very well in the sheep business. He finally sold out and returned to his native country, Germany, where he died. It was currently said that when he left Roswell, he took with him $60,000 in gold.

32

Trail's End for the Cow King

WITH ALL THE IMPROVEMENTS that were under way at the South
Spring River ranch, Uncle John was kept there pretty constantly
until the summer of 1884. Intermingled with his interest in the
development of the place on the magnificent scale indicated and his
enjoyment of his well-earned prosperity and ease after so many
years of hard work, was considerable concern regarding his health.
Worrying him most was a malignant tumor which had developed on
his neck. He suffered no pain, but the growth was so large and
uncomfortable on the left side of his neck, just over the shoulder,
that to avoid discomfort he had let his right shoulder sag down and
incline his head in that direction. He suffered more from it in his
mind, because both his father and grandfather had died from the
same trouble, and he was inclined to feel sure his was to be a similar
fate.

For several months he had been fighting to conceal the anxiety
that was growing upon him. He would not talk much about his
condition, for fear that he would show how pessimistic he was
about himself, and that would alarm those about him who were
so largely dependent upon him. Without much ado about the course
he proposed to take, he decided to go get the best medical treatment
available, and very quietly announced his determination to those
of us then at the ranch.

When Uncle John left on the 7th of July, 1884, he seemed to

feel a premonition that he would never return, and was so overcome at leaving that he almost broke down and cried. The rest of us felt much the same way, and I remember I wrote my sister shortly afterwards, saying that I felt I would never see Uncle John again. He drove away in his buggy, accompanied by Mr. Anderson, one of the neighbors. He declined to allow any of the family to accompany him on the trip. Midsummer was always a busy time on the range, in fact a large roundup was in progress and Uncle Jim had to be on hand at it. Uncle Pitzer was just then very busy building a new house and looking after the new orchard.

After reaching Las Vegas, Uncle John stayed long enough to take part in an important conference of cattlemen concerning the location of shipping pens at Bernal, and then he went by train to Kansas City. I do not believe it was his original intention to get treatment at Kansas City; I rather think his plan was to go on to Chicago, or even to New York if needful, for he wanted the best possible medical knowledge of that time. It seems probable that he stopped in Kansas City simply to consult some doctors, and finding that they took a serious view of his condition, he consented to an operation then and there at their hands.

The first news about his operation came to Mrs. Robert in the following letter:

Kansas City, Mo.
August 30, 1884

Mrs. Sallie Robert
Dear Niece:

I came here about the 16h inst. and on the 24th I had an operation performed on my throat or jaw about where the rising was on my jaw. Some 10 months ago this last spring it began to grow but was not sore but a hard solid lump and it grew very fast and got so large that it became very troublesome and began to shove my head to one side and was still growing very fast so I had it cut out. It was about the size of a beef's kidney. It was a very dangerous operation but it is over now and I am getting well and can leave for home in a week. Your Pa and Willie had just left here before I got in, so I did not get to see them. I was told that he was going to Arizona but I got a letter yesterday from Anderson who came here with me. He went back home and he wrote me from Jim Lains and said James was at the Lain's branding cattle. From that I suppose he has changed his notion and was going on the Pecos but I only judge so by his being at Lain's. Robert is at the Ranch looking after matters while I am gone. I regretted to leave home but was compelled to have this pet cut out. The doctor says if it had not been cut out it would have killed me in about six months more. He says it was the enlargement of the glands.

My best wishes with regards to all.

Yours as ever,
John S. Chisum.

As the foregoing letter shows, the operation was supposed to be successful, and in the strength of this hope, Uncle John started back to New Mexico. But by the time he got to Las Vegas the trouble reappeared and he returned immediately to Kansas City. The outcome of this second visit is detailed in the following letter addressed to me, which I believe is the last letter Uncle John wrote:

Kansas City, Sept. 18/84

Miss Lillie Casey,
My Dear Lillie:
I would have written to you long ago but was so weak and poorly and it gave me so much pain to write I would put it off from time to time hoping I would feel better next day. I had the tumor out on the 24th of July. It was a very delicate operation, and a very dangerous one but I had a good surgeon and I came through all safe but was very weak, from the loss of blood having lost a water bucket full, and was kept under the influence of chloroform for one hour. I finally recovered so I thought I could make it home though I was very weak. I got to Vegas and by that time another tumor had made its appearance and was growing very fast and gave me great pain, so I was compelled to return to this place again. The doctor thought it not best to cut it out until he could put my system in a shape so another would not form. He says he cut this without first cleansing the system another one would form, so I am taking medicine by the wholesale and applying the battery twice a day, but as yet no change in the tumor. It is about as large as the one I had cut out. This one will have to be cut out before I get shut of it. I am now in good fix for courting the girls as I cannot speak above a whisper. I am very tired of this place and would be glad to get home again but I cannot tell how I will stand the next operation as I am much weaker then when the other operation was performed. As my neck is giving me such pain I will close hoping this will find you in good health and happy. I know you are a good girl as well as a good friend of mine. Yes, Lillie, when I think of you, which is very often, I think of you as one of my very best friends and no one wishes you more happiness than I do. Do you think of me? I hope so. Don't write me as I am liable to go East.

Yours as ever,
John S. Chisum.

Acting upon the advice of his physicians, Uncle John went to Eureka Springs in Arkansas to submit himself to a course of baths and treatments that might prepare him for another operation. Realizing the seriousness of his condition, he sent for Uncle Jim Chisum to come and be with him. For a time he seemed to improve at Eureka Springs, but about the middle of December, he grew rapidly worse. On the 20th* of December he died, and in fulfilment of his

*Accounts differ on the date of death, but this is regarded as most accurate.

own request, his body was taken by his brother to Paris, Texas, and buried in the Chisum lot there on Christmas Day, 1884.

The death of Uncle John Chisum took away from the helm the steersman who had developed and guided the large business he had built up. While his brothers were in many respects capable enough, they did not possess his rare business ability. They tried to keep the business intact, but in spite of all that could be done, it began to drift slowly but surely toward the rocks.

The property fell into the hands of Uncle Jim Chisum and his children, Mrs. Sallie Robert, and his sons, Walter and William. His son-in-law, William Robert, was also interested in the business. Thus the Jinglebob Land and Cattle Company became a sort of family affair. Uncle Pitzer Chisum had, at the time of his marriage, sold out to Uncle John and he had no interest in the later phases of the business. But he did hold in his hands the means of bringing about the wreck of it.

When Uncle John felt he must protect himself by putting his property in the name of his brothers, he had selected Uncle Pitzer, who had been with him for so many years, as the one to whom he could most safely turn over his property. In this connection he had given Uncle Pitzer his note for $100,000, but he never expected it to be collected. When Uncle John bought Uncle Pitzer out, he paid him a fair sum for his interest in the business; but the note for $100,000 still remained in Uncle Pitzer's hands. Uncle Pitzer still lived on the part of the ranch that had been turned over to him.

About that time there came into that part of New Mexico M. J. Farris who was connected with a bank in Danville, Kentucky. As it was understood that he was willing to take loans for bond on New Mexico cattle and land, the Jinglebob Company arranged a loan for $64,000 so as to secure funds with which to run the outfit. About the same time Uncle Pitzer Chisum determined to leave New Mexico and go back to Paris, Texas. So he sold out his place to the Jinglebob Company, and in addition, he sold to M.J. Farris the $100,000 note of John Chisum. I do not know what amount Farris paid him, but I suppose it was a mere fraction of the face value. Whatever it was, M.J. Farris came into control of the situation by virtue of his bank's holding an indebtedness of the Jinglebob Company for approximately $164,000 with perhaps a considerable amount of interest. It was not long before Farris took advantage of his power and proceeded to close the company out. The story of how this was done I shall give in the account of Walter Chisum who knew more about the matter than anyone else.

In the latter part of May or the early part of June, 1890, M. J. Farris said to me, "If you can buy the interests of the other members of the Jinglebob Land and Livestock Company, I will let you have stock in the new company, provided you will sign your shares in the Jinglebob Company, which amount to $33,333⅓ over to me." Farris also said that if he could buy out the other members in the Jinglebob Company, he could form a new company.

M. J. Farris also said during the above conversation that he intended to buy the stock range on the north of the Jinglebob Land and Livestock Company's range, and asked me how it would suit me to manage the concern for him. I said I would accept the position provided there was money enough in it for me to undertake the handling of such a concern. Farris then said to me, "The handling of such a concern will give you a big name." I said to Farris, "I'm not working for a name neither do I expect to, for my parents gave me all the name I care for. Money is what I will work for."

Farris then told me that William Robert could not manage or was not managing the business of the Jinglebob Land and Livestock Company successfully and it would eventually become insolvent under his management. Farris also told me that he would see if he could make a deal during the year 1890 by which he would become owner of the property then belonging to the Jinglebob Company, by which deal he hoped the stockholders of the company would be able to come out in good shape. Farris made a deal with the Jinglebob Land and Livestock Company about the 26th of August, 1890. William Robert, W. J. and W. P. Chisum were present when this was made for all of the real estate together with 300 head of mules and horses consideration $75,000. The horses were estimated, if my mind serves me correctly, at $30. per head.

M. J. Farris came to me on the 5th of September, 1890 and said, "Walter, you go ahead and tally all the horses in the U brand, and I will allow your company $40 per head for them, as that is what I am valuing them at in my report to my company at Danville, Ky.; for I fear my company will think I paid too much for the real estate of the ranch and I want to make a good showing with the horses." So I tallied for the Jinglebob Company 300 head of mules and horses, which were turned over to M. J. Farris. I had tallied but a few horses up to September 6, 1890. Farris instructed me to put a small — (called a bar) just above the U, thus U̅.

Farris then left for Danville, Ky., or for Kansas on September 6, 1890, and did not return until in the early part of April, 1891.

When Farris bought the real estate and 300 horses for $75,000 in August 1890, he also agreed to buy all the cattle belonging to the Jinglebob Land and Livestock Company at $10 a head, excepting the calves of 1891. The cattle were to be tallied and delivered at three places on the Jinglebob Company's range; one place of delivery was to be at South Spring River ranch, the second place of delivery was to be at Buffalo Valley, a distance of thirty miles south of South Spring River ranch, and the third place was to be decided upon later. Farris agreed to attend to the construction of pens and pounds so that everything might be in readiness to begin delivering the cattle in the spring of 1891 as soon as I could gather the first herds.

As Farris did not return in the fall of 1890, I wrote to him urging the necessity of having the pens and pounds ready by spring. Farris did not answer my first letter in regard to the above matter, but after writing again, he wrote me to commence gathering the cattle when spring came and that he would be on hand in due time. He stated that in the event he did not arrive in time to receive the first herds he would make all damages and expenses good.

I began my gathering of the cattle early in the spring as per agreement. I left South Spring River ranch with my outfit March 8, 1891, and went to gathering cattle belonging to the Jinglebob Company that were at that time on the plains on the Littlefield Cattle Company's range. I began my work about a hundred miles from South Spring River ranch. When I finished my work on the plains, I left my herd of cattle under the care of another man to bring to South Spring River ranch, and I came into the ranch to see Farris and to find out where I was to take my first herd to be delivered.

When I arrived at the ranch I was very much surprised to learn that Farris had not come. When my herd came in, I turned it loose on the west side of the river, and then I took my outfit down the river to begin to gather another herd of cattle. Farris arrived at South Spring River ranch between the 1st and 11th of April, 1891. I asked him about the deal and he said, "Walter, I have just received word from the Citizen's National Bank of Danville, Ky. (of which at that time he was president) that they will not take any more notes of the Jinglebob Land and Livestock Company as a company for money to pay running expenses, unless you folks sign the notes individually."

I said to Farris, "Mr. Farris, you know I told you last year I had signed my last note for our company individually, and you also remember you agreed last August to furnish the Jinglebob Land and Livestock Company money with which to pay running expenses while gathering and delivering the Jinglebob cattle for you until we had delivered enough to you to pay you what was due you from the company. After a sufficient number of cattle at $10 a head were turned over to you to pay all the company's indebtedness, you were then to pay in cash $10 a head as you received the Jinglebob cattle until all the cattle had been delivered; calves of 1891 not to be counted."

Farris said, "Yes, I know that was the agreement, but the bank says it will only do just what I have stated. Walter, the bank looks upon your company as being insolvent, and wants no more company notes." I said, "Mr. Farris, I am satisfied there are today over 20,000 Jinglebob cattle exclusive of the cattle of 1891." This conversation took place, I think, on the 11th of April, 1891.

Farris said, "Walter, you are way off. You are mistaken and you put the number far too high. I have been over the range considerable and I know there is nothing like what you number." I said, "Mr. Farris, you have only been up and down the river in your buckboard and have no chance to know how many cattle there are in the Jinglebob brand. What authority, then, have you for disputing my estimate on the cattle?" Farris replied, "Mr. Lutes of the firm of Lewis, Lutes, and Lewis of Las Vegas said the tally of the Jinglebobs had been run up, or, in other words, that calves had been put on the tally books that were never branded."

I said, "Mr. Farris, any one telling that tells a lie! I have been range foreman for this outfit from the spring of 1885 up to today, and I have been keeping the tally books myself all this time and I know they have not been run up. Neither you nor any other man knows about the number as well as I do or has had a better chance to know the number of cattle on the Jinglebob range, as I have been on the range almost constantly since the spring of 1885."

Farris said, "Walter, I'll tell you what I'll do. I will give you $1,000.00 for your interest in the Jinglebob Land and Livestock Company, and will settle with all the other stockholders of the company accordingly. I'll take the cattle on the range for what your company owes me, and you just slip down and out, and I'll take charge of the concern and cancel all the debts of the company." I said, "Mr. Farris, this is too small an amount to talk about. Maybe I had just better let you take the outfit and let you keep your $1,000." Farris then quit me for the day without saying what he would do.

About the 15th of April, 1891, Farris proposed to the stockholders of the Jinglebob Land and Livestock Company — James Chisum, W. J. Chisum, Mrs. Sallie N. Robert, and myself — that he would turn over all the notes that he held against the company and also pay all the debts of said company, including the running expenses up to that date, together with $9,000 in cash, which was to be paid as follows: James Chisum, $3,000; Wm. Robert, $3,000; Mrs. Sallie L. Robert, W. J. Chisum and W. P. Chisum, each $1,000. It was understood that Farris was to save 9,000 head of Jinglebob cattle, or, in other words, that Farris was to take charge of the Jinglebob cattle and handle them at his own expense, Farris getting the calves from the spring of 1891. Farris, however, agreed to sell the cattle as soon as possible and tally them when he sold them and pay the Jinglebob Company in cash at whatever price he sold the cattle at for all over the 9,000 head exclusive of the calves from the spring of 1891.

It was further agreed that Farris should not be compelled to tally the cattle in the year 1891 owing to the condition of the range and the cattle. It was very dry, and cattle were thin up to the 15th of April, 1891. So it was thought best for all parties concerned not to attempt such an undertaking as the tallying of such a large stock of cattle under the then existing circumstances. The above is the reason why Farris was not to be compelled to tally the cattle in 1891 should he succeed in selling them in 1891. Farris was to have the benefit of all credit for the company.

Farris bought the V brand of cattle owned in the spring of 1891 at $10 per head. Farris asked me how many I thought I had on the range. I said, "There are about 250 head." Farris paid me $2,500 for my cattle without a word as to my over-estimation of the number, at the same time disputing my word as to the number of Jinglebob cattle and saying I was entirely too high, when the V cattle were not the Jinglebob cattle and had been always handled by the Jinglebob outfit on the same range. On the average I could not see more than one V animal to where I could see a hundred Jinglebob cattle. Farris disputed my word in one case, and in the other he paid me in full for all I claimed and did not say one word as to my estimate of the number.

33

Characteristics and Opinions

THERE ARE STILL CERTAIN PHASES of John Chisum's character and personality needing emphasis, and to them I wish to devote this chapter. It is easily seen that Uncle John was a man of large ideas and wide vision — his plans were always on a large scale. His rise from a small beginning in the cattle business to the pinnacle of being possibly the largest individual cattle owner in the United States at that time was mainly because he had vision and ambition to conduct business on a large scale.

His imagination held before him a picture of his thousands and thousands of cattle on the vast stretches of Texas and New Mexico; and toward the ultimate realization of this he bent his energies tirelessly. The elaborate scope of plans for the South Spring River ranch was but one evidence of that quality. That place was to be the finest, if not the largest, establishment of the times that the country could make possible.

Accompanying these big ideas was the strain of lavish generosity. Uncle John was always furnishing poor people with supplies from his store, on credit or upon the remotest possible chance of payment. In some cases he simply gave outright what was needed. Often I have heard him say to Mrs. Towry something like this, "So-and-so's family is hard up and ought to have some supplies. You go to the store, pick out what you think they need, and have it sent over to them." At another time he would say in regard to another family, "They look to me like they need clothes. Won't you run over to the store and get what goods you think they need and have some clothes made up for them?"

I think it may be said without contradiction that no worthy person ever came to Uncle John asking a favor of any kind which he did not grant if it was in his power to do so. One instance of this comes to mind. A widow with five children, who had a farm but no wagon or team to use on it, let Uncle John know of her plight. He at once bought a nice team of black horses and a wagon, and sent them to her, asking as a favor to him that she use and take care of them until he called for them. He never called for them, and in all probability never intended to do so when he sent such a message along with them.

In many cases it was not material aid that he gave, but rather helpful advice from his wide experience in business affairs. My own mother might be cited as a case in point. When she was harassed and perplexed in her efforts to manage the property Father had left, she frequently went to Uncle John for advice, and never came away empty handed. In my possession is a sheaf of letters he wrote to her which clearly show the willing and kindly interest with which he replied to her frequent inquiries and his desire to be as helpful as possible to us.

Side by side with generosity naturally went the characteristic of being a warm-hearted man full of the quality indicated by the old word "sensibility." This was apparent in the strong affection he showed toward members of his family. His own mother and a sister had died many years before I knew him; yet, when talking of them I have seen tears come in his eyes. Unlike many another whose frontier life of hardship and danger tend to make them austere and cold hearted, he remained to the last "a soul whose master-bias leaned to home-felt pleasures and gentle scenes."

In this connection there is the story of the little silver ring that Uncle John wore on one of his fingers. I often wondered why with all his wealth he continued to wear a cheap ring. One day I asked him about it. "Why, Lillie," he said, "there's a story to that ring. When I first came to New Mexico, I had in my employ a young man — he was just a boy, in fact. After we got the cattle up into New Mexico his mother wanted him to come back to Texas. I had grown very fond of him and had begun to feel a very fatherly interest in him. I was, of course, sorry to have him leave me, but as his mother wanted him and was set and determined about the matter, there was nothing to do but pay him off and let him go.

"The boy wanted in some way to show his appreciation of all I had done for him, but he was way off from any store where he could buy anything. So he took a dime, and with a punch, he managed to make a hole in the center of the dime. With this as a start, he battered and pounded away all day until he had worked that dime into a ring. This he brought to me when he came to say good-bye, and with tears in his eyes, he gave it to me, saying, 'Uncle John, this is all I have to give you to show my appreciation of your kindness to me.' The ring is not worth much, I know, but I cherish it because of the way it came to me. The boy said he wanted me to wear the ring as long as I lived, and I always shall." I am confident that Uncle John lived up to that intention. I saw that ring on his finger the day he left the ranch the last time when he went away for medical treatment, and I would dare to say that it was still on his finger when the mortal mist finally enveloped him.

Another illustration of Uncle John's tenderness of heart may be found in his buying the two Negro boys, Frank Chisum and his brother, and his subsequent treatment of them. Uncle John used to laugh about the way he acquired what he called his family* while living at Bolivar, Texas. Frank was four years old, and his brother about two. Uncle John went after them horseback and brought them back, the younger one astride a pillow placed across the front of the saddle, and the older one perched up behind Uncle John. When they crossed a creek, little Frank fell off and got a soaking.

Uncle John brought up these boys, showing almost a fatherly interest in them. When the Negroes were freed, these two, of course, became their own masters, but they remained with Uncle John, working for wages. They both came out to New Mexico with him. Frank was always the horse wrangler at the Chisum place, and when Uncle John was stricken with smallpox he showed his devotion in a signal way, as I have told in a preceding chapter.

Uncle John always had a great esteem for womanhood. His ideals in regard to marriage were the highest, so high in fact that I have sometimes wondered if his fear that he could not exemplify

---

*There are other versions of his acquisition of the two Negroes.

them did not have something to do with holding him back from marrying. He felt that a man could tough it out alone under almost any sort of conditions, but before any man persuaded a woman to marry him he should be able to provide a good home for her, and so avoid bringing her down to hardship and sorrow. For the man who mistreated his wife, Uncle John had the utmost contempt. He used to say that if disagreement arose which could not be adjusted, then the man should say, "Good day, Madam," and leave. I recall hearing him express this attitude in the following way, "Me fuss and quarrel with a woman? Why, I'd be ashamed of it. I'd nevermore have respect for myself or call myself a man, much less a gentleman."

Uncle John enjoyed the company of ladies. He liked greatly having with one or more of them a bantering conversation, full of jokes and raillery and even teasing, but he never descended to coarseness or roughness. He seemed especially to like ladies who were lively, jolly, and high strung, yet not inclined to sentimentality. He once impressed upon me a valuable piece of advice concerning the importance of trying to hold my own with people and having a "comeback." On a certain occasion I had come to feel that I was too much teased or "picked on" as we used to say, by the various ones at the Chisum ranch, and had let Uncle John see that my feelings were hurt. Calling me to him, he asked what the matter was. When I told him, he laughed and said, "Lily, you are wrong in thinking the people here don't like you. It's just the other way. They like you and I'll tell you why. It's because you scrap them back." It was this type, the sort that scraps back, that Uncle John enjoyed selecting for his lady friends.

There was nothing Uncle John enjoyed better than a good joke and a hearty laugh, long and deep, right from the heart. The sort of laugh he had has become a stock feature in all accounts of him, but it is sometimes misrepresented. It was not at all the kind of guffaw that some have made it out to be; it was a laugh, not of the face and diaphragm only, but of the whole man from head to heel.

His great fondness for a joke was also well known. Once when he was in New York on business he became conscious that he was attracting attention as a cow king from the West. So, in order to have some fun with the easterners, he decided to enact the part. He struggled hard with his turned-down collar to get it on upside down, then walked into the hotel lobby and went to the desk to ask the clerk something. Before Uncle John had said a word, the dapper little clerk remarked, "Pardon me, sir, but your collar is wrong side up." "No, I guess not," replied Uncle John, and went into the dining room and took a seat at a table by himself. Some ladies at other tables looked intently towards him, then began to whisper to one another, and finally to giggle noticeably. But Uncle John appeared oblivious to their amusement, and when he had finished his meal, he added consternation to their amusement by snatching off altogether what he called the "plaguey thing." Then he went out and sat in the lobby in that collarless fashion. In telling the incident Uncle John liked to add that when calling on businessmen in New York he always wore a collar because the businessmen knew a man when they saw one, but he was entirely willing to be disregardful of a collar when around a hotel where they judged a person by his clothes.

Another example of his fondness of a joke was his method of disposing of a carload of ribbon wire he happened to buy. The first barbed wire brought to New Mexico well deserved the adjective "vicious" as it was very heavy and had four pointed barbs. Such wire was really dangerous to animals, especially horses, which have a tenderer skin than cattle. At first, the stock knew nothing about a wire fence; in fact they knew nothing about fences of any sort. Consequently they frequently ran into the wire fences, generally cutting themselves up badly as well as tearing the fence down. The fence, of course, could be fixed, but a good horse cut by wire and crippled for life was a dead loss.

On a visit to Las Vegas Uncle John discovered what was called ribbon wire, which was about a half inch wide with a slight twist in it, and no barbs. He thought he had found just the thing to prevent further injuries to his stock. He bought liberally of it. In his enthusiasm he planned to fence the yard, the corrals, the garden, and everything else that was fenceable on the South Spring River ranch, with ribbon wire. To have enough required buying in carload quantity, a familiar practice of Uncle John's.

He had a lot of good cedar posts brought down from the mountains and awaited the arrival of the carload of ribbon wire. In due time it came, and Uncle John promptly fenced the yard, the orchard, and the garden, its use for the corral being dependent on the outcome of experimenting on these other plots. In a short time he discovered that this sort of wire would not hold stock or turn even the very gentle milch cows or the old work oxen, to say nothing of the more unruly ones.

Realizing he had duped himself into this purchase, he proceeded to get his fun out of the situation by passing on to his friends the remainder of that carload. If any of them came to the ranch, he expressly called their attention to the new-fangled wire and sang its praises, pointing out how it removed all danger of wounding and crippling the stock. This generally enlisted their interest, and led to a request to sell them some of it. After some hesitation and remarks about needing it for his own use, he would finally consent as a great favor to let them have a few spools of it, adding that if he deprived himself of enough for his own use, he supposed he could get another carload. In this way he eventually got rid of the ribbon wire. But the neighbors found it as unsatisfactory as he had, and sometimes came back with complaints. These he was always able to turn aside by his unfailing good humor, and then or afterward, he saw to it that the investment in his ribbon wire was made up to those who fell victim to his clever salesmanship. As the whole thing had been done in the spirit of a joke, Uncle John would have been the last man in the world to want one of his friends to suffer loss in such an affair.

This purchase of the ribbon wire was one of the stock jokes among the Chisums and their friends, and it reminds me of another occasion when Uncle Pitzer made a wholesale purchase to the consternation of Uncle John. This happened at a somewhat earlier date than the ribbon wire episode. When Uncle John could not get to Las Vegas to buy supplies for the store at the South Spring River ranch, he would send someone else to purchase from the commission houses there and see that the goods were properly loaded on the freighter's wagons and started down to the ranch. On this occasion, he sent Uncle Pitzer. One of the articles needed was jumpers, as they used to be called, a sort of short jacket the cowboys liked to wear. Uncle Pitzer was instructed to buy fifty of these but somehow got confused about the matter and came back with a bill for 500 jumpers, enough to stock the store for a lifetime! Uncle John took the situation with good humor for he had become accustomed to expecting freakish behavior from Uncle Pitzer. All the country got to talking about the large stock of jumpers the Chisum store was carrying, and the cowboys who patronized it fixed on Uncle Pitzer for the time being the nickname of "Jumper" Chisum.

Life at South Spring River ranch was always full of pranks and fun. If Uncle John did not start the joke, he was ready enough to aid and abet anyone who did. In this way he became *particeps criminis* to several jokes I conceived and engineered. One day I happened to walk with Uncle John down to his timber claims, and as we passed an irrigation ditch in which were growing a number of pond lilies and cattails, I stopped and pulled some. The roots came up with the stems, and I was at once struck by the similarity these roots bore to Uncle John's favorite multiplying onions (shallots). This resemblance at once gave me an idea.

Uncle John had a friend, a Mr. Anderson, who always liked to tease me and play jokes on me. Knowing that he was very fond of onions, and knowing also that he was to be at Uncle John's that night for supper, I suggested that I take some of the cattail roots up to the house and have them served for Mr. Anderson's supper. Uncle John, seeing the chance for some fun at Mr. Anderson's expense, said, "Good, Lily! I'll help you pull them." So we gathered a lot and carried them to the house. I peeled them nicely and even went so far as to get real onion tops to stick on top of the cattail roots. I took them to Negro Dick, the cook, and got him to play his part by telling him that Uncle John was in on the joke. I placed the dish at the table where Mr. Anderson usually sat, and awaited the results.

When everybody was seated and the meal had begun, Mr. Anderson promptly helped himself to some of the onions, and began to eat them. Of course the cattail roots were as tough as could be, so all he could do was to chew and chew. Finally he gave up on the attempt, remarking, "John, I don't seem to come often enough to eat up your onions. These are so old they are getting pithy and hard." "Yes, yes," said Uncle John with his face as grave as a judge's, "but try some others. Maybe you'll have better luck next time." Mr. Anderson took the suggestion and helped himself to several more from the dish, but he fared no better than before. By that time those at the table who knew about the joke or suspected it was a joke, began to laugh. Uncle John said, "Oh, those girls and their jokes! You have no idea what I have to put up with from them. They intended whatever is in that dish for me, and you went and got into them first, so you brought the joke on yourself when it was intended for me." Then he broke out into a great fit of laughing, the rest of us joining in, too. Even Mr. Anderson indulged in a laugh at his own expense.

Uncle John made Old Man Felix McKittrick, one of his most reliable herd bosses, the butt of many a joke. While they were employer and employee, they had been in that relationship so long that they were more pals than anything else. They were very congenial, especially in this matter of playing jokes, and did not hesitate to pull off some pretty stiff ones on each other. Once when Uncle John attempted to saddle McKittrick with a prospective wife, McKittrick nearly turned the tables on Uncle John. It happened this way. Uncle John had purchased a new wagon and team of mules for it in Las Vegas. How to get the outfit to the ranch was the problem. Uncle John heard of a party of emigrants planning to follow the route down the Pecos to Texas; he thought it very likely he could get someone in the party to drive the new wagon down. On inquiry he learned the party included a widow with five children, traveling in the wagon of her brother-in-law. Here, then, was just the chance he was looking for and also an opportunity to have some fun with McKittrick.

So he called on the woman and proposed to her that she drive the wagon down to his place. "I'll provide you with an outfit and provisions," he said. "When you get down to my place you'll find a very good man in charge of things. I'm afraid the poor man has more to do than he is able to handle, especially in regard to all the cooking and housekeeping matters. Now, if he wants to get you to stay as cook and housekeeper, and to relieve himself of these matters, it will be all right with me. I might also add that I recommend him highly as a perfect gentleman, although he's a little over-crazy on the subject of getting married. I am sure that he'll give you some sort of a chance to stay at the place. As I said, any arrangement you two make will be all right with me, even to something in the way of a matrimonial alliance. If you go to that point, I'll gladly give you a job and do the best I can by you."

Then having lighted the fuse in this manner, Uncle John forthwith dispatched a letter to McKittrick, which reached the ranch before the woman did. In this letter Uncle John told him about the wagon and mules he was sending down, and then said he was sending them in charge of a charming widow and five helpers — he did not say children. He then went on to say that the woman seemed anxious to get married but disclaimed any intention to annex himself. "You know," he wrote, "I have no business with a wife for I have to be gone all the time from home. But with you fellows who stay at the ranch the case is different. You ought to be provided with such a luxury, and I think that now is your chance. I've paved the way for you. Remember that such good luck doesn't always knock at the door of a poor man. Take advantage of it when it does come your way."

The effect of this letter, however, was different from what Uncle John expected. It served to put McKittrick on his guard, and he arranged to be off the scene when the woman arrived. He fixed it up with one of the men helpers to tell the woman that McKittrick had gone down to Fort Stockton and would not be back for some time. The woman remarked, "Well, I'm sorry he is not here, for I wanted very much to see him. I suppose though that I'll see him there, for that will be right on my way to Texas. But what will I do about some way of going on? Mr. Chisum told me that if I didn't get employment at the ranch some arrangement would be made for me to go the rest of the way to Texas."

This man who was acting as go-between reported the situation to McKittrick, who continued to hold himself in the background. McKittrick saw his chance to turn the tables on Uncle John. "You go back and tell her," he said, "that she can rest up here a few days, and then we'll send her on. Say to her also that she can help herself to all the provisions she needs from the store, and that you'll have a team ready for her in a few days."

The helper carried this message to the woman, giving a color of plausibility to it by explaining, "We happen to have a team of Mr. McKittrick's here that he wants brought down to Fort Stockton and I'm sure, he'd be glad to have you drive it down." A few days later the woman was presented with an old wagon and a team of horses belonging to Uncle John, and she went on her way rejoicing, liberally provided with supplies from the store, and with hope high in her heart of eventually meeting and entrapping McKittrick into matrimony when she arrived at Fort Stockton.

When Uncle John came back from Las Vegas he found himself minus a wagon and team and a liberal supply of provisions. He took the loss good-naturedly, comforting himself with the fact that he had succeeded in getting his new wagon and team down to the ranch without cost. When he heard McKittrick's explanation that he had charged the wagon and team and all the rest the woman had taken off with her to the profit-and-loss account, Uncle John laughed his characteristic laugh, and said, "Young man, the next time I try to marry you off, you'll know it."

I must tell another instance of Uncle John's practical joking, even at the risk of taking up too much of this chapter with such examples. That they are very characteristic of Uncle John is my only apology. Jimmie McDaniels, one of the Chisum cowboys whom Uncle John liked very much, was courting the daughter of a man by the name of Fredericks, who lived on our lower place. Uncle John could not resist having a little fun with this pair of lovers by setting himself up as a rival to Jimmie. The young woman was about fifteen or sixteen, a mere girl, in fact; but in a country where marriageable girls were as scarce as hen's teeth, she was very popular. Jesse Evans, Frank Baker, Marion Turner, and a number of others were in the running, but somehow Jimmie seemed to have the lead. But Uncle John planned to give him a good run for his money, for a short while, at least.

On his way up to Lincoln, Uncle John stopped at the Fredericks and met the girl. When he found the chance he presented himself as a suitor. He pointed out that Jimmie McDaniels was too young and unsettled for such a heavy responsibility as establishing a home and taking care of a wife and children. Then called her attention to the fact that he could give her a nice home, a fine buggy and team of horses, and everything else she might want. He admitted Jimmie was a good boy and all that, but he harped steadily on the fact that he was not able to take care of her. He promised that if she would marry him, he would place her mother and father on his ranch so that they would be near her, something that Jimmie could not do as he had no ranch.

The poor girl was somewhat dazed by this deluge of offers from a man old enough to be her grandfather, but she would not give him any definite answer just then. She said she thought Jimmie loved her very much as evidenced by the candy, and more especially the green delaine dress he had given her. When the old folks learned of Uncle John's offers they were inclined to favor him, especially the mother. But John had to go on his way, taking with him only the girl's inconclusive answer that she would have to talk over the matter first with Jimmie McDaniels.

Jimmie turned up at her home a short while afterwards, and when he learned what Uncle John had been saying to her, he promptly and emphatically assured her that Uncle John was only flirting with her. "Why, Flo," he said, "that old man — it's true he's got a ranch, but he's never at home. If you go down there with him, you'll have to stay by yourself, except for the cowboys. Besides, he's too old for you. He'll surely want you to give up dancing of which you are so fond; and I know he won't go horseback riding with you as I've been doing. Pretty soon the old fellow will be decrepit with age, and all that'll be left for you to do'll be to wait on 'im. You don't want to become a nurse for an old man, do you, even though he's got money?" This side of the argument had its weight with the girl, but between the two offers she was almost *locoed*. Finally she decided to stick to Jimmie.

On his way home Uncle John stopped again at the Fredericks' place to see if the girl was ready to give her answer. The girl's mother met him and told him that her daughter had decided to reject his offer. "Poor Florence," she told him, "says she just can't break her own heart and that of Jimmie, too, by taking you instead of him. But she says she's awful sorry she didn't meet you first and if anything happens to Jimmie so that he gets killed in this rough and tumble life out here, you'll surely come next."

Uncle John carried the joke still further by pretending to take his turning down very seriously, saying with the gravest face, "Mrs. Fredericks, you don't know how badly I feel over what you have just told me. I do feel very badly about it, I assure you. I guess her decision is final, and so there is no need for me to stay with you longer. I believe I'll turn back and go up to the Caseys and stay for the night."

"Why, no, Mr. Chisum, do by all means stay all night here with us!"

"I'm sorry Mrs. Fredericks, but under the circumstances I do not feel that I could. I'm really too much cast down by your daughter's refusal to be good company. I really think I'd better go back to the Caseys."

"Well, Mr. Chisum, we'd like mighty well to have you stay at least for supper."

"No, Ma'am, I am afraid I can't. The fact is that I'm so upset I couldn't eat anything."

"Oh, Mr. Chisum, I'll be only too glad to fix you something to eat that you like. What shall it be?'

"Well, Ma'am, since you're so kind I think I might eat some chicken broth if you have a young chicken."

"I certainly will, and I'll fix you some custard, too."

"That's kind in you, Mrs. Fredericks, but don't go to that trouble. I couldn't eat a thing but a little broth. I'm feeling mighty bad, mighty bad, over your daughter's turning me down."

Mrs. Fredericks was as good as her word, and Uncle John kept up his pretense of invalidism all through the meal. Then he told us all about the joke he had played on the Fredericks, laughing all the while and repeating with especial relish the girl's anchor to windward in her message that if she had only seen him first or that if anything happened to Jimmie, she might accept him.

Mother felt Uncle John had gone somewhat too far in the matter, and took him to task for it, saying, "Mr. Chisum, don't you think it is dangerous to try to fool a girl as young as that?"

"No danger, I should say," he answered, "she was too much wrapped up with Jimmie. If I'd seen any indication on her part of taking me up on my proposal, I'd have called a halt then and there, and given her some good fatherly advice on the inadvisability of December mating with May."

To wind up the story, I will add that she and Jimmie McDaniels did not get married. He went to Arizona, and the people in our section of the country lost track of him. He was not the sort to settle down, and Uncle John was right in that respect. The girl's family moved off our place, and she afterwards married someone else. Uncle John was left with a good story to tell, and often have I heard him relate the whole episode, laughing all the time over this "court-ship" as he called it, of Jimmie McDaniel's girl.

Uncle John was a man of intense likes and dislikes. In the eyes of some people, these might savor of eccentricities, but I think they simply came from the general independence of both thought and action that marked the old-time cattleman. One peculiarity was that he would not live in a two-story house. Neither would he stay in a second-story room for even a single night if it could be avoided.

When he went to a hotel in Las Vegas, or Santa Fe, or even in New York, he always insisted that his room be on the first floor. If his wishes could not be met, he never stayed more than one night, moving next day to a hotel which could supply a room on the ground floor. He explained this as having a horror of both fire and steps so he felt safer on the ground floor.

He had a violent dislike also for weeds in general and for cockleburs in particular. Such a dislike as this is much easier to understand than his attitude about first-floor rooms, for anyone who has lived in the West knows that cockleburs, sunflowers, and grass burrs are the bane of existence in an irrigated country. Without question the cocklebur is the worst of the lot. A most prolific weed, it shows an especial aptitude for getting into the manes and tails of all animals, causing them serious discomfort. An animal with its tail all matted up with cockleburs is without defense against flies and mosquitos.

In waging unrelenting warfare on this weed pest, Uncle John insisted that the cowboys clean the cockleburs from the manes and tails of each horse in their mounts regularly every two or three days. This brought double satisfaction — it not only destroyed multitudes of the pestiferous things, it also gave the cowboys something to do in their spare time. But Uncle John went even further, believing he could rid the ranch of them by having the plants pulled up, and he kept not only the cowboys but everybody else about the ranch, even the girls and women, occupied in weed pulling. I can testify from experience that it was not such hard work at first when the morning was young and the sun not up to its full New Mexico warmth, but by midday when the sun's rays came straight down, the extermination of cockleburs was far from being a pastime. It always greatly amused Uncle John when anyone whom he had set to the job or had inveigled into trying it would seem ready to give up. He would urge such a person on to the work by saying in a laughing way, "Just stick to it longer; it gets very interesting after awhile."

I must not fail to mention Uncle John's bravery and courage. His whole life was passed on the frontier sections of Texas and New Mexico when they were hotbeds of lawless characters, whose pride was the skill with which they handled firearms and whose boasts were constantly of the number of men they had killed. Uncle John never went armed and never avoided such men nor did he seek to conciliate them. He always said a six-shooter would get a person in more trouble than it would ever get him out of, and he acted upon that theory all his life. He felt that if he could talk two minutes to a man who might hold a pistol on him, the man would never pull the trigger. The truth of this belief was exhibited soon after the end of the Lincoln County War when Billy the Kid threw a six-shooter down into his face and threatened to kill him if he did not give him $500. The Kid claimed this amount as reward for killing the leaders of a gang that was stealing from Chisum herds in wholesale fashion.

Uncle John displayed his remarkable self-control by first reaching in his vest pocket for his pipe and tobacco sack, and then in his slow, drawling way he addressed the Kid as follows: "Let me get a smoke, Billy, so I can talk better. Now, Billy, listen. You could talk to me about that $500 until your hair was as white as mine, and you couldn't convince me that I owed it and ought to pay you."

Now that was a clever appeal to Billy the Kid who had always boasted that he respected and protected two things — one was women and children, the other gray hair. So Uncle John's reference to his white hair made the Kid hesitate and lift his finger from the trigger where it had been resting while Uncle John was speaking. This was the entering wedge which Uncle John was quick to follow up.

Without flinching or changing his voice, but with his eyes fixed steadily on the Kid, Uncle John continued, "Billy, you surely wouldn't shoot an honest man while he was looking you square in the eye. You've killed a few men, I know, but they needed killing." This remark pleased the Kid, for he had boasted often that he had never killed an honest man but only those that needed killing.

When he saw the Kid beginning to weaken, he pressed the matter to a victory by reminding the Kid that during the Lincoln County War he had allowed him and others of the McSween party to hide out in the vicinity of South Spring River ranch. He also reminded him that he had let them have whatever they wanted from his store on credit and that very few of them had ever paid for what they got.

The outcome of this conversation was that the Kid put his pistol back into its holster, even though he did not relinquish his claim. It is sometimes said that the Kid closed the discussion by saying that if Uncle John wouldn't pay him, he would steal from the

Chisum cattle until the amount was paid and more than paid. This may possibly be true, but it is not correct to state, as some do, that thereafter the Kid stole only from the Chisum herd; as a matter of fact he took cattle from a good many others.

The last characteristic of Uncle John Chisum that I shall mention was his thorough honorableness in all business matters and private affairs. The business he was engaged in would have failed if it had been founded on anything less than the solid rock of business integrity. His sense of justice was keen and his decisions in any course of action were always colored by the respect for the viewpoint of the other person concerned in the matter. He had no use for a crooked man. I have heard him say many a time that it was against his religion to employ knowingly a thief, and he endeavored to practice what he said in this regard. For that reason, I am inclined to reject the stories that make Uncle John sympathetic and helpful towards Billy the Kid and others of the lawless ones in Lincoln County. The character of that young desperado and others of the same type was too clearly known by Uncle John for the latter to have had a desire to help him.

At the same time, Uncle John did not hesitate to waive aside finely drawn distinctions about rights regarding property. This attitude is well shown by a remark I once heard him make: "I've got a lot of horses on my range, and I know they don't all belong to me. As long as the boys ride them and use them, I don't care who they belong to. Anyone who comes along claiming to be the owner, he can have them. But in the meantime I've had the use of them, and so make them pay for the grass they have eaten and their care." This remark shows his sense of fairness that he should have some return for the pasturage and care, and at the same time a willingness to recognize rightful ownership when it became necessary.

The same attitude manifested itself in the advice he gave the county commissioners who were thinking of buying the old Murphy & Dolan store building from Dowlin & Delaney. One commissioner, a Mr. Lawton, had discovered that the title was faulty, and was objecting to going into the transaction. At the same time the chance to secure the building at a bargain price of about $2,000 was very appealing to the commissioners. Uncle John carried the day in favor of buying the building by saying, "The county is already in the soup and nearly bankrupt. Here's a fine chance to get a courthouse cheap.

Let's take it up. As long as nobody bothers us about the title we are all O.K. The Rustlers always figured on the range that as long as they got the calf it matters little who got the cow."

(Editor's note. It should be remembered that Mrs. Klasner died with the manuscript of her book not only unpublished but incomplete. What her reaction might have been in her later years is conjecture, and need not be attempted by those who undertook to put the manuscript into form for publication.)

Index